Plans, pragmatism and people

Changing Eastern Europe

Editors:
David M. Smith
Queen Mary & Westfield College
University of London
R. Antony French
University College London

Plans, pragmatism and people

The legacy of Soviet planning for today's cities

R. Antony French

University College London

UCL
PRESS

First published in 1995 by UCL Press.

UCL Press Limited
University College London
Gower Street
London WC1E 6BT

The name of University College London (UCL) is a registered
trade mark used by UCL Press with the consent of the owner.

ISBNs:1-85728-415-1 HB
1-85728-416-X PB

British Library Cataloguing in Publication Data
A catalogue record for this book is available from the British Library.

Typeset in Times New Roman.
Printed and bound by
Biddles Ltd, Guildford and King's Lynn, England.

To Vivian

CONTENTS

PREFACE AND
ACKNOWLEDGEMENTS

A decade and a half ago, the present author, in collaboration with Dr F. E. I. Hamilton, published the view that there was indeed a definite socialist city (French & Hamilton 1979). In their introductory overview, the editors expressed their judgment that there was a distinct socialist city, although with some qualifications as to that distinctiveness (ibid.: 4). If that judgement were correct, one would expect that the successor States to the Soviet Union would necessarily be facing an urban legacy which differs from the endowment of the past in non-socialist developed countries. In fact, further work since then inside and outside the Soviet Union, the greater availability of information and, above all, the generously helpful reactions of Soviet colleagues to what he then wrote, have all modified this author's view. In broad terms, the thesis of this book is that a socialist city did indeed develop, but that its characteristics and thus its distinctiveness are an amalgam, on the one hand of socialist features deriving from Marxist theory which postulates a very high level of centralized state power and planned operation of the economy, and on the other hand of surviving elements of earlier capitalism and new elements of rediscovered capitalism, the whole amalgam being heavily affected by those uncontrolled and surely ideologically uncontrollable elements, the individual and technology. Moreover, the theoretical concept of a "City of Socialist Man", and the plans drawn up to bring it into being, have at every stage been forced to yield to pragmatic decisions taken to achieve immediate, shorter-term goals. This modified view, if correct, still means that the ex-Soviet cities today face a special set of circumstances that differ in a number of respects from those occurring in "capitalist" cities and which vitally affect the appearance of the city, its functioning and the way of life of its citizens.

In the development of the author's views, in addition to his own researches in libraries and archives and decades of long tramping around Soviet cities, he has relied heavily on the very substantial volume of work which exists on the Soviet city both within and outside the USSR. A comprehensive and wide-ranging bibliography of material published up to 1970 was compiled by Chauncy Harris as part of his seminal book, *Cities of the Soviet Union*. A full, if by no means totally comprehensive, bibliography of works consulted, as well as those cited, has been included in this volume as an up-dating of Harris's work. To all the researchers, Soviet and non-Soviet, the author owes a debt of gratitude. There are so many that it is not possible to list them all here; their names recur in citations and the bibliography. But without their work, this book could not have been written, although they are in no way responsible for its errors and shortcomings.

Within this large group there are colleagues and friends whose work over the years and whose advice and comments in discussions have much influenced this book. My acknowledgements and heartfelt thanks go most especially to Greg Andrusz, Natasha Barbash, Jim Bater, Gyorgy Enyedi, Revaz Gachechiladze, Bob Gohstand, Chauncy Harris, Gary Hausladen, David Hooson, Pavel Il'in and Ella Kagan, Sergey Kovalev, Yuliy Lipets, Mervyn Matthews, Yuri and Olga Medvedkov, Judy Pallot, Yevgeni Pertsik and Sofiya Kabakova, Vadim Pokshishevskiy, Pavel Pol'yan, Alex Rondeli, Denis Shaw, Leonid Smirnyagin, David Smith, Andrey Treyvish, Yuriy Vedenin and Il'ya Zaslavskiy. A special and affectionate tribute is due to the late Professor Yulian Glebovich Saushkin, who supervised the author as a postgraduate student at Moscow University and who was one of the first in the USSR to grasp the importance of social geography, at a time when most Soviet urban geographers were compiling endless taxonomic classifications of towns in a rather naïve branch of economic geography.

In undertaking the research for this book, the author has been substantially helped by a number of bodies. In the first place, much of the initial development of the book and literature research took place during a period at the Kennan Institute for Advanced Russian Studies, as a Fellow of the Woodrow Wilson Centre in Washington. For that period of strongly supported research and the opportunity it afforded to discuss and debate that research, the author is deeply grateful. In particular, he would like to thank most warmly his research assistant, Miss Cathy Love, whose hard work, endless patience and perceptive initiative produced much valuable material from the Library of Congress. Thanks are also due to the British Academy, the British Council and University College London for their financial support in making many visits to the Soviet Union, and to the Institute of Geography of the Soviet Academy of Sciences for its sponsorship on most of those visits. Colleagues in the Institute and in the Irkutsk and Yekaterinburg divisions of the Academy of Sciences, in Moscow State University, Leningrad State University, Tbilisi State University, the Georgian Academy of Sciences and the Culture Fund gave generously of their time, knowledge and hospitality to assist the author. Special warm gratitude for much logistical organizing goes to Sergey Artobolevskiy of the Institute of Geography and to those young members of that Institute, Natasha Steglik, Vera Sidorova and Yelena Sidorova, who acted as couriers on various tours around the USSR and whose tireless efforts, persuasive charm and ferocious partisanship made it possible to achieve far more than the author could have hoped to do on his own. The staffs of the Lenin Library and INION Library in Moscow and the Saltykov–Shchedrin Public Library in St Petersburg also gave much help on many occasions.

This publication was prepared in part under a grant from the Woodrow Wilson International Center for Scholars, Washington DC. The statements and views expressed herein are those of the author and are not necessarily those of the Wilson

Center. An earlier version of Chapter 8 was published as an Occasional Paper of the Kennan Institute for Advanced Russian Studies of the Wilson Center and the author is grateful for their permission to reproduce the greater part of it here.

INTRODUCTION

The search for a Soviet city

The revolutions of 1917 brought to power in Russia a party that based its principles on the ideas of Karl Marx, as interpreted by Lenin. The avowed aim of the new regime was to create ultimately a communist society from which all traces of the previous capitalist economic system had been eradicated. This new, unprecedented society would enjoy totally different, just and egalitarian relationships between its members and these would be reflected in their living and working environments.

Since then, nearly three-quarters of a century have elapsed. Lenin wrote copiously, putting his own gloss on Marx's theories and seeking practical ways to implement them, although all he achieved was the ideological compromise of the New Economic Policy. His death and succession by Stalin saw the formulation of what was then termed Marxism–Leninism–Stalinism and creation of a fully planned or "command" economy. The Stalinist element in the theory and much of the practice was rejected after Stalin's death, but by 1960 Khrushchev was claiming that the intermediate stage of socialism had been achieved in the USSR. He produced a twenty-year plan, which would bring the Soviet Union to its final communist goal. His target date of 1980 came and went without the faintest sign of such an achievement, but by the beginning of the 1980s the accepted official view was that the USSR had reached a stage of "developed socialism" and that such a society was clearly distinct from, and potentially better than, societies in capitalist or, in practice, mixed economies including elements of both the market and State control to varying degrees. The ultimate goal of communism was by then far over the horizon and there was little effort to estimate when it might be achieved. By 1985, it was widely perceived and at last officially admitted that the socioeconomic system that had been created was very far from progressing towards its goals and not even working satisfactorily in an economic sense.

Throughout the changes of leadership and interpretations, the constant was a belief that Soviet society under the unchallenged and unchallengeable rule of the Communist Party was based on Marxist principles and that the Party leadership was correctly interpreting those principles of socio-economic organization and social justice. This was still true in 1985, when the dying out of the old guard and the coming to power of Gorbachev ushered in the era of *perestroyka*, restructuring or economic change, and of *glasnost*, relaxation of the secrecy practised by the

1

Communist Party. The methods were intended to bring about change and it was acknowledged that there would have to be a limited and strictly controlled element of capitalist private profit in the form of co-operatives, but all within the framework of Communist Party dominance and Marxist doctrinal guidance. Gorbachev's initial aims were acceleration (*uskoreniye*) of the economy by updated technology, increased efficiency and quality of management, but not by political change.

The speed with which these officially sponsored developments took on a life, impetus and direction of their own astounded the world and the decade of the 1990s opened to the general disintegration of communist parties and Marxist systems. The year 1991 saw the end of the Marxist experiment in planning a society in the USSR, as had happened in the countries of eastern Europe a little earlier. The Communist Party was abolished after the failed coup of August 1991 and the year ended with the legal abolition of the Union of Soviet Socialist Republics itself. Four of the former constituent republics, Estonia, Latvia, Lithuania and Georgia, went their own ways as independent entities. The remaining republics, equally claiming full independence, agreed to remain tenuously linked as the Commonwealth of Independent States (CIS). At the time of writing, this body too seems destined to disappear in the wake of the USSR. The principal role envisaged for the CIS was to form a body controlling the former Soviet armed forces; with each republic moving towards establishing its own defence forces, this role has now little significance and the CIS has already become no more than a shadow. There is a possibility that some or most of the republics might join some kind of economic union or that some might voluntarily rejoin Russia, but at the time of writing this is highly uncertain. It is unlikely that many people, if any, in the successor States of the USSR today actually believe that the perfect society, promised 70 years ago by the Communist Party, is ever really achievable and fewer still believe that the way forward can be based on the ideas of Marx. The personnel of the Communist Party in the former Soviet republics, as in the ex-socialist lands of eastern Europe, are in some cases surviving in power, but with at least an outward rejection of the Party, if only by changing its name.

There can be little doubt that the present time is seeing, surely has seen, the end of an experiment with a new and different socio-economic system. At the same time, since the advent of *glasnost* there has been, not just greater openness and truthfulness about the situation in the dying years of the USSR, but equally importantly, greater realism in assessing what has actually happened over the period of its existence. For some years the Soviet leadership had been compelled to admit, and the Soviet population at large had gradually assimilated, the many ways in which the country failed to achieve, or even move towards, the bright optimistic goals of the theoreticians behind the Revolution. This then is surely the moment to take stock of the achievements and failures over the seven decades of the Soviet period and to assess what has been created to serve as basis for advance into the future. In the context of the social geography of the city, such is the purpose of this book.

The society of the Soviet Union, as it developed after 1917, required a living environment for work, residence and leisure. From the start, this living environment was seen by nearly everyone as an urban one. This is hardly surprising in view of the pre-eminence of the urban industrial proletariat, both in Marxist theory and in the actual events of the Russian Revolution. The natural, or at least rural, environment might provide health and recreation (and of course food), but the prime production task of society was to make the material goods needed for a satisfying quality of life. The centre of production and the place where full cultural satisfaction could be provided was the town. But the town was in itself an expression of social organization and relationships and if, therefore, there was to be a new society founded on new principles, inevitably a new town would be required, one moulded by and expressing those socialist principles.

Capitalist society had used the market as the regulator of activity and development and the inherent contradictions of such a system led to sub-optimal consequences, urban chaos, inequality and squalor. Socialist development would have to be thought out and controlled in order to achieve optimum benefit for all society. The Revolution made the State responsible for organizing the advance to communism, up to the point where it would itself no longer be necessary and would wither away. Meanwhile, the State had acquired ultimate responsibility for urban development to a degree never before experienced anywhere on a nationwide scale. It had to decide on and control the rate of growth of towns in number and size, the location of new towns, the allocation of functions to towns and the ways of evolution of individual towns as geographical, economic and social entities. The State had to decide priorities for all these processes, and distribute resources, financial, material and human. To accomplish this massive task, a mechanism was required and throughout the Soviet period, the correct and indeed only mechanism was seen as the plan.

The characteristics of the urbanization process – growth in number and size of towns and the allocation of functions – are directly linked to the overall development of the economy. They were therefore controlled by the national economic plans, the sequence of five-year plans and their annual subdivisions – the process known in Russian as *planirovaniye*. The features of the towns themselves, the geography of their layouts and location of their functional elements were controlled by physical general town plans – the process of *planirovka*. In the words of a former chief architect of Moscow, "City planning in the Soviet Union is the process of integration of knowledge and action into a single controlled effort, the object of which is to achieve harmony between man and his environment" (Posokhin 1974: 13).

Planning as *planirovaniye* started to operate in 1928 with the First Five-Year Plan, whereas *planirovka* in practice began in the early to mid-1930s. One may fairly ask therefore what some 60 years of planning have actually achieved in the way of creating a new urban environment and ask if there now exists a distinctive "City of Socialist Man" and, if so, what are its characteristics, and assess the degree to which the plans have succeeded in their aims and the degree to which other factors have asserted influences on urban growth and brought about consequences unwanted and unforeseen by the plan. These then are the questions that this book seeks to examine. Finally, the book seeks to survey the benefits and the problems the socialist period has bequeathed to its successor regimes.

Urban places in the USSR were defined in a statistical sense, although the definition varied somewhat from one republic to another. In the RSFSR, to qualify as a town, a place required a population greater than 12 000, with more than 85 per cent of the employed labour force engaged in manufacturing or the tertiary sector. For the lesser urban category of "settlement of town type" (sometimes referred to as "workers' settlement") the minimum population was 3000, again with 85 per cent employed in manufacturing and services. In other republics, both thresholds could vary, down to a minimum in the Tadzhik Republic, where a town needed only 5000 people and a settlement of town type no more than 1000 inhabitants, in both cases with 66 per cent employed in the urban functions. In fact, as the 1989 census made evident, many towns and urban districts in the Soviet Union were far below these legal thresholds and it is not clear how and why they managed to cling on to their status.

The question "Is there (or was there) a socialist city?" is not, of course, a new one. The years that followed the 1917 Revolutions saw much theoretical consideration and prolonged argument over this very question, as Chapter 2 outlines. The ideas then put forward had antecedents dating back in some cases to the nineteenth century or even earlier. Although Stalin brought debate on the nature of the City of Socialist Man to a halt, by characterizing the theories as Utopian, the belief that there *was* a socialist city remained. Thereafter, Soviet literature took for granted that the city in the USSR was qualitatively different from the Western city of capitalism. The question in the post-Revolutionary period up to the early 1930s was rather, "What will, or should, such a city be like?"

Once Stalin had simplified the definition to the extreme – a city under control of the Communist Party – subsequent analyses by Soviet writers were almost all *post hoc* characterizations of what had been brought into being by the needs of his policy to fulfil the drive for heavy industry. The passage of time, above all the termination of the rigid Stalin regime, brought changes in policy and different practical aims for the planning of the city, but the expressions of the theoretical, ideal socialist city continued to be *post hoc* justifications of what practical policies (by then focused mainly on housing) had actually achieved.

The non-Soviet participants in the debates of the 1920s – Walter Gropius, le Corbusier, Ernst May, Hannes Meyer, Mies van der Rohe and others of the Bauhaus group – spread the concepts of that exciting, imaginative period throughout the world. Although they were by no means universally, or even generally, accepted, many of the ideas generated at that time were enormously influential and several other countries saw experiments in turning the theories into reality. In France, le Corbusier built his *maison l'Unité d'habitation* in Marseilles. In the USA Gropius expressed communal living in the Graduate Centre of Harvard University. Ultimately, in the 1960s, some watered down, merely superficial versions of these experiments started to come back to the Soviet Union in the guise of high-rise blocks and neighbourhood units. Ironically, about this time the Western world was beginning to question the social desirability of some of these developments and to move away to newer concepts.

If in the Soviet Union little was done to create a theoretically and qualitatively new urban environment, at least the belief remained that to do so was the final goal. Towns had plans. The cities that were to be built according to these plans were intended to be better than capitalist cities in specific, worked out ways. Thus, there was a body of theory as a basis for town planning. It was not very sophisticated, but it incorporated certain principles, often deriving from the intellectual furnace of the 1920s. However, the decades following the 1920s saw, for one reason or another, even the more limited aims of the city planners at best only partially achieved or, more commonly, totally ignored. Stalin's priority for heavy industry was succeeded under Khrushchev and Brezhnev by a priority to rehouse the populace that Stalin had neglected.

It is, therefore, the aim of this book to examine the past and present of the Soviet city in terms of its physical layout and social geography. It seeks to discover how far the existing present realities reflect the conscious aims of planning over the years, how far they are the result of *ad hoc* pragmatic decisions taken in response to the pressures of events and interest groups, or how far they arise from the uncontrolled actions of individuals. The analysis hopes to determine whether it is possible to consider the Soviet city as an expression of urbanism *sui generis*, as "the City of Socialist Man", responding in its form and functioning to distinctive political, economic and social constraints.

Alternative characterizations of the Soviet city are certainly possible. It can be seen as essentially a lagging version of the "Western" city in advanced capitalist or mixed-economy countries; as it developed, it therefore displayed ever more signs of convergence with the Western "capitalist" city. Such a view has been strongly supported by the Hungarian geographer, Gyorgy Enyedi; "*Socialist urbanization. . . is not a new model of modern urbanization.* It replicates the stages of a global process." (Enyedi 1992: 106). Finally, the actuality may be seen as an amalgam of the two foregoing situations: as a city shaped by a socialist system, increasingly modified as the system itself changed, and modified also by the problems posed by technical rather than political developments – above all the car. Such modifications have made the Soviet city ever more like its Western counterpart and the present political and economic developments are speeding up such convergence.

Given the objectives of the Soviet system, it is perhaps a matter of considerable surprise that the overwhelming bulk of Western literature on town planning, urban sociology and urban geography totally ignores the largest-scale experiment in history to bring about a new form of town. Peter Hall, who included Moscow in his study of world cities and in his writings took account of events and ideas in the Soviet Union, was one of the very few exceptions (Hall 1966, 1984). Interest otherwise has been largely confined to those involved in area-specific Soviet studies, but over time this group has produced a not inconsiderable body of literature on the Soviet city. Yet, for all the valuable contributions made by researchers within and without the Soviet Union, there are still enormous lacunae in the study of Soviet urban geography. In part this has resulted from the relatively narrow lines of approach to the field, followed for so long by Soviet urban specialists, especially where social geography and its interplay with planning were concerned. These approaches were opened up only gradually, first by the efforts of the early pioneers Saushkin and Pokshishevskiy; then, from the late 1960s, the next generation developed a much faster advance, spearheaded by the Laboratory of Human Ecology in the Institute of Geography of the Soviet Academy of Sciences, under the inspired leadership of Yuri Medvedkov. The closure of that laboratory a decade later was a disaster for urban geographical scholarship and was a prime cause of so many of its powerful team eventually ending up in the USA. It also left the task of developing urban social studies very largely in the hands of sociologists. Only in the 1980s did surviving members of that generation of geographical urban specialists in Moscow, such as Barbash (also later in the USA), Pertsik, Petrov and Vasil'yev, begin to rebuild serious, academically sophisticated, social geographical research on towns, backed up by the end of that decade by the young generation pressing behind them, such as Sidorov and Zaslavskiy.

Meanwhile the torch was carried by the sociologists and some of the economists, and by geographers in other republics, most especially in the Baltic States, where Tiina Raitviir has long been in the vanguard of a large and productive group, and in Georgia with an active and pioneering group in Tbilisi. The relative newness and underdeveloped state of the field was long acknowledged by Soviet writers themselves: "Soviet urban studies are taking only their first steps. Until now works about towns have been of a scrappy, uneven nature" (Aitov et al. 1982: 3).

One of the hindrances to deep analysis of the social geography of Soviet cities has always been the paucity of basic statistical data. Soviet specialists may often have had access to material not in the public domain and denied to Westerners, but even they have been handicapped by the non-availability of other needful statistics; when such material was available to them, the censorship (which persisted up to 1990) refused to allow publication of the resulting analysis. A classic example of this is provided by Zaslavskiy's work on determining spatial social differentiation in Moscow, using subscriptions to journals as an indicator. His paper (Zaslavskiy 1984) on the methodology was permitted to be published, but the accompanying map was suppressed because it was based in detail on Moscow postal districts and therefore showed up the Moscow postal district where the KGB censorship office was located (personal communication from the author).

For the Western writer, the deficiencies were appalling. The three standard sources of raw material for the urban geographer, survey on the ground itself, questionnaire surveys, and large-scale topographical maps and aerial photographs, were all rigidly "off limits" to the foreign researcher. Censuses have never been fully published for towns. Even in those of 1959 and 1970, which were published for high-level administration units (republics and oblasts), basic population

6

figures for urban places below certain thresholds were omitted, as was all other information for individual towns, with the occasional exception of Moscow and Leningrad (St Petersburg). Basic sourcebooks such as directories, even telephone directories, have rarely if ever been available for any city other than Moscow. These deficiencies of data inevitably make the outside researcher heavily dependent on work undertaken by native specialists. Yet, in relation to the size of the country and its great regional and ethnic diversity, the number of the latter has really been rather small. The scope for interpretation is considerable.

A particular problem arises in that, at the time of preparing this book, place-names in the former Soviet Union were in process of constant, but irregular change. Even the area of the former USSR has now no comprehensive term. Since the theme of this book is set in the Soviet period, the area is referred to herein as the Soviet Union or USSR, unless the present situation is actually under discussion, when "the former USSR" or the names of individual republics in their new form are used as appropriate. Where towns have reverted to their pre-revolutionary names, these are used with their sometime Soviet name in brackets, for example Tver' (sometime Kalinin). In other cases the book uses the name appropriate to the period under discussion, with any later or previous names in brackets, if necessary for clarification.

CHAPTER 1

The legacy of the pre-Soviet past

The outbreak of revolution in Russia in 1917 and the eventual establishment of the world's first nation State based on Marxist principles, have generally been seen, both at the time and since, as a sharp break with the past. Certainly, many of the initiators of Soviet planning concepts in the 15 years or so after 1917 believed that a new world had begun and they therefore devised plans and planning theory as if starting from nothing. In fact, the Soviet Union throughout the 70-odd years of its existence displayed far more continuities than discontinuities with its predecessor Russian State. This is as true for town planning as for the broader aspects of national policies and social developments. A heritage of past towns and established urban populations from the previous era existed, refused to disappear and remained to affect deeply the nature of the Soviet city ever since and the post-Soviet city today. It is pertinent then to begin with an examination of that inheritance, to study the lineage from which the Soviet city sprang and the consequences of bygone times for that city. One particular physical aspect of the past heritage – the survival and treatment of historic buildings – is examined in some detail in Chapter 8.

Stages and patterns of urban growth

THE MEDIEVAL TOWN

The oldest urban forms, which developed on the territory that formed the Soviet Union, were not Russian. In Central Asia, urban cultures based on irrigation were well established in the first millennium BC Perhaps the best known is Afrosiab, later Macaranda, and today known as Samarkand, which was founded about 500 BC. Equally old were the Greek colonies founded along the northern coasts of the Black Sea. The first of these was set up on Berezan Island in the Dnepr Estuary in the middle of the seventh century BC. By the mid-fifth century BC there were over 30 Greek cities between the mouth of the Dnestr in Moldavia and that of the Rioni in Georgia. Many of these were major cultural and economic centres, including Panticapeum, where Kerch now stands on the Straits between the Sea of Azov and the Black Sea; it was for long the capital of the kingdom of the Cimmerian Bosphorus. Other key Greek cities included Tyras on the Dnestr, Olbia on the Yuzhniy Bug, Theodosia on the south Crimean coast and, most important and most enduring of them all, Chersonesus near modern Sevastopol (French 1983: 250–52).

Of early Central Asian and Greek towns alike, little remains today other than the finds of archaeology, rich though these have often proved, and the sites or ruins of buildings. The significance of such places in the wider Russian–Soviet urban context is primarily as sources for the diffusion of urbanism to Russian lands. Other areas too saw urban development as early as, or earlier than, among the Slavs. Around the north and northwest shores of the Caspian Sea, a number of fortress-towns marked the heartland of the empire of the Khazars in the sixth to ninth centuries AD. In the Transcaucasus, the Georgian and Armenian cultures established flourishing urban centres hundreds of years before the Russians.

Compared to the Central Asian towns and the Greek colonies, Russian urbanism is young, with a history stretching back only to the period between the sixth and ninth centuries AD. At that time, the East Slav tribes were colonizing the mixed forest zone of what is today the European USSR. Tribal and clan centres developed as central-place foci of authority and acquired thereby wealth accumulated from tribute, craftsmen to process the raw materials given in tribute, patronage of chiefs and princes, surpluses for trade, and defences to maintain authority and safeguard the increased wealth (ibid.: 253–7).

As the East Slav tribal settlement gradually developed into the first Russian State of Kievan Rus, deriving its name from its capital at Kiev, the number of towns grew. The evidence provided by chronicles and archaeology for this early stage of urbanism among the Russians is thin and often unclear, but it seems that by the time of the Tatar invasion of 1238–40 there were up to 300 towns in Kievan Rus. At least two of these, Kiev itself and Novgorod the Great, ranked among the larger and more important towns of Europe at that time and had extensive, well established trading links.

Thus, even before the Tatar invasion, the oldest element in the Soviet urban inheritance had been established. If authority was initially the prime central-place function and cause of urban foundation, and if economic life expressed in manufacture and trade was the engine of advance, from the very beginning defence was the *sine qua non* of continued existence. The pre-Tatar towns that were to survive (and many that did not) all had kremlins: fortified enclosures containing the princely palaces and cathedrals – temporal and ecclesiastical power (Fig. 1.1). Originally, the garrison, the traders and artisans all lived within the kremlin, but, as population grew, the town expanded into further settlements, "fore-towns", outside the walls. Into these extensions of the town moved the economic activities, leaving the kremlin as the seat of secular and religious power.

This second element in the town's growth, usually known as the *posad* in distinction from the kremlin, in due time was also walled. So too were subsequent extensions of the urban area, in a series of fortified "cells" spreading outwards as a town's importance and population grew (ibid.: 268–72). From the kremlin (the

Figure 1.1 The Moscow Kremlin: the kremlin maintaining its function to the present day.

original focus), streets radiated outwards to gates in the outermost set of defences. Minor streets connected the main radials in an annular pattern. The "ring and radial" pattern of the earliest Russian town, with the kremlin at its hub, has left its mark on the inner areas of many of the oldest Soviet cities today (Fig. 1.2). Nowhere is this seen more clearly than in Moscow, where two ring roads – the inner semi-circle of the Boulevard Ring and the outer full circle of the Sadovaya (Garden) Ring – have been laid out on the lines of the successive medieval fortifications, marking today the outline of the cellular stages of growth.

In Moscow, the Kremlin has maintained to the present its function as the seat of authority and in consequence it has kept and added to the buildings expressing that authority, from the palaces and cathedrals of the later medieval period, through those of imperial Russia, to the modern 1960s expression of authority, the Palace of Congresses. In other towns there is usually little left today of the kremlin, other than the archaeological site and perhaps a museum in a surviving building; this is usually the cathedral, which generally maintained its function long after the rest of the kremlin had lost its purpose. Nevertheless, the kremlin site still occupies the central point, the original nucleus of the first cell, or stage, in city growth. In Rostov Velikiy, Novgorod, Pskov, Suzdal, Kazan', Rostov-na-Donu, Astrakhan and many other towns, reasonably substantial traces of the kremlin survive to be seen. Quite commonly, the walls, or the banks on which walls once stood, still remain, as well as the principal churches. Often, as in Novgorod, the kremlin is still the area where the radial roads converge.

In the *posad*, the commercial quarter, the focus was the market square. In the market place the traders, merchants and craftsmen had their stalls, most frequently

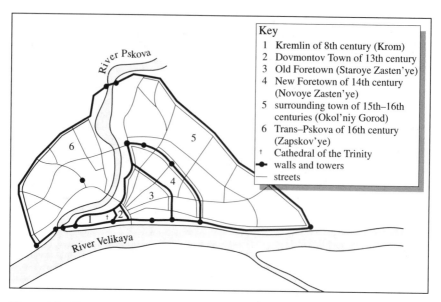

Figure 1.2 The medieval ring and radial pattern.

in rows, each of which was devoted to a single trade or commodity. Once again, Moscow is outstandingly the best example of historical continuity in its layout. Its *posad*, known to this day as the Kitay Gorod and with part of its medieval wall still standing, was centred on the Red Square beneath the Kremlin walls. Where the medieval trading rows stood, in the nineteenth century after the 1812 fire enclosed trading rows were built . These in their turn were replaced in 1888 by a department store, now GUM (State Universal Shop); its interior is laid out in three parallel rows of boutiques on two storeys, a ground plan strongly recalling the medieval layout. Even the name "Red Square" derives from the seventeenth-century Russian word originally meaning "beautiful".

If the market place was the focal expression of the mercantile functions of the pre-revolutionary city, its role in the Soviet city was transmogrified into the political focus, the scene of the biannual parades on May Day and on the anniversary of the October Revolution. In consequence, new towns that have been created since 1917, from largest to smallest, have invariably been given their central square. In Moscow, the focal political significance of the central square was reinforced by the location in the Red Square of Lenin's mausoleum, the supreme shrine of the regime, not just for the city but for the entire country and for the communist system worldwide (Fig. 1.3).

The Tatar invasion was a disaster for Russian urban development. Some of the sacked towns never reappeared on the map; others were not refounded for centuries. Yet others struggled to re-establish themselves, only to be sacked over and over again in the period of the Tatar yoke. Economic activity was slow to recover. Nevertheless the Russian town did survive, did struggle ever more successfully to build its economy and its defences. In time the tide turned and the Russian State, now based on Moscow, began steadily to expand. In the years of the Tatar hegemony and in the succeeding years of expanding Russian settlement, which by the seventeenth century had reached the Pacific, defence remained a prime consideration for the Russian town. Scores of places, indeed almost every present-day town that was in existence before 1700, began as a fortress-town, perhaps on the series of southern defensive lines protecting Russia from attack by the Crimean Tatars, perhaps by the confluences and portages along the thousands of miles of river routeways through northern Russia and right across Siberia.

From the fifteenth century, as the core area of Muscovy became safer from external attack, small undefended townships also began to appear. Their *raison d'etre* was purely economic and they tended to be located on trade routes, selling their wares to passing merchants. The pattern of such settlements was often linear, along the trade road, a pattern reflected in the name of this type of township, *ryad* (a row) or its diminutive, *ryadka*. In general, their lifespan was limited; the majority eventually died out or declined to become mere villages. Those that did flourish tended in time to acquire the defence functions of older towns and to build walls. For example, Tikhvinskiy Posad (nowadays Tikhvin, east of St Petersburg), was originally a trading settlement outside the walls of a fortified monastery; in time it too became fortified sufficiently strongly to resist a determined Swedish siege in 1613.

Thus, from the beginning of Russian urbanism to the reign of Peter the Great and the end of the medieval period in Russia, there tended to be a persisting coherence in the structure of the town, a structure of walled cells extending outwards,

Figure 1.3 Red Square: the focal centre of medieval and Soviet city.

13

most usually in a circular or semicircular pattern, but also occasionally in a row of cells, as at Vladimir. The frequency of common structural layouts has led some urban historians to detect a "Russian planning tradition" in the pre-modern town. Tverskoy (1953: 198) sees it even in the tenth-century town, because its defensive location was selected, not accidental! Such locations may have more to do with the requirements of function in relation to the possibilities offered by geography, than with planning in any modern sense. After all, mistakes in the form of badly located towns could be, and often were, destroyed in enemy attacks; very frequently indeed new frontier fortress-towns were subsequently moved to newer and better sites nearby, in some cases several times. The present site of Orenburg, founded in the first half of the eighteenth century, was chosen at the third attempt. In other words, the frequency of a pattern is largely a matter of the survival of the most apt for defence.

Nevertheless, Tverskoy is justified in pointing out that the existence of a frontier defensive system, steadily expanding outwards across a huge area over a period of several centuries, meant that a very large number of Russian towns were founded as part of that system. In consequence, they came into being, with conscious deliberation, on surveyed and selected sites, with drawn plans approved by the central government. Few countries have such a large proportion of "plantation" towns, for which the original site and layout were centrally determined. Already in the seventeenth century, early examples of linear and rectangular geometries were appearing in new foundations, more often than not fortress-towns on the expanding margins of the State (Savarenskaya et al. 1989: 99–100). The fortress-town of Taganrog, founded on the shores of the Sea of Azov in 1698, was laid out on the plan of the "ideal" fortress-towns of seventeenth-century Italy (Kirillov 1986: 18). Indeed, Tverskoy (1953: 198) goes so far as to claim that "the flowering of the principle of planned town building" came in the second half of the sixteenth and the seventeenth centuries, when it "reached such grandiose levels as were never known in the history of town building in any country whatsoever." One might query whether the Romans at least did not outdo the medieval or early modern Russians in this respect; indeed, the rectangular plans of the fortresses of Zaraysk, Mokshany and Belgorod (ibid.: 55, 67) and pre-eminently Samara (sometime Kuybyshev), which was founded on the Volga in 1586, are highly reminiscent of the Romans (Kirillov 1986: 19). Nevertheless, one must concede both the high level of centralized State decision-taking and control involved in the establishment of Muscovite towns and also the consequent frequency of repetition of patterns.

THE BAROQUE AND NEOCLASSICAL CITY

With the end of the pre-modern age and the onset of the reign of Peter the Great, the element of planning design in the layout of towns was reinforced. The later seventeenth and eighteenth centuries were a time throughout Europe when new towns and new developments in existing towns were designed with classical regularities, straight streets in rectangles, or diagonals with focal squares, often containing monuments or monumental buildings, or circles, ovals and crescents. Kirillov (1983: 127–9) sees a first beginning of such classical regularities in Russia in the triumphal arches and facades along processional routes to celebrate Peter's victories at Azov and Poltava. Far more significantly, Peter's victory over the Swedes led to his foundation in 1703 of St Petersburg, to become his new capital.

From the start, under Peter's strict personal control, St Petersburg was a planned city. The initial sequence of construction was intentional, first the Peter and Paul fortress to protect the newly acquired site, next the Admiralty dockyard to create Russia's first Baltic fleet, and only then the residences of the incoming population. Peter himself initially lived in a log cabin, preserved to this day as a museum. Nobles, merchants, craftsmen and labourers alike were ordered to take up residence; palaces of the aristocracy were commanded to be built of stone.

For the new city, a planned layout was required. While still in Moscow, Peter had taken up residence outside the Kremlin in the foreigners' quarter of Lefortovo, with regular straight streets and houses of west European style. To this day, the gridiron street pattern of the Lefortovo area shows up as a local anomaly in the otherwise ring and radial pattern of pre-revolutionary central Moscow. Peter's travels in Europe furthered his knowledge of Western cities and reinforced his determination to introduce the form of the absolutist city, as part of his efforts to drag Russia out of the Middle Ages; it was to Europe therefore that Peter turned for his architects and planners. The first overall city plan for St Petersburg by Leblond in 1717 envisaged a classical, "ideal" city of rectangular street pattern, with focal squares linked by diagonals, the whole enclosed by an oval of massive fortifications. The oval encompassed the bifurcation of the Great and Little Neva rivers and therefore comprised three separate sections; the largest section, with Peter's palace, was to be on Vasil'yevskiy Island.

Leblond's plan was not adopted; the focus of the city shifted to the mainland section, known to this day as the Admiralty Side, but the determination to develop and maintain a regular planned layout continued, with a new plan in 1720 and further one, by P. Yeropkin, in 1737. The last included the key feature of St Petersburg at the present time, the three main avenues, or prospects, radiating out from the Admiralty and intersecting a more or less semicircular pattern of drainage canals and streets. On Vasil'yevskiy Island, a rigid gridiron pattern of streets was laid out and to this day those streets running perpendicular to the Great Neva are called "lines" and are distinguished by number. Strict adherence of houses to the building lines along streets had been specified by decree as early as 1719. Perspectives along streets to major buildings were planned and achieved (Kirillov 1986: 4). Houses were to be of stone or brick and the architects' plans had to be approved (Jones 1973: 324).

Peter the Great ordered the extension of the regularities of street plan and building line from St Petersburg to other cities, to Moscow as it made good the damage of the great fire in 1712, to Novgorod after its fire of 1723 (Jones 1973: 324–5). This initial impetus of Peter was not immediately adopted throughout Russia and traditional forms tried to hold out against the new trends. But Peter's successors also showed a predilection for the fashions of Europe rather than Russian traditionalism; their reigns saw the extension of the long sequence of foreign architects that had started under Peter – Domenico Trezzini, Bartolomeo Rastrelli, Antonio Rinaldi, Giacomo Quarenghi and the Scot, Charles Cameron, a follower of Palladio and the Adam brothers. Russian architects went to study abroad. Inevitably the planned geometries of classical city design began to appear more widely in Russian cities.

That process culminated in the reign of Catherine the Great, which set the pattern of urban development for the next hundred years. Catherine began in 1775 with the Statute of Provincial Administration, directing the reform and modernization of the old regional network of provinces into administrative governorships and districts, together with the reform of the legally defined status of the urban population (Hittle 1979: 198–212). A revised system of policing and magistracy was established. This statute involved confirming or conferring urban status on places designated as centres of new administrative units at each level, thus setting up a planned hierarchy of central places, at least where authority was concerned. This hierarchy survived until after the 1917 Revolution.

The Statute was followed up in 1785 by Catherine's Charter of Rights and Privileges given to the Cities of the Russian Empire. The Charter identified categories of townsfolk – house and property owners, merchants (organized into three guilds on the basis of amount of capital), craftsmen-foreigners and out-of-town merchants, eminent citizens (those possessing over 50000 roubles capital, magistrates, burgomasters, etc.) and finally the *posad* people, ordinary people who lived and worked in the town (Hartley 1984: 63–4). The Charter also set up municipal administrative institutions, headed by a six-man council or *duma*. The town was also required to have a coat of arms.

The Charter had considerable shortcomings in terms of organizing social structure and administration, not least in the large sections of the urban population that were not included in the six categories (ibid.), but it had a major significance in the history of Russian urban planning. In addition to the enactments concerning the social structure and economic activity of towns, it required every town to have a development plan which had to be approved by the crown. The central agency controlling these plans was initially the Commission on the Building in Stone of St Petersburg and Moscow, set up in 1762, which now took on additional responsibility for the planning of all other towns. In all, the Commission considered 416 plans and approved 306 of them (Schmidt 1989: 28). After the disbanding of the Commission in 1796, the duty of overseeing plans eventually in 1806 became the responsibility of the Building Committee (Lavrov 1977: 49).

The standard plan called for a focal centre. This was often the pre-existing historic core of kremlin or cathedral. Proskuryakova (1985: 43) lists over two dozen major towns where the historic core was preserved, including Kazan', Nizhniy

Novgorod, Novgorod, Pskov, Tver', Voronezh, Yaroslavl', Smolensk and Tula. Often, the historic core was set in a newly created square, in turn surrounded by principal buildings in the fashionable classical style. From this square main avenues radiated out fanwise, transecting a background gridiron pattern of streets. Such a central focus was not necessarily the kremlin. At Kostroma the plan established a new focal square, flanked on its Volga river side by a large, regularly laid out, commercial centre of trading rows. The old kremlin site and cathedral stood just off-centre from the focal square, from which radiated no less than twelve main streets (Fig. 1.4).

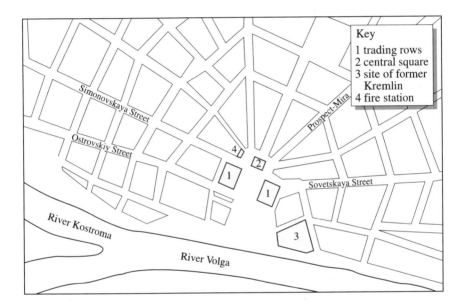

Figure 1.4 The baroque planned city of Catherine the Great – Kostroma.

Buildings in the central zone of a town were to be of stone and, if not public, were constructed by nobles and merchants. Around this was a second zone, where wooden houses were permitted but were spaced out to minimize fire risk; beyond that was a third zone on the outskirts, of meanest housing (Jones 1973: 339–40). Catherine was also concerned that the service structure of her towns should be properly developed, with schools, hospitals, homes for the old and for orphans, all to be built under the supervision of a Board of Public Welfare (Jones 1973: 328). For the first time, town planning was consciously including services with the physical layout. A feature of Kostroma is the classical eighteenth-century fire station, with its imposing lookout tower, on the west side of the central square (Fig. 1.5).

Street plans and architecture alike reflected the eighteenth-century fascination with absolutist and triumphal grandeur. It was expressed in extravagant use of space and vistas, with broad prospects flanked by buildings in Palladian or baroque styles. The ratio of street width to the height of buildings along it ranged from 2:1 to 4:1 (Schmidt 1989: 6). The motto of Peter the Great, "For a new, ordered state, an ordered capital" (Kirillov 1973: 138), not merely epitomized the town in general in the eighteenth-century, it laid foundations for a grandiose "imperial" expression in the urban landscape which was eventually to flower once again under Stalin.

It has more than once been suggested that the grand imperial design of St Petersburg, as in other centres of eighteenth-century autocratic power, was a conscious expression of that autocratic power and the fear which it felt of the oppressed populace. The straight prospects were lines of artillery fire, and the location of military barracks at the outer ends of the prospects allowed troops to come quickly to the aid of the Autocrat. This theory seems more than a little dubious, especially if one considers that the inhabitants were located *between* the Autocrat and his troops and that the troops hastening along the prospects would be the ones most exposed to enfilade fire. Rather, the location of the barracks at the then outer limits of the city, on the radials leading towards the Western frontiers (but *not* on the radial Nevskiy Prospekt pointing to Moscow), would appear to have more relevance to the protection of the capital from external enemies. Imperial power in the eighteenth

Figure 1.5 The eighteenth-century fire station, Kostroma.

18

century felt little need to fear the *hoi polloi*, but wished to express its strength, wealth and splendour through magnificent architecture, displayed in extravagant use of space.

At the time, the degree to which the town plans drawn up and approved as a result of Catherine's Charter were actually carried out varied from place to place. Tver' (sometime Kalinin), which had been largely destroyed by fire in 1763, was the first place to be reconstructed according to plan (Jones 1973: 333). At Kostroma the basic plan of the centre was one of the most fully achieved of all Catherine's towns, also as the result of a major fire in 1773 that cleared space. The layout that was created remains to the present day. The Kostroma office of the Culture Fund is fighting valiantly to get a conservation order for the city centre, to protect this splendid example of eighteenth-century planning from modern high-rise developments. But nowhere, not even in Kostroma, was the application of the plan total; at times the work accomplished was minimal. Regional centres lacked sufficient architects and even though the government sent architects to assist, they were unable to cope with the massive reconstruction involved in the plans (Timofeyenko 1984: 199).

Mumford (1938: 127) in *The culture of cities* has commented that "a baroque plan was a geometric achievement: it must be laid out and built up at a stroke; if possible under the guidance of an architectural despot." The despot in Russia was the Tsaritsa, with other matters of State to attend to as well, rather than an architect. Circumstances rarely permitted the fulfilment of the new plans at a stroke. Of Moscow's 1775 master plan, almost nothing was accomplished, despite the burning of considerable central areas in two fires in 1773. Indeed, during Catherine's reign and afterwards, architects produced a series of draft plans for Moscow (Schmidt 1989: 36–59). Even in the aftermath of the great fire of 1812 during Napoleon's occupation of the city, the Commission of Reconstruction achieved only limited parts of its plan (including the Bol'shoy Theatre and the square in front of it). Most of the rebuilding was left to individuals, who employed traditional materials and styles on pre-existing street layouts.

Yet in many towns, especially in places newly raised to urban status, not a little was achieved. In general, the requirements of planning imposed by Catherine on the Russian town left on it a permanent mark to form an element in the make-up of the town today. The central squares, forming the focus of Party celebration during the Soviet period, in many towns were originally laid out in the eighteenth or early nineteenth centuries; so too were the gridiron or semicircular street patterns. In one place after another, of those given an eighteenth-century plan, one sees the triple radiating avenues imitating the three outward-fanning prospects of St Petersburg. Not infrequently, the partial implementation of the new regular plan resulted in towns having a mixed layout, fusing the new gridiron with the traditional ring and radial pattern, as at Dmitrov, north of Moscow (Khokhlov & Yakuta 1979: 87).

Where towns were completely new foundations, the influence of the classical city pattern was unalloyed and remains to shape the inner areas of such places

19

today. Nowhere is this better seen than in Catherine's new Black Sea port of Odessa, founded in 1794. The site, on the high bluff above the shoreline, broken by gullies, imposed physical constraints, but the planned rectangular street layout, devised by the Dutchman de Voland, was still achieved by adopting two intersecting gridirons meeting at an angle (Herlihy 1986: 12). The streets were 100 feet (30m) wide and, when the Duc de Richelieu took over as Governor in 1803, he actively concerned himself in planting trees, especially acacias, along them (ibid.: 36). The symmetry and architectural merit of streets and buildings were greatly admired by visitors (Skinner 1976: 140). After 1826, the wide Primorskiy Boulevard was laid out along the top of the bluff, lined with majestic buildings and linked to the waterfront by the great flight of steps immortalized in Eisenstein's film, *The battleship Potemkin*. Nevertheless, as Skinner (ibid.: 146–8) has pointed out, the planned magnificence of Odessa was only a facade for a town where the infrastructure was entirely inadequate.

Even the factory settlements of the Urals, consisting of an ironworks and housing for workers, were laid out in regular geometric fashion; they were usually surrounded by protective fortifications, making their layout strongly reminiscent of the frontier fortress-towns such as Taganrog, built in 1698 early in Peter the Great's reign (Kirillov 1986: 14). In the southern steppelands north of the Black Sea, settled by the Russians only at the end of the eighteenth century, almost all the towns were new and were laid out on compact gridiron patterns (Timofeyenko 1984: 217).

Although the accomplishment of new town layouts was so often only very partial, nevertheless the regularities of the classical period left a huge mark on almost all towns of the time, in the form of individual buildings, administrative offices, hospitals, trading centres (formally laid out market areas), houses of the nobility, and churches. The yellow-painted stucco and white porticoes of the Moscow classical style frequently survive to witness the imprint on the city of architects such as Bazhenov, Kazakov and Bove. Moreover, the classical style continued to dominate Russian architecture throughout almost all the nineteenth century, even as new forces were arising to affect the nature and appearance of the towns.

THE INDUSTRIAL CITY

The end of the eighteenth century and the dawn of the nineteenth saw the Industrial Revolution in full flood in the major countries of western Europe and North America. It brought with it the dominance of private, individual enterprise, emphasis on profit rather than planned principle and, in consequence, fast and largely uncontrolled urban development. Only here and there did factory and mill owners build planned settlements for their workers. In Russia the very tardy arrival of the Industrial Revolution, which only got fully under way in the last three decades of the nineteenth century, meant that in most towns the plans from the Catherine period continued to be significant for most of that century.

When at last the pace of industrialization did accelerate, in the relatively limited number of towns seriously affected, features began to emerge which were comparable with those that had earlier appeared in western Europe. Some towns grew very rapidly. Kiev, only 65 000 in 1861, had reached 248 000 by the 1897 census and 626 000 by 1914 (Hamm 1986a: 83). Odessa grew over the same period from 110 000 to 655 000 (Skinner 1986: 217). The growth of new industries brought in large numbers of migrants from the countryside and provision of housing was usually far less than adequate, leading to overcrowding and slum conditions. This typical process of the Industrial Revolution was in many Russian instances exacerbated by the shortage of skilled management and the few sources of capital, which encouraged the growth of very large industrial enterprises, bringing in considerable numbers of workers. As the number of in-migrants from rural areas increased, especially after the Stolypin agrarian reforms of 1906–11, the planning controls on town development weakened. In the words of Bater (1984: 136), "any remaining hope for an orderly development of the Russian city evaporated."

If there were similarities in the overall process of industrialization and urban growth in Russia and in the countries of western Europe and North America, the differences were perhaps even more strongly marked. The relationship between industrialization and urbanization in Russia has been a matter of controversy (see, for example, Rowland 1976: 122–3; Thiede 1976: 137). Some, like Lewis and Rowland, have seen a very low level of correlation between the two processes, in sharp contrast to the west European situation. This view rests on, first, the frequent establishment of industrial enterprises in rural areas, on the estates of the landowning class. Such rurally located factories were particularly common in the textile industry of the Central Industrial Region east of Moscow, and again in the sugar-beet refining industry of the Ukraine.

Secondly, the large influx of population from the village to the town, more especially after the Emancipation of Serfs in 1861, was by no means wholly or even principally linked to industrial development. Service employment, including domestic service, pulled in large numbers. Many of the in-migrants did not form a permanent stable urban population, but migrated seasonally between town and home village. This was usual with those serving in the households of the nobility, who also moved between winter season in town and summer season on their estates. Many village families sent a member to find work in the towns, while the rest of the family continued to operate the family share in the village lands; the absent member commonly returned each year to help at the busy harvest time. Bradley (1986: 14) has calculated that the median period of residence in Moscow at the end of the nineteenth century was only seven years. In St Petersburg in 1900 and still in 1910, only just over 32 per cent of the population had been born in the city (Bater 1986: 53).

This assessment of a weak relationship between industry and the growth of towns has been challenged by Thiede, who has shown that, in New Russia between 1860 and 1910, industrial towns, based chiefly on mining and metallurgy, grew much faster than towns that were local commercial centres (Thiede 1976:

125–37). But his area covered the Donbas coalfield and the Krivoy Rog iron mining area, the only modern heavy industrial regions of Tsarist Russia and therefore very much an exception to the general situation.

One must also remember that the statistically "rural" textile mills of the Central Industrial Region were, by the beginning of the twentieth century, in large settlements, urban in every respect other than legal status. Not all such factory "villages" were textile producers. Along the Oka were metalworking and glass-making "villages". Some had populations of 5000–6000 in the 1860s and 10000–12000 by 1914 (Vodarskiy 1972: 9, 159) and some of the textile centres were larger still. For all, their development was essentially industrial. Nevertheless, it is difficult to deny that the connection between urban growth and industrialization in Russia was far weaker than in other industrialized countries in the nineteenth century.

In relation to the organized evolution of Tsarist Russian towns, a more important difference from Western counterparts was the extremely feeble development of local urban authorities with the power to control what happened in their towns. Only in 1846 did St Petersburg, the capital, get its own *duma* or city council; its franchise was so tightly restricted that it covered less than two per cent of the total population (Hanchett 1976: 93). Moscow received an only slightly less restrictive power of self-government in 1862, but in 1870 the General Statute, spreading powers of local government to other towns, much improved the situation. But although the franchise was widened to all who owned any property or paid any taxes, the voting age was raised to 25 (ibid.: 100) and in 1884 Moscow's electorate, like St Petersburg's, formed no more than two per cent of the population (Bradley 1986: 24). Then in 1892 a further statute both restricted the franchise again, principally by raising the property qualification, and placed additional burdens on the local *duma*, such as paying for the quartering of troops. In Moscow there were only some 6000 voters in a population approaching a million (ibid.: 111).

The improvement in the degree of urban self-responsibility, however slight, often did lead to some improvement in the provision of a functioning infrastructure. Odessa received its reform statute in 1863 and the effect was immediately seen in the increased frequency of town *duma* meetings, raised city income and increased expenditure on city facilities, notably the harbour (Skinner 1976: 149–50). In 1866, gaslights were installed and in 1880 the first horse tramway was commenced (Herlihy 1986: 269).

In the period between 1870 and 1892, a number of other local authorities made some real efforts to modernize, to develop infrastructure and services, and to put up public buildings to enhance the appearance, status and quality of life of their towns. Yet even in the period of relative opportunity for town councils to act, little was done. The financial base was usually inadequate and councils ran up huge debts. The situation worsened as the powers of self-government declined. The finances of Odessa between 1897 and 1913 were in the red every year but one and the total debt reached 8 284 240 roubles (Skinner 1976: 154).

The greatest proportional share of representation in urban government lay with the nobility, whose principal residences and principal interests were usually in their estates out in the country and who therefore had limited interest in spending money to improve infrastructure in the towns. Moreover, what was done was done piecemeal, with no effort at overall planning or control. Bater (1986: 44) comments of St Petersburg, "Factories, workshops, markets, retail stalls, pedlars – all were to be seen throughout the central city and beyond, in defiance of the zoning, land-use, and licensing controls of an earlier era."

All aspects of public services were weakly developed. Most towns, even the largest, had either no piped water supply or an entirely inadequate one. Few had any form of sewage disposal, with all the consequent hazards to health. Medical services were rarely sufficient to meet the health problems arising from the urban environment. Khar'kov in the mid-nineteenth century had a population of 50000 and a police force of only 50 men (Brower 1990: 15).

Above all, the housing situation in the larger towns, and in the towns where industry played a dominant or major role, was as bad as or worse than that in the industrialized cities of western Europe. Individuals and whole families occupied "corners" in rooms or slept in rows on low platforms running the length of doss-houses.

The level of crowding was made worse by the slow development of cheap public transport. Odessa got horse-drawn trams in the 1880s, but steam and electric trams only made their appearance in the 1890s (Skinner 1976: 152). In Kiev, although horse trams had been discussed in 1869, they were only introduced in 1890, two years before the first electric tram (Hamm 1986a: 88). St Petersburg, the capital, was particularly slow in developing its public transport. The first horse-drawn tram ran in 1860, but the first electric tram came only in 1907; even in 1914 most of the tramlines in outer city areas were still horse-drawn (Bater 1973: 92). In those towns that did have tram systems, networks were limited and fares, although generally cheap, were not cheap enough for the low wages of Russian workers. The proletariat had therefore to live within walking distance of their place of employment.

The need for the poorest to cram themselves into the central urban areas, together with the large numbers of domestic servants and household attendants, meant that different social groups tended to live in much closer proximity than was usual in the more widely spread English town. Often, social distinction was as much by floor of the building as by building, street or quarter, with the lower orders living in basements and attics (Bater 1984: 138).

Overall, the period of development of the modern and industrialized towns of Tsarist Russia was characterized by a near total lack of co-ordinated planning, whether in the layout of the expanding city or in the provision of service infrastructure. As Starr (1976: 224) has commented, "State agencies whose city-planning activities under Catherine II had once made Russia the European leader in deliberately conceived town construction, had atrophied even before large-scale industrialization began."

Even the "imperial principle" of planned city grandeur, which had been so evident in the eighteenth and first half of the nineteenth centuries, now languished.

Imposing buildings were indeed built, by State, by local authorities, by large companies and by wealthy individuals. It was a period dominated architecturally by both the Revivalist movement of perceived traditional and medieval Russian styles and the "Style Moderne" or Art Nouveau. But the buildings erected existed in individual isolation, without any efforts at spatial coherence. Ideas such as Fomin's "New Petersburg", a large residential area on a classical layout, remained paper plans (ibid.: 227). Only in the socially "best" part of Moscow, west of the Kremlin, did the concentration of wealth produce an otherwise fortuitous grouping of large private houses in the fashionable "Style Moderne". Most have survived and many are today foreign embassies.

Only here and there did enlightened land or factory owners make an effort to establish planned workers' settlements; Prozorovka, near Moscow, was a "garden city" for railway workers, inspired by Ebenezer Howard. Such examples were exceptionally rare, although they do provide an interesting continuity, linking back in time to the planned iron foundry settlements of the Urals in the eighteenth century and forward to the planned microregions of the Soviet period.

The pre-revolutionary inheritance

There were then a number of aspects of urbanism existing in 1917, which the new regime took over and which it discovered to be deeply rooted. Some of these aspects have, very slowly, been modified; others have proved resistant to change. For the present-day city in the former Soviet Union (as for cities throughout the world) few elements of the past have proved more stubbornly enduring than the street patterns of inner areas, whether the ring and radial layout of medieval times or the geometric patterns of the baroque city. These, and indeed all the legacies, have in varying degrees modified the process of urban development since the Revolution and many, perhaps most, have been constraints on the fulfilment of Soviet town planning aims.

Starr (1976) has pointed out that many of the planning concepts which were important in the post-revolutionary era (discussed in the next chapter) owed their origins to debates and theories promulgated in the preceding period, notably the ideas of Howard and the Garden City movement. Long before, there were concepts of physical town planning, which date back at least as far as Peter the Great, but there are reasonable grounds for seeing deliberate organization of urban layout in even older towns, founded as frontier fortresses in the course of Russian expansion. Tsarist Russia in 1917 was a country where it was the norm for town plans to be commissioned, drawn up and approved by central government authority. If Peter the Great launched the process to create his new capital of St Petersburg, Catherine the Great made a development plan a requirement for all towns. In this sense, Russia was perhaps uniquely placed in having central and local authorities accustomed to this concept, despite the shift away from planning control in the

half-century before the revolution. One might, cynically but not altogether unjus-
tifiably, add that the pre-revolutionary situation had equally accustomed people to
think that such plans were not put into practice to any very great extent, beyond a
certain initial construction of monumental public buildings, wide central squares
and axial roads; there was never serious expectation that such plans would be
wholly carried out.

Some Russian writers, such as Tverskoy (1953) and Lavrov (1977), have
detected long-established planned geometrical patterns in the layout of the
Russian town. To a large extent these regularities are really universal rather than
Russian, and they demonstrate consistencies in the sites, development processes
and functions of towns everywhere, rather than conscious planning. Nevertheless,
it is certainly the case that a sizeable proportion of Russian towns established
before the nineteenth century were set up as part of a deliberate process of frontier
colonization and protection and thus had a strong element of planning in their siting and layout.

There was undoubtedly a strong and deep-rooted tradition of "Russianness",
which in the period preceding the Revolution had undergone a major revival,
expressed in architectural styles. In the time following the Revolution there was a
reaction against this nationalist inheritance. The Revolution was seen as only the
start of a worldwide transformation; its commencement in Russia was in large
measure fortuitous and unexpected. But the national sentiment was strong enough
to survive the period of international socialism and it revived powerfully as "world
revolution" gave place to "socialism in one country".

Stalin, in the Second World War, was to lean heavily on patriotic nationalism,
if not indeed to encourage a new imperialism. If the planners and architects of the
1920s were for the most part consciously rejecting everything of the past, by 1945
Bunin and his co-authors were holding up the oldest Russian towns such as Tver
(Kalinin), Uglich, Suzdal and Vladimir "to serve as an historical example to
Soviet architects and source of inspiration in their great task of restoration and
construction of towns destroyed by the fascist barbarians" (Shvarikov 1945: 319).
In the late 1980s, the Russian tradition was again expressed, if ultimately unavail-
ingly, in the Russian opposition to separatist tendencies in the non-Russian republics, and even more strongly in ultra-nationalist groups such as *Pamyat'*
("Memory"), which supports the preservation and restoration of the architectural
monuments of the Russian past. In the early 1990s, this Russian imperialism was
being expressed by politicians such as Zhirinovskiy, demanding a return to Russia
of the newly independent republics of the "near-abroad".

The physical legacy included, as well as street patterns and architectural glories
of various periods, the beginnings at least of the modern industrialized town. For
many places the industrial profile had been shaped before 1917. The railway
network was reasonably well developed, at all events in the European part; railway towns had grown up to join the older-established port cities. Main-line ter-
mini marked the edge of the densely built-up areas of Moscow and St Petersburg
of their day, just as they did in London or Paris. In the Donbas there was a thriving

concentration of heavy-industry towns, to rival the Ruhr or South Wales. Compared with the leading capitalist countries of the West, the number of towns with Industrial Revolution structures – factories and mass housing – were limited, but they did exist. In many cities, areas of substandard, overcrowded slum housing had grown up. If there was minimal development of local urban self-government to foster municipal pride with town halls, art galleries and universities, at least provincial bureaucracy made a number of attempts to leave its architectural mark in similar ways. Most importantly, there was an urban industrial proletariat, slowly but surely growing in political consciousness. It would in due time ensure that the Revolution that succeeded was primarily an urban uprising, unlike the failed 1905 Revolution, which was most active in rural areas.

Yet when the pre-revolutionary urban developments are weighed up, one must conclude that the greatest legacy of the old regime to the new one was a population largely non-urban in number, location, character or spirit. Very narrow franchises and strong central control gave few people experience in town autonomy. The role of the State in town finances was already in place and remained after the revolution and until the present day. The limited degree of urbanization resulted in a lack of urban consciousness. Many of those who did inhabit towns felt no sense of permanence in doing so. Richest and poorest alike moved seasonally from countryside to town and back again, and perhaps for most the first loyalty was to the village. The *mir*, the village commune, provided a focus for the sense of belonging that the town could not readily match. In the hard times immediately following the revolution, millions left the towns to return to their native villages.

There was in consequence a lack of separateness of town and country. Andrusz (1987: 481) has pointed out that even the houses looked alike – wooden, 99 per cent of them single-storey. His claim that town and village served the same function might be qualified "up to a point"; it is a fair comment on the small local centre with little industry other than *kustar* handcrafts and with minor administrative functions; but even then, its chief role was as a minor market. Pre-revolutionary Russia was unusual in Europe for the emphasis given in the exchange of goods to the transient fair and itinerant pedlar (Gohstand 1983). To a great extent the same social structure was supported in both town and village. Estate factories put industry into many rural areas, with employer and worker in direct line of descent from boyar and serf. Yet the similarity of function scarcely applied, despite the continuing links of individual people with the countryside, in the larger towns where industry had assumed a major or dominating role. In consequence, it was the small minority of truly urban, factory-employed workers who made the 1917 revolutions, to which large-scale support of the rural dwellers was attracted only by the non-Marxist promise of "land to the peasants." This small urban proletariat faced the task of urbanizing the population as a whole. As it did so, the structure of Soviet society did indeed change, but, as the events of the late 1980s and early 1990s have made abundantly clear, the urban society which developed in the 70-odd years after 1917 is by no means that envisaged by Marx or Lenin, or the early Soviet city planners. It is, at one and the same time, in the line of traditional

Russian culture (or, as appropriate, the cultures of the various non-Russian areas) and in the line of urban culture of other non-socialist developed countries.

CHAPTER 2

"The City of Socialist Man"

If the centuries leading up to the October Revolution bequeathed a series of physical and human conditions to the urban areas of the new State, these legacies did not necessarily carry much influence in the planning thought of the immediately post-Revolutionary period. For almost everyone, it was a time when all things were new, or at all events were to be made new. If Russian town planning had a history going back at least to Peter the Great, now the State found itself responsible not just for urban layout, but for every aspect of urbanization and urban life, for the care of the process of urbanization and for the development of the layout and functioning of each individual town. At the same time, although the new Soviet State inherited a population overwhelmingly rural in location, lifestyle and attitude of mind, the Revolution gave primacy to the town and to its inhabitants. They, after all, had been the principal actors in making the Revolution and it was on the urban population that the Bolsheviks chiefly depended for their support, more especially after the peasants had adopted the slogan "All land to the peasants" as meaning their private ownership, and after the sailors of Kronshtadt had risen in revolt. Significantly, when in due time the Soviets began to restructure the old administrative network of *guberniya* and *uyezd* (province and district) into the present system of *oblast'* and *rayon*, it was laid down that every oblast should have its proletarian urban centre. The practical political reliance on the town proletariat reinforced the Marxist attitudes towards the inequality and backwardness of rural life; the Marxist requirement to abolish the distinction between town and country meant essentially raising rural living standards to those of urban areas.

The first steps, which laid a basis for the assumption of State responsibility for towns, followed on the morrow of the October Revolution on 28 October 1917 (OS), when all land was nationalized. This was followed up by a further law on the socialization of land on 18 February 1918 and by a decree on 20 August 1918 taking all urban property into the hands of the State or local authorities. Large houses of the rich and the bourgeoisie, and empty houses, were commandeered and subdivided into apartments and rooms for the proletariat, bringing about at least some immediate amelioration of the chronic cramped living conditions. Except in the larger cities, the improvement was limited and the average amount of living space per urban dweller rose only from $6.3\,m^2$ in 1913 to $6.4\,m^2$ in 1923 (Andrusz 1984: 17). As early as April 1918, an Architectural Studio was set up for the replanning of the centre and outskirts of Moscow (Glushkova & Fedorov 1986: 139).

However, the chaos of the Civil War period and War Communism did not permit any practical measures of town planning or development to be taken at that time. Labour was engaged in the armed struggle, and resources were desperately scarce; but, even if labour and resources had been available, no-one yet knew what should be constructed. Until Gosplan was established in 1921, there was no plenipotentiary organization to draw up and implement plans. Thus, the first stage in the story of urban development in the Soviet Union was a consideration of what should be planned, what in fact should be "the City of Socialist Man". In the words of one of the leading figures in the discussions, L. M. ("El") Lissitskiy (also transliterated as Lissitzky), "to determine the direction in which the housing of a socialistic society should develop . . . represents one of the central tasks in the reconstruction of our architecture" (Lissitzky 1984: 42). The group of Constructivist architects, OSA (Association of Contemporary Architects), declared that, "Modern architecture must crystallize the new socialist way of life" (Khan-Magomedov 1983: 347).

The fierce and wide-ranging debate on the nature of the new city was to last into the early 1930s. Although the discussion was then abruptly and dismissively terminated by Stalin, it did succeed in evolving a number of principles and, perhaps more importantly, attitudes of mind, which became deeply embedded in Soviet town planning thought ever since. The 1920s saw the affirmation of the concept of *planning* a city for socialism, a concept accepted as fundamental throughout the Soviet period.

Sources of influence – architectural and planning movements

The architects and planners, who devoted themselves to consideration of the future environment of work and life in the new society, were by any standards an unusual, talented and imaginative group. They sought new concepts, explored new techniques. Nevertheless, their ideas emerged out of antecedents in urban and social planning and were influenced by developments that had already taken place in political, economic and sociological thought and in technological advance.

The concepts and principles of the new social order more often than not derived, or were believed to derive, from the principles of Marxist doctrine. In the words of Aleksey Gan, author of *Constructivism* (1922), "Constructivism . . . is actively and consciously fighting for communism" (Cooke 1983: 36). Milyutin (also transliterated as Miliutin) was a party member before the revolution. Hannes Meyer was a sufficiently committed follower of the party to be able to accept the Stalinist diktats after 1931, even in contradiction to his own earlier concepts (Richardson 1991: 121). Often enough, however, the inspiring concept was not so much Marxism as revolution in and for itself. At the same time, the making of a new social order was paralleled by the availability of new building materials, especially concrete and glass.

For a number of people the past was a significant negative influence, simply engendering a reaction against what had gone before. Inevitably, the Revolution expressed a revulsion from the Tsarist city, with its social inequalities, its poverty and the dreadful living conditions of so many of the working classes. For some, the reaction against the previous social order meant the rejection of all its aspects, including even the family as the basic unit of society. Equally, in bricks and mortar, many turned away from the flamboyant traditionalist architecture of the Revivalist movement and from the bourgeois "Style Moderne", which seemed to them to epitomize the old regime. Not all, however, rejected the recent past. Some of those building neoclassical houses for rich merchants before 1917, such as I. V. Zholtovskiy, were later in the Soviet period to become increasingly influential, as the rise of Stalin brought about a swing away from the avant-garde back to a version of classicism.

Starr has rightly pointed out that town planning must not be seen as only beginning in 1917 and even the architects of the traditional neoclassical and baroque schools had drawn up plans for a new St Petersburg (Starr 1976: 227–8) and, although nothing came of them, the concepts of planning and laying out *de novo* were already enunciated.

Initially, as one would expect, it was the more radical ideas of the pre-revolutionary period that most inspired the planners of the Soviet city, and none more so than those of Ebenezer Howard and the Garden City movement. Howard's influence had already reached Russia before the Revolution. His book, *Tomorrow: a peaceful path to real reform* (first published in 1898 and later re-issued as *Garden cities of tomorrow*), was translated into Russian and a Russian branch of the International Garden City Society was set up in St Petersburg in 1913. Although the branch lapsed in the aftermath of the Revolution, significantly it was refounded in Moscow in 1922 (ibid.: 236). The reformist nature of Howard's proposals obviously held great appeal among revolutionary groups, but the link was made much closer by the association between Howard and the revolutionary Prince Petr Kropotkin (ibid.: 230–35). Howard's view that "Town and country *must be married, and out of this union will spring a new hope, a new life, a new civilization*" (Howard 1965: 48) expressed in effect the prime Marxist aim of abolishing the distinction between town and country. Howard also saw his proposed new type of urban environment as bringing about social change. His Garden City, as a Soviet city would have to be, was a planned entity: "The essential thing is that before a sod is cut, or a brick laid, the town must in its broad outlines be properly planned" (Macfadyen 1970: 160). Moreover, Howard believed that planning *ab initio* would be more effective than attempting to adapt old cities (ibid.: 33).

The emphasis of the Garden City movement on space and greenery for psychological and physical health was to become common ground to all the participants in the 1920s debates and to remain so in Soviet planning thereafter. When in the early 1920s the People's Commissariat for Internal Affairs issued a set of "Rules for planning and building towns", they ordered that a tenth of the residential area be left for parks and that every dwelling must be within 2000 feet of a park (Bliznakov 1976: 245).

31

Starts had been made to build garden cities before the Revolution, notably the Kaiserwald suburb of Riga in 1911 and, flagship of the movement, the railway workers' dormitory of Prozorovka on the Moscow–Kazan' Railway outside Moscow. The designer of Prozorovka, V. N. Semenov, was later to be in charge of drawing up Moscow's first officially adopted General Plan in 1935. Various other schemes incorporating garden city principles were drawn up, if not implemented, in the period before the Revolution.

After the Revolution, in 1922 a garden city for 500 people was proposed near Moscow. In various cities, workers' cooperatives designed and built garden city suburbs – in 1924–5 for Tver' (sometime Kalinin), Ivanovo and Bryansk (Miliutin 1974: 4–5). Other places where such efforts were started included Vologda, Nizhniy Novgorod (sometime Gor'kiy), Saratov and Shcheglovsk in Siberia (Khan-Magomedov 1983: 273). K. Karasov designed a "Red Garden City" for the Istomin Cotton Mill near Smolensk, modelled on pre-revolutionary Prozorovka (Starr 1976: 236).

If the ideas of Ebenezer Howard were the most widely influential, there were other architects and planners whose concepts were eagerly taken up by some, if not all, the post-revolutionary planners, for example Frank Lloyd Wright in America and Soria y Mata with his *ciudad lineal* in Spain. Not only in the USSR but around the world, exciting and radical new approaches were being proposed and tried. In Germany during the 1920s, the Bauhaus group headed by Walter Gropius flourished, first in Weimar, then after 1925 in Dessau, and finally in Berlin; its Russian links were close and included the Suprematist painter Malevich. Architects influenced by the Bauhaus went to the Soviet Union to participate in building the socialist city, notably the Swiss Hannes Meyer and the Germans Ernst May and Bruno Taut, the last of whom had designed large-scale housing complexes in Germany, described by Commissar Lunacharskiy as "built socialism" (Kopp 1990: 180). Mies van der Rohe exhibited at the first exhibition in Moscow of the Constructivist group at VKhUTEMAS (the Higher Art and Technical Studios). From France, le Corbusier came to the USSR three times between 1928 and 1930 to play an active role in the debate and, perhaps more than anyone, to turn its thinking into architectural realities in the world at large. For him, Moscow was "a factory of ideas, a promised land for specialists" (Ikonnikov 1988: 117).

Art, sculpture and architecture

The participants in the debate were not just architects and planners; perhaps primarily, they were artists and sculptors. Commonly enough, the one individual played all four roles. They moved easily between two and three dimensions, drew no distinction between artistic creation and practical design, and were not merely committed to social, usually socialist, change, but felt a sense of duty to bring about such change.

Not surprisingly under such circumstances, quite as important perhaps as the ideas of the social planners such as Howard were the preceding trends in the creative arts. Ikonnikov (1988: 79) refers to the influence of Piranesi and there can be no doubt that, among others, Golosov's design for a columbarium (Khan-Magomedov 1983: 94) was taken directly from Piranesi's "Carceri" series of engravings. One might well see a beginning with the Futurist group and with Sant Elia's "New City"; after all, Mayakovskiy's painting entitled "Self-portrait" is a pattern of interlocking multi-storey houses (exhibited in London in 1989; Elliot & Dudakov 1989: 115). But of immediate and direct importance was the UNOVIS (Affirmers of New Art) group, centred in Vitebsk; it was led by Malevich and the Suprematists who brought into sharp focus the concept that creative art and practical design for living were inseparable. Perhaps best known of the group in the town planning context was El Lissitskiy, author of *Russia: an architecture for world revolution*. He, with Vladimir Tatlin (most famous for his 1919–20 design of a colossal monument to the Third International, which never progressed beyond the stage of a model) and Aleksandr Vesnin, led the way from Suprematism to Constructivism, where the barriers between art and practice to all intents and purposes entirely vanished. As the name of the group implies, its members were not concerned with representation by art, but with construction. For them, it was the same people who expressed forms and patterns in art and then used them for practical buildings and city plans.

Malevich's famous painting of about 1915, "Black Square", reappears in many Constructivist paintings, for example in Lyubov Popova's "Pictorial architectonics" of 1916 (exhibited in London 1989; ibid. 1989: 117). The title of this painting underlines the links between artistic creations and planning and building designs. Even more directly, so does Lissitskiy's picture, "Proun (City)" of 1920–21, which embodied Malevich's "Black Square" and which was intended, as were Lissitskiy's other "Prouns", as a design for use in architecture (Khan-Magomedov 1983: 31–2).

It might be claimed that, for all their intent, these designs were only two-dimensional paper or canvas expressions. This was not true of Lissitskiy's "Prouns", nor could it be said of Malevich's "Arkhitekton" series, three-dimensional models intended to express volumes, shapes and buildings; the influence of these "Arkhitektons" can be clearly and frequently seen throughout the work of the 1920s. It is but a short step from Malevich's "Planit" dwelling to Khidekel's building design (ibid.: 765, 766). Malevich strongly influenced the artist and architect I. I. Leonidov, especially in his 1928 design for a film studio in Moscow (Shvidkovskiy 1971: 126).

Similarly, the engineering-like "Spatial Constructions" of Stenberg and Klutsis inspired designs for factories and hydroelectric plants. Ladovskiy's drawing, "An example of a composed structure" could well be an inspiration for Lissitskiy's 1922 design for a restaurant on a cliff or for M. Korshev's 1926 sectional drawing of a stadium grandstand (Lissitzky 1984: 77, 47). In Lissitskiy's words, "'engineer' equals 'architect'" (ibid.: 70). Lissitskiy's own "Prouns" have been described by Khan-Magomedov as "a symbiosis between painting and architecture" (Shvidkovskiy 1971: 10).

Gradually, from the welter of ideas, dreams, experiments, models, drawings and paintings, there emerged concepts and designs for actual buildings and, by the late 1920s, specific plans for towns. In particular, the artistic works emphasized certain geometries, which were utilized, not only in designing new buildings, but also in laying out city plans, although this echo of the eighteenth century's "ideal" city was scarcely acknowledged as such. The circle, glowing vividly in Klyun's paintings, was favoured in much of the architecture of Melnikov, including his own house in Moscow, which was of a double, interlocking drum shape; it appears in Grinberg's 1930 scheme for a House of Soviets in Nizhniy Novgorod (Gor'kiy), in many other Constructivist buildings, in T. Varentsov's design for a ring and radial town (ibid.: 77) and, superlatively, in Shestakov's plan for a Greater Moscow, which extended Moscow's pre-existing ring and radial pattern outwards on a colossal scale.

So too, the parabola, which defined Bunin's 1930 house design and Ginzburg's third-round entry in the Palace of Soviets competition, appeared in Krutikov's concept of "The Flying City" and above all in Ladovskiy's basic plan for a town, later worked up as a plan for the open-ended growth of Moscow to the northwest. Ladovskiy's parabola was subsequently to be taken up by Constantinos Doxiades in his Dynapolis (ibid.). At times, circle and parabola might be combined, as in Ginzburg's 1933 design for the Nemirovich–Donchenko theatre (Khan-Magomedov 1987: 471).

The form that appeared most frequently in the creations and concepts of the time was the linear pattern, whether in Rozanova's painting "Untitled (Green Stripe)" of 1917, Klutsis' "Construction" of 1922–3 (Lodder 1983: 27, 29), or in the many linear buildings, such as Khidekel's design in 1927 for a collective dwelling or the 1931 project by Afanas'yev, Kornfeld and Milinis for a House of Industry in Sverdlovsk (Khan-Magomedov 1987: 223, 430). A fundamental expression of linearity in the new society was the factory assembly line, where work was collective and where the building needed to be linear to accommodate the line. Ultimately, the linear pattern culminated in the linear city designs of Lavrov and Milyutin, in the latter case finding at least some concrete expression in the towns of Volgograd (originally Tsaritsyn, sometime Stalingrad) and Magnitogorsk.

This last point reminds one that, in addition to the influences of art and sculpture, there was yet another set of factors which powerfully affected the architects and planners – those things that were "new" and therefore apt for the new world about to be created. The automated factory assembly line was only one of many developments of engineering and science that had to be reflected in the design of buildings and cities. There were the new forms of transport made possible by the internal combustion engine: the car, or preferably the collective omnibus, and the aeroplane. The relatively "new" means of communication, the radio, appears in innumerable architectural schemes; for example, the Vesnin brothers' preliminary scheme for the Palace of Labour competition was topped by an elaborate radio aerial network which formed an integral part of the design (Khan-Magomedov 1986: 116–27). Electricity was the relatively "new" power and designs for power stations included the overhead high-tension cables as elements in the overall aesthetic theme. But it was above all the exploitation of the possibilities of the new building materials, concrete and glass, that led architects to incorporate curves rather than right-angled corners into their buildings, to the point where circles, drums and curved corners (often of glass) are well nigh infallible indicators of a Constructivist building (Fig. 2.1).

Figure 2.1 Constructivist architecture: the Zuyev Club, Moscow, designed in 1929 by I. Golosov.

The great debates

If the architects and planners shared common ancestries or sources of inspiration, their ideas of how to proceed varied very widely. The decade of the 1920s was marked by endless discussion and controversy. Many Western commentators (Bater 1980: 22) have seen these debates as between two clear and opposed "schools" of planning, "Urbanist" and "Disurbanist". Although there is some truth in this as a simplifying clarification, the reality was far more complex, with much overlapping of views and cross-relationships between the many groups.

The first great set of arguments arose in 1922–3 over the concept of the "Green City". The adherents of this idea were, not surprisingly, those most strongly influenced by Garden City theories. For them, the use of greenery, the conservation of natural areas and the rejection of geometric patterns were part of the overall vision of the "natural beauty of a town" (Khan-Magomedov 1983: 274). The development of more flexible, yet fast, forms of public transport – primarily the motor bus – not only was an expression of the all-embracing modernity and technical advance of the coming new world, but also in practical terms obviated the need to concentrate population in close juxtaposition to places of work. Towns would be small, not over 32000 population (a figure deriving from Howard), and linked to central administrative towns not over 58000. People would usually live in small individual cottages. In 1923, Markovnikov commenced construction of a "village" suburb of such cottages in the Sokol district of Moscow. One of those most influenced by Garden City ideas was the German architect Ernst May, who devised a plan that kept only the inner core of Moscow within the Garden Ring and replaced the rest of the city with a dispersed scattering of small satellite garden cities (Kirillov 1976: 235–7).

At its extreme, some members of this school of thought saw the achievement of the Marxian goal of abolishing the difference between town and country through the total disappearance of the town as it had existed – the group known as the Disurbanists or Deurbanists. They envisaged people living in an ultimate form of ribbon development along roads through the countryside, with public bus services taking them to work in nodes of employment at road junctions.

One of the leaders of the Disurbanist school was M. Okhitovich. He planned triangles, with factories at the apices, with dwellings along the sides of the triangles, bordering park strips; agriculture or extractive industry occupied the centre of the triangle (Fig. 2.2). His plan for Magnitogorsk in 1930 called for eight rib-

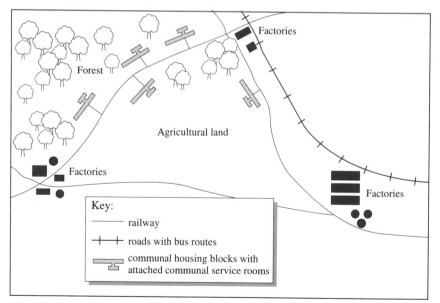

Figure 2.2 The Disurbanist city: Okhitivich's concept.

bons, each 25 km long, converging on the metallurgical plant (Khan-Magomedov 1983: 335). The outstanding figure among the Disurbanists was M. Ya. Ginzburg. He envisaged all Moscow's population and factories gradually being moved out, leaving only the old historic core as an administrative centre, set amid parks. The population would be resettled in long zones of new communal houses through forests, with bus stations at regular intervals and zones of services, recreation and sport. The slogan "Not greenery in the town, but the town in green plantations" (Kirillov 1976: 222) was the inspiration for his entry, with M. Barshch, in the 1930 competition for "Green City", where they proposed a line of houses in forest to the northeast of Moscow.

Extreme, even fanciful, as some of the Disurbanist views might seem, Khan-Magomedov (1983: 272) makes the very pertinent point that the colossal shrinkage of urban population during the period of the Revolution and Civil War, as people fled back to their family villages in the hope of finding food supplies and stability, gave a not unreasonable impression of the fragmentation or even approaching disappearance of large cities.

Generally opposed to the Disurbanists was the group which Bater (1980: 22–3) and others describe as "urbanist" and which is often referred to as the "Sotsgorod" (Socialist Town) group, from their own name for the ideal city they sought to achieve. This "communal" group embraced many of the outstanding architects of the time, including the brothers Viktor, Leonid and Aleksandr Vesnin, the brothers Panteleymon and Il'ya Golosov and, as leader of the group, Leonid Sabsovich. This set did not expect towns to disappear entirely, although they did believe that towns should be small and generously endowed with greenery. In 1928–30, Sabsovich produced his design for a compact, communalized Sotsgorod, focused on a large industrial enterprise or even a state farm, with a norm of 40 000–50 000, at the very most 80 000–100 000, population (Khan-Magomedov 1983: 284).

Most of the "urbanists" believed in the break-up of the family unit and its replacement by communal living, but this in fact was a belief held equally widely by proponents of Green City and the Disurbanists. Whether in towns or in individual buildings along roads through the countryside, the ideal house of the future would comprise separate sleeping units, or "cells", in buildings accommodating in some schemes up to 2000 people; under the same roof or in separate buildings would be communal kitchens and eating halls (Lissitskiy's "mechanized superkitchens"), separate crèches, kindergartens and schools for the nurture of the young, and separate houses for the care of the aged and incapable. Extreme proponents of communal living, like Kuzmin, planned that the life of each age group would be separately and precisely regulated, minute by minute through the day (ibid.: 389). Competitions were held for designs for communal houses, for Khar'kov in 1924–5, for Moscow in 1925–6, and for Leningrad in 1930.

From the concept of the communal house developed the "superblock", a grouping of four- to six-storey blocks of flats arranged around a quadrangle; this was used frequently for housing during the five year plans before the Second World War, although without the originally envisaged features of communal living. In its turn, the "superblock" led to the concept of the *mikrorayon*, the microregion. This concept was elaborated considerably later in 1961 by Academician S. G. Strumilin in the period of vast expansion of housing under Khrushchev. Frolic (1964) has given a full account of Strumilin's iteration of the microregion idea and it is interesting to see that Strumilin was still envisaging it as based on communal living, at a date when the family was acknowledged as the basic unit of society and when, indeed, microregions based on family units were actually under construction. In this context Strumilin can be considered a "throwback" to the 1920s period, and his description of the ideal microregion reflects the concepts of that earlier period. In brief, the microregion expanded the communal house into neighbourhood units of communal housing blocks, together with all the services needed for communal life.

Further expressions of communality were the ideas of standardization of buildings, building techniques and materials; such ideas were said to be derived from the traditional standard wooden house of Russia (Lissitzky 1984: 35). Whether that was so or not, they were the forerunners of the standardized prefabricated techniques of the 1960s and later.

Throughout the 1920s the debates continued. New groups and subdivisions of groups were constantly forming and re-forming in a kaleidoscope of acronyms. In addition to the original UNOVIS in Vitebsk, in 1918 two early, rather traditionalist foci were the Moscow and Leningrad Associations of Architects (MAO and LAO). In 1920 appeared the Higher Art and Technical Studios (VKhUTEMAS). From the latter in 1926 until 1930 there developed VKhUTEIN (the Higher Art and Technical Institute). The faculty of VKhUTEMAS was a roll-call of the leading figures in the disputations and included A. Vesnin, M. Ginzburg, I. Golosov, I. Zholtovskiy, N. Ladovskiy and A. Shchusev (Shvidkovskiy 1971: 31–5).

In 1923 Ladovskiy, leader of the Rationalist group, which laid stress on new building materials and techniques, founded the Association of New Architects, ASNOVA, but only five years later he and others broke away to form the Association of Urban Architects (ARU). Meanwhile, the Constructivists Ginzburg and the Vesnins had established the Association of Contemporary Architects (OSA). Opposed to OSA was the traditionalist All-Russian Union of Proletarian Architects (VOPRA) (ibid.: 21–4).

The multiplicity of associations and the cross-currents of ideas and conflicting theories created a vitality and vigour in the debate, which still comes through to us today. So too does the sense of excitement. All participants shared Lissitskiy's "unshakeable confidence in the future" (Lissitzky 1984: 59) and all shared, as they did with their Bauhaus colleagues in Germany, the belief that they were free to devise the City of Socialist Man. The State, which in any case was to wither away as communism was achieved, was merely the enabler. All believed that the new city that was to arise would of itself bring about social engineering and the desired society. In Milyutin's words, "The new way of life must be born as a natural result of the new organization of labor and housing" (Miliutin 1974: 79).

Equally, they all shared belief in the appropriateness and symbolism of new construction materials and, above all, in the power of new technology to fulfil their wildest imaginings. Chernikhov wished to celebrate its triumph in his Palace of the Wonders of Technology, designed as an inverted pyramid (Cooke 1983: 69). Technology would free the planners from all constraints. Lissitskiy declared, "Reality will surpass the most daring prophecies" (Lissitzky 1984: 62). Beyond question, imagination was boundless. Lavinskiy conceived a "City on Springs" to reduce the vibration of traffic, while Malevich's "cosmic city", floating in space, was taken up by Krutikov in his "Flying City". Lissitskiy foresaw "the conquest of gravity as such" and asserted that the task of technology was "to make sure that all these elementary volumes that produce new relationships and tensions in space will be structurally safe" (ibid.: 66). His own scheme envisaged "horizontal sky-scrapers" (sometimes translated as "skyhooks") resting on vertical building shafts and forming, as it were, a second layer above Moscow's major street intersections. Little wonder that, when Commissar Lunacharskiy visited VKhUTEIN in 1928, he should comment that the young "already dream of the city as it will be in fifty years time, but how they do dream!" (Khan-Magomedov 1983: 282).

The fervour of the arguments was kept going by the many competitions launched by the various architectural and other bodies, all of which attracted innumerable entries. In 1922–3 the competition for a Palace of Labour in Moscow brought entries from the Vesnins, Ginzburg and Golosov. The latter two also submitted entries for the House of Textiles competition in 1925–6. In 1930 the competition for "Green City" evoked, as we have seen, a major entry from the leader of the Disurbanists, Ginzburg, as well as others from Ladovskiy and Melnikov. The 1928 competition for the Central Trade Union Building was exceptional, in that the winner, le Corbusier, actually saw his design built. A number of competitions focused on the design of a communal living house.

Perhaps greatest of all the competitions were, first, for the Soviet pavilion at the 1925 Paris Exhibition, which evoked many imaginative entries and did much to convey the excitement of the time to a world audience, and, secondly, the last of them all, in 1929–32, for a central showpiece of the new regime, a Palace of Soviets in Moscow, to occupy the site of the former Metropolitan Spasskiy Cathedral. Most of the leading architects, including Ladovskiy and le Corbusier, submitted entries.

Increasingly, as time went on, there was acrimony between the various opposed groups. In a letter to Ginzburg, le Corbusier referred to the Disurbanist view as a "false interpretation of Lenin's principle" and said, "THE FACTS WILL NOT ALLOW THIS TO BE DONE" (his capitals; Kopp 1967: 305). Considerably harder things were said by the VOPRA group about Constructivists and Rationalists alike. But, in addition to all the shared concepts, there were compromise and intermediate positions and, often enough, collaborations. M. Barshch, a leading advocate of communal living, collaborated with the leading Disurbanist, Ginzburg, in their entry for Green City.

In particular, the concept of the linear city is generally seen as intermediate between "disurbanism" and "Sotsgorod". N. A. Milyutin, the outstanding propo-

nent of the linear city, declared that, "there can be no controversy about urbanization or deurbanization" (Miliutin 1974: 60) and the linear principle itself was
equally characteristic of the Disurbanists. In 1930, I. I. Leonidov came up with
"Magnitogorye", a linear plan for Magnitogorsk in which a central residential strip
of buildings of various heights included a series of high-rise tower blocks (Kirillov
1976: 224–7). Milyutin's famous scheme of parallel strips of residence and factories, separated by an amenity green belt, was based on theoretical concepts of the
new town as producer: "If the pivot for capitalist economy is the market and its
laws, then the pivot for socialist economy must be production and its planning"
(Miliutin 1974: 62). For him, the fundamental planning principle was the assembly line – "a flowing functional assembly line system is the absolutely necessary
basis for new planning" (ibid.: 65). The zone of industry within the linear town
would reflect production, as plants involved in primary production, in processing
raw materials, secondary working and finishing lay in sequence along the longi-
tudinal rail link (Lubetkin 1933: 71). This therefore determined the linear layout
of the city, although not necessarily in straight lines but in linear zones adjusted to
local topography (Fig. 2.3).

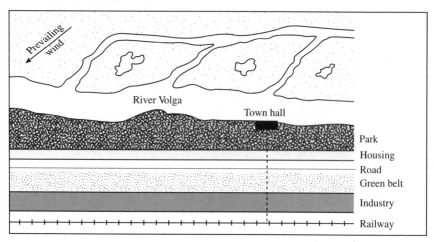

Figure 2.3 The linear city: Milyutin's design for Stalingrad (now Volgograd).

If Milyutin's Sotsgorod was first a centre of production, it also must be constructed so as to optimize the living conditions of the workers. The parallel strips
would allow short, easy movement on foot between residence and work, through
the intervening green belt at least 500 m wide. Social buildings, clubs and sporting
facilities would lie on the far side of the housing belt from the factories, but technical colleges would be located near the relevant factories to allow sharing of lab-
oratories and workshops (Lubetkin 1933: 71). Housing would be placed up wind
of the factories and their pollution. Every dwelling should have access to sunlight
and should look out onto forest, field or water (Miliutin 1974: 80).

Milyutin believed that communal living should characterize the linear city;

"the present influence of the family on upbringing must be gradually replaced by the influence of the collective" (ibid.: 66). This, *inter alia*, would free women from domestic drudgery. He recognized the importance of greenery, expressed in his plans by the buffer zone of trees between houses and work-places and by the parallel zone of parks and open spaces beside the housing zone. Yet he rejected the ideas of the Garden City, which "in spite of all their alluring qualities, are a pure, and what's more, evil Utopia, creating the illusion (false representation) of a possible escape from the situation without doing away with the capitalist system" (ibid.: 54).

The flexibility of Milyutin's scheme, allowing as it did both Urbanist and Disurbanist variants, caused it to be the concept that came closest to being given expression in reality. Milyutin's city, in its ideological content and in its practicality, appealed to Ladovskiy and the Rationalist group at ARU, one of whom, V. Lavrov, also designed a linear town. Ladovskiy's own 1927 plan for Kostino near Moscow used three zones of industry, housing and park. This design he worked up first in a parabolic form which he then adapted for the open-ended development of Moscow to the northwest. The central axis of the Leningrad Highway, which formed a service core, was flanked on either side by zones of housing, in their turn flanked on the outside by industrial zones, with a green belt in between. Outside the industrial zones lay agricultural land.

A plan for Moscow, drawn up by the VOPRA group headed by S. N. Gornyy, was vaguely linear, in that all industry lay northeast, down wind of a northwest–southeast railway axis, while housing spread in a gridiron pattern to the southwest; the central area within the Boulevard Ring was retained as a cultural and administrative centre (Kirillov 1976: 233–4).

Another plan, which substituted a ring and radial pattern for the linear, was the vast project put forward for Moscow in 1925 by S. S. Shestakov, who assumed that Moscow as centre of the new world order would become the largest city in the world. Beyond the existing ring and radial city were to be two huge industrial areas to northwest and southeast; beyond these would be four even larger residential zones to north, south, east and west, separated and surrounded by tracts of forest and farmland. Colossal as this scheme was, it was only part of a plan that covered the whole of Moscow Oblast and included a double ring of new satellite towns (Kirillov 1976: 217–20).

The end of the debate

By the time that Milyutin and others were designing the linear city, surely the most practical of all the many proposals of the period, the political and economic environment was already changing rapidly. Stalin was firmly in control and in 1928, two years before Milyutin promulgated his Sotsgorod, the First Five Year Plan had begun. Already hundreds of new towns and settlements of town type were rising on greenfield sites beside new sources of raw materials, while in existing towns new factories were pulling in ever larger numbers of migrants from rural areas. There was no longer any reality in fostering the dissolution of urban areas. A decade of discussions and arguments had produced no blueprint for the city of the future, but the need was immediate. For example, in Kuznetsk, the heart of the newly developing Kuzbass coalmining and heavy metallurgical region, in 1931 after three years of the Plan there were still 2500 people living in clay huts and only four bathhouses for the total population of 70000 (Lubetkin 1933: 73). In Magnitogorsk, thousands were living for the early years in tents, even through the bitter winters.

Time had run out and there had been failure to achieve results. Ginzburg commented in 1928 that "a great number of new buildings do not satisfy present requirements and thus have to be classified as failures" (Lissitzky 1984: 156). In fairness, much of the failure to produce solid results can be attributed to the disturbed times, to the lack of organization with the retreat of centralized control during the NEP (New Economic Policy) period, and to the shortages of readily available materials.

Moreover, Stalin was above all a political realist and if on the one hand he had urgent goals in building up military strength, on the other it is highly unlikely that he had the faintest belief in the ability of architecture and planning to achieve social engineering; after all, one could not unreasonably argue that such a belief is a version of environmental determinism, anathema to Marxism–Leninism. By 1930, the architects were coming under attack. On 16 May 1930, Sabsovich, a leader of the communal Sotsgorod group, was criticized by name in a resolution of the Party Central Committee which described his plans as "quite baseless, half-fantastic, therefore extremely dangerous experimental efforts" (Miliutin 1984: 124).

In 1931 at the June Plenum of the Central Committee, Stalin and Kaganovich completed the assault. Shestakov, Sabsovich and Milyutin were all singled out for criticism. Kaganovich said of Shestakov's plan for Moscow that it was "a mere paper plan drawn up without any regard for economic and social conditions" (Miliutin 1984: 10). Sabsovich's proposition (for houses to accommodate 2000–3000 people) was "absurd and impossible" (Kaganovich, n.d.: 86). The ideas of the City of Socialist Man were rejected as Utopian; the cities of the USSR, it was averred, were socialist by virtue of their take-over by the Communist Party.

Kaganovich (ibid. 82) poured contempt on the theorists, "There are at present many who decline in every possible declension the formula 'we must build a socialist city'. They forget one little trifle: that the cities of the USSR already are socialist cities. Our cities became socialist from the very moment of the October Revolution, when we expropriated the bourgeoisie and socialized the means of production." Those who had advocated communal living were designated "leftists" who "advocate the artificial implantation of the domestic commune, the compulsory liquidation of the individual kitchen, etc." (ibid.: 85).

In 1932, final mopping-up operations were completed. A decree of 14 July specified the type of housing to be built – in separate family apartments (Blizna-kov 1976: 249). All the various groups were wound up and incorporated into a single government-controlled Union of Artists, which set about the imposition of socialist realism throughout the creative arts (Shvidkovskiy 1971: 181). A government body, ARPLAN, was established by Kaganovich to approve all master plans (Bliznakov 1976: 253). Architects such as le Corbusier left the USSR while others like Milyutin recanted. It is instructive to compare Grinberg's 1931 model for a theatre in Novosibirsk with the one he actually built, which overlaid the simplicities of the original structure with elaborate neoclassical decoration including a huge portico (Khan-Magomedov 1983: 467). The many exciting and imaginative plans submitted for the competition to design the Palace of Soviets in Moscow were passed over in favour of a grandiose and ponderous 300m high neoclassical tower topped by a 75m statue of Lenin. Seemingly this was designed chiefly to overtop the capitalist Empire State Building in New York. Mercifully, it was never constructed and the site, formerly that of the Saviour Cathedral, is today occupied by a huge open-air swimming pool.

The bringing down of the axe by Stalin and Kaganovich was ruthless. Yet there was more than a grain of truth in their charge of Utopianism, even if one disregards the more *outré* visions of cities on springs and flying cities. Far too many schemes were based on *ab initio* planning; perhaps one might see in this the influence of the painter, who starts with a blank canvas. As Lissitskiy commented, the plans were "intended for a flat terrain" (Lissitzky 1984: 60). Le Corbusier's plan for Moscow (1930) involved the wiping away of the entire existing city except the Kremlin, to be replaced by his "town as machine for living", an ideal geometrically patterned city of skyscraper blocks (Kirillov 1976: 231).

Certainly, many if not most of the theoreticians assumed a new society and made little or no effort to understand the working of social groups in reality. The facile rejection of the family was a supreme example of such disregard. Of all the bodies, only the Rationalist ARU of Ladovskiy made some efforts in this direction with the establishment of a "psychotechnical laboratory". As Ernst May acknowledged, "It is no secret that the great majority of the Russian working class rejects the collective dwelling" (Lissitzky 1984: 187). It is scarcely surprising that it should do so; Kuzmin's communal plan, in which the lives of the inhabitants were regulated by the minute, is frighteningly reminiscent of Aldous Huxley's *Brave new world*.

The achievements of the period

The 1920s saw little enough of the theory turned into real buildings and even less into accomplished town plans. Nevertheless, enough was done for Kopp (1967: 279) to sum up the 1920s as "a period when, in less than ten years, all the ideas, which have nourished contemporary architecture, were put forward, where innumerable projects saw light of day and when a not insignificant number of build-ings – some remarkable – were erected in spite of poor technical and material conditions." Most of the architects did design and carry through actual buildings. Perhaps not surprisingly, the largest number of Constructivist buildings are in Moscow. Its re-assumption of the role of capital in 1918 made it the main focus of activities of all sorts and also created a strong demand for new offices to house its new or re-acquired functions. Leningrad (St Petersburg), with ministries and ancillary activities moving out, had a surplus of public buildings.

In Moscow the combination of the desire to improve facilities for the workers and the belief in communal activity led to the building of a number of Construc-tivist clubs, Houses of Culture and Palaces of Workers. Leading examples include the Rusakov Club by Melnikov, who put up in all five clubs for the capital, and the Zuyev Club, built by Golosov. Other cities too acquired new clubs. Other buildings intended for the communal social life were schools, public baths, depart-ment stores (including one by the Vesnins for Moscow's Krasnaya Presnya dis-trict) and mass kitchens.

New office blocks were needed for the ministries and government departments moving into the new capital, and housing for their personnel. Prominent among these were the Narkomfin Building to house workers in the People's Commis-sariat of Finance, and le Corbusier's "Tsentrosoyuz" House of Trade Unions (Fig. 2.4). G. Barkhin in 1925–7 designed the new offices for the newspaper *Izvestiya*, while Panteleymon Golosov produced the *Pravda* offices in 1930–5. Offices for local Soviets were built for Bryansk in 1924–6 by Grinberg, for Nizhniy Novgorod (Gor'kiy) in 1930 also by Grinberg, for the Narva Gate district of Len-

Figure 2.4 Dom Tsentrosoyuza, Moscow, designed by le Corbusier, 1929–36.

ingrad and for Novosibirsk.

Major government complexes were created in 1929–33 for Minsk, the capital of the new Belorussian SSR, on Lenin Square, and for Khar'kov, the first capital of the new Ukrainian SSR before it was moved to Kiev. This new administrative role for Khar'kov and consequent demand for office space caused the construction of a number of new Constructivist buildings, including the Post Office, the Telephone Building, a Palace of Labour and, in 1925–8, one of the largest and architecturally most famous buildings of the period, the House of State Industry, forming two-thirds of a circle around Dzerzhinskaya Square. Similarly, Alma Ata (formerly Vernyy, now Almaty) as capital of the new Kazakh Republic was given a Government House designed by Ginzburg and a Telephone Building by Gerasimov.

Another town with a number of buildings from this period was Ivanovo–Voznesensk to the east of Moscow. This was one of the textile centres of the Central Industrial Region, which had developed out of estate serf textile workshops and which had never been granted town status before the Revolution. With a population of 111 000 (in 1926), its urban status was acknowledged and new buildings were put up, including a collective house by Golosov, a bank by Viktor Vesnin and a combined theatre and circus. In the Urals, the old metallurgical city of Yekaterinburg (sometime Sverdlovsk) was rapidly expanding and it too has a number of Constructivist buildings in the city centre.

In relation to the great effort made by the architects to design the ideal house for the new society and the countless plans that were drawn up, comparatively few housing blocks and complexes were erected and most of those were in Moscow. Best known is Boris Iofan's building on Bersenevskaya Naberezhnaya (1928–30), immortalized by Trifonov in his novel *The house on the embankment* (Fig. 2.5); this huge complex included shops, a theatre and the subsequently named "Shockworker" cinema. Lying across the river from the Kremlin, it became a house for the privileged and, for a time, its theatre was used for sessions of the Supreme Soviet.

Although several estates of houses were built, in only two cases were the concepts of the period put into practice as town plans, and then only very partially. Milyutin's linear city, modified by Ernst May, was used as a basis for the original town plan of Magnitogorsk, the new metallurgical centre in the Urals. The severe constrictions of the site, between the River Ural and nearby hills, made the linear development impossible in reality, and the new town soon spread across the river. Not least of May's problems was that the Soviet government decided on which bank of the River Ural the town should be built after work on the plan had been carried out (Kopp 1990: 196). Milyutin's scheme, modified this time by Vladimir Semenov, was also used for Stalingrad (formerly Tsaritsyn, now Volgograd) on the River Volga. In this case, its growth along the right bank of the Volga has inevitably given the city a linear pattern, although Semenov planned the extended town along the river as four separate *sotsgoroda* or independent linear town complexes (Ikonnikov 1988: 113). However, the Semenov/Milyutin design envisaged the

45

Figure 2.5 "The house on the embankment", by B. M. Iofan, 1928.

housing complexes along the river with the outlook on water and on the upwind side. In practice it was the all-powerful industrial ministries that demanded and got sites along the river, with wharfage facilities. The houses were built down wind to the west. Even after the near-total destruction of the town in the 1942–3 Battle of Stalingrad, the very rapid post-war reconstruction followed the pre-war layout. The present-day Volgograd is in actuality less an expression of Milyutin's concept than a travesty of it.

The heritage of the 1920s in planning

If buildings actually put up were relatively few and the application of town plans almost non-existent, the great debates did articulate or refine a number of principles of planning as a framework for subsequent town development. Even if many of these principles were ignored in practice through the Stalin years, they remained in theory and in the plans conceived. They also spread to other countries and, in the post-Stalin era, they have seen at least some application in the USSR.

Bater (1980: 27–30) has identified ten such principles, as expressed in the 1935 Moscow master plan:

- limited city size
- State control of housing
- planned development of residential areas
- spatial equality in the distribution of items of collective consumption
- limited journey to work

46

- stringent land-use zoning
- rationalized traffic flow
- extensive green space
- symbolism and the central city
- town planning as an integral part of national planning.

However, not all of these are products of the 1920s period and some can be seen as aspects of the same overall principle. Very few of them have been practised to any great extent and none of them has been fully implemented. Moreover, the principles that have been consistently regarded as crucial in theory, if less satisfactorily followed in practice, are those that were derived from earlier theory.

The first, perhaps obvious, principle and one that subsumes the majority of principles listed by Bater, is that a city must be planned, and planned as a whole; this principle derives from Ebenezer Howard, among others. The functions acquired and their developments must be controlled and matched by the planned provision of a labour force and of facilities to give the workers an optimum life-style. This may not have happened to any great extent, but not only was this principle accepted by all the disputants in the 1920s, it was for ever after the fundamental goal of the Soviet city planner and was paid at least lip service by all Soviet political theorists.

Equally derivative and again largely from Howard, but equally universally and continuously accepted, was the principle of creating an aesthetic environment for the physical and mental health of the city dwellers, with an emphasis on greenery and green space. At the time, this reached its peak of expression in the competition for "Green City". To this day no township in the former Soviet Union is so small that it does not have its Park of Culture and Rest. Of all basic tenets, the greening of towns is probably the one that has been most widely and successfully implemented.

The principle of a close relationship in space between residence and workplace – ideally within walking distance – remained firmly in Soviet planning thought, although real life saw this goal recede rather than approach. Planners have continued to call for the length of journeys to work to be reduced, if only to the maximum set by planning norms. To achieve this aim has always meant the juxtaposition of the two main forms of urban land-use, residence and employment, rather than the separation sought by Western town planning or "zoning" regulations, even if the two uses were intended in the Soviet context to be divided by belts of greenery. To the very end of the Soviet era, planners were trying to spread industry and employment throughout urban areas rather than concentrate them in zones away from residences.

Standardization was a generally accepted principle among the architects and planners of the early Soviet period. Some saw it as deriving from the wooden peasant home; all saw it as egalitarian. Subsequently, its justification has been, rather, the greater economies and speed it permits, especially with prefabrication. Standardization of the appearance of buildings at any given moment, right across the vast country, has been the hallmark of Soviet urban development. Another expression of the standardization principle was the legal establishment of planning norms – of space per capita, of levels of provision of every kind of service and of lengths of journey to work.

The principle of a maximum city size certainly lay behind the thinking of everyone in the 1920s. All regarded megalopolis with horror, as the ultimate expression of capitalism (although such anti-metropolitan views were often shared by those in the capitalist world). The idea that towns should not exceed the variously stated maxima of 30000, 50000 or even 100000 people was already a lost cause in the 1920s. It reflected the widespread belief that the socialist town was to be created *ab initio* to replace rather than reconstruct existing towns. As a principle, it continued in later decades to be proclaimed by planners in ever higher figures that trailed hopelessly behind reality, until by the 1980s, or even the 1970s, it had been tacitly allowed to lapse.

The principle of symbolism and the central city, as described by Bater (1980: 29–30), arose in connection with the 1935 master plan for Moscow, supposedly as a contradiction to 1920s ideas. Much of it has been expressed in the universal provision of central squares as venues for the May Day and October Revolution commemorative parades. In fact, one might see this as part of a principle, often unexpressed or not consciously acknowledged, which has persisted without a break from before the Revolution to the present time – what might be termed the principle of "imperialism". The Soviet Union and its capital in Moscow were seen as centres of the coming new world order, as the Tsar and St Petersburg had been of the old Russian Empire.

Lissitskiy did indeed disapprove of the expression of grandeur in the new buildings such as the House of State Industry in Khar'kov and the State Trade Centre and offices of the Supreme Economic Council, in Moscow; he remarked acidly that, "the huge dimensions of these massive buildings are an expression of new power rather than one of new ideas in design" (Lissitzky 1984: 51). Yet he himself subtitled his book "An architecture for world revolution." Shestakov planned the world's largest city; he recognized the imperial principle, even if he did not term it such.

Others, whether they recognized it or not, designed on scales of colossal grandeur. If Chernikhov designed an "Architectural Fantasy – a Gigantic Building" (Khan-Magomedov 1984: 208), architect after architect drew up plans for no less gigantic buildings to be constructed – Tatlin's 400m high "Monument to the Third International", the Vesnins' and Ginzburg's submissions for the Narkomtyazhprom (People's Commissariat for Heavy Industry) building and, above all, nearly all the submissions for the Palace of Soviets competition.

Certainly, the theme of imperial grandeur appealed immensely to Stalin and was put into practice by him, especially after the Second World War, when Moscow emerged as the capital of one of the two world superpowers. His seven massive skyscrapers of Moscow were matched in later Soviet history by the giant Rossiya Hotel and the avenue of skyscrapers along Kalinin Prospect.

If "imperialism" was a principle that survived the turmoil of the 1920s, so was "traditionalism". Although the world at large identifies that period with the Constructivists and Rationalists there were architects who never lost sight of the traditional styles that had preceded the Revolution. On the one hand the Revivalist movement, an expression of Russian nationalism, had sought to adopt what were seen as traditional Russian styles. On the other, there was the classical architecture that had completely dominated Russia from the eighteenth century to 1917. These established, familiar forms were favoured especially by MAO and VOPRA, the members of which saw themselves as expressing popular aspirations and, above all, as Russian. In contrast, the ideas of the Constructivists were alien and non-Russian.

Among leaders of "traditionalism" were Shchuko and Gelfreykh, who with Iofan won the Palace of Soviets competition with their colossal but never completed tower, and who actually did build the Lenin Library with its array of colonnades and classical statuary. Also outstanding among the older traditionalists were I. Zholtovskiy and A. Shchusev who led the way into the new Stalin era after 1931. The eclectic Shchusev had begun as a major figure in the Revivalist movement before the Revolution, had then turned to the Constructivists and had designed the Lenin Mausoleum on the Red Square and had now adopted Stalinist neoclassicism. Zholtovskiy in contrast had always strongly opposed Constructivism and maintained a classical approach.

The period from the Revolution to 1931 can be regarded as the initial phase in Soviet urban development. It was a period when little was accomplished in practice, but when theories were elaborated about the way in which future town planning should go. The Revolution inspired ideas of change, of novelty, ideas that were reinforced by developments in technology and materials. The arguments were fierce, lively and imaginative. But, at the end of the day, what was left, other than some Constructivist buildings, was a reversion to classicism, now sadly distorted by giganticism, and a set of town planning principles that had individually first been enunciated well before the Revolution.

CHAPTER 3

The realities of the Stalin period

The start of the First Five Year Plan in 1928, or at the latest the Central Committee Plenum of 1931, can be considered the opening of a second phase in Soviet urban development, when the emphasis shifted from theory to practice. The three years between those two events represent a brief period of transition, as the debates were wound up and as the actual need for rapid provision of urban fabric accelerated day by day. If, previously, little of the theory had been made manifest, the new phase and its successors up to the present time have experienced urban change on the largest scale and have indeed witnessed the urbanization of the country. At the census of 1926, the 26 314 114 urban dwellers constituted 17.9 per cent of the total population, almost exactly the same proportion as before the Revolution. By the census of 1989 that one-fifth share had become two-thirds, but even by 1956 (the first year in the period after Stalin's death when an official estimate was issued) the urban proportion had reached 43.4 per cent. This was the process which most of the planners in the first phase had foreseen and desired as part of the transformation of society. Yet the nature of the urban place that developed was in most respects very far from that which they had envisaged. The Soviet town was in reality formed under unforeseen pressures, whether of government policies with differing priorities or of outside events such as war.

The early Five Year Plans

The second stage in town development is essentially co-terminous with the Stalin era. Stalin was already firmly in control during the transition from phase one to phase two, between 1928 and 1931, and it was only after his death in 1953 and the coming to power of Khrushchev that a further third phase emerged. The second phase falls into three periods, the early five year plans between 1928 and 1941, the Second World War, and the final Stalin years from 1945 to 1953. The last of these three periods can be extended to include the immediately succeeding years up to 1957, during which Stalin's policies continued under their own momentum, while the Party leadership engaged in the struggle for succession.

During the opening years of the first Five Year Plan urban construction was still dominated by those who had figured largely in the debates. Most examples of Constructivist architecture actually date from after 1928. So too do the two rather loose adaptations of Constructivist town planning, the linear city plans for Magnitogorsk and Stalingrad (Volgograd), together with the linear plan for Karaganda, which was not even started. Nevertheless, with the commencement of the plan, and, more especially, with the launching of Stalin's effort to catch up the industrial lag behind the advanced capitalist countries, a completely new climate was created for urban development. Ideas requiring vast capital investment and construction capacity and long lead times were no longer wanted or tolerated, let alone Utopian dreams. In practice, if not in theory, everything, including quality of life for Soviet citizens, had to be sacrificed to achieve the fastest possible growth of industry and, above all, of the heavy and armaments industries, together with their essential props, the extractive industries and energy production.

This goal of fast industrialization, of course, required urban development in both the growth of existing towns and the foundation of new ones. The city was seen primarily as a base for industry. In particular, the nature of the industries receiving priority and the desire to achieve economies of scale meant that many of the new plants were very large, contributing accordingly to the speed of urban population growth.

The period between the censuses of 1926 and 1939 saw a rapid rise in the number of urban dwellers and their share of the total population (Table 3.1). Precisely how great that rise was cannot be accurately calculated, because of the falsification of the published 1939 population figures. Figures for the census of 1939 were never given out at the time, and when they were finally quoted 20 years later, along with the figures for the 1959 census, they were certainly overstated; in this way the population losses from the period before 1939 were hidden in with the losses from the Second World War and the post-1939 period. The deaths during collectivization and the famine which followed, and from the purges, were on such a huge scale that they would certainly have shown up; that they did happen is now officially admitted, leaving no question but that the 1939 figures were false.

Table 3.1   Urban growth in the USSR.

	Number of places			Urban population	
	PGT	Towns	Total	Millions	% of total
1926	1216	709	1925	26.3	17.9
1939	1450	923	2373	56.1	33.0
1959	2940	1679	4519	99.8	47.9
1970	3599	1935	5504	136.0	56.3
1979	3852	2062	5914	163.6	62.3
1989	4026	2190	6216	188.8	65.8

Source: census of given years.

Thus, the rate of urban growth over the 13-year period between 1926 and 1939 is exaggerated in official figures, but however much allowance is made for this, there can be no doubt that the increase in urban population was very rapid and large.

After all, it is possible that the distortion might be less severe in urban areas, as a very large share of the population losses before 1939 was borne by the rural population as a result of the collectivization campaign and famine. Here, 1939 figures are given *faute de mieux*, but these reservations need always to be kept in mind.

The spread of industry to new centres throughout the second phase meant a substantial increase in the number of urban places. After the Revolution a rationalization of places possessing official urban status took place. Some towns, given that status in Catherine's reform, had maintained their rank, although never developing in size or range of urban functions. These were now downgraded. Of the 675 towns inherited from the Tsarist period (excluding the protectorates of Khiva and Bukhara), 106 were downgraded to villages and a further 36 were reduced to settlements of urban type. About half were in the central region of European Russia and included several places that had been important in medieval times, such as Sudislavl', Yarenska and Vorotynsk. All had under 4000 population at the 1926 census and most had under 2000; only 19 of the 106 were on railways and, of those, nine later rose again to town rank (Konstantinov 1947: 13–16).

Other places, especially those in the Central Industrial Region that had grown out of estate textile manufactories, had never been granted town rank, despite their size and function. Others in the same situation were Urals metallurgical centres such as Nizhniy Tagil. A total of 182 such settlements were correspondingly upgraded to towns. As a result of the rationalization, by the census of 1926 there were 1925 urban places (within pre-1939 boundaries), of which 709 were full towns and 1216 settlements of town type. By the census of 1939, the overall number had grown to 2373 and the military occupation of eastern Poland and the Baltic Republics in that year brought the total to 2759, including 1191 full towns (Table 3.1).

Of the 448 new urban places appearing by 1939 nearly half (214) were towns and the rest settlements of town type. Many, especially those in the latter category, were small, on greenfield sites and based on newly opened up mineral resources. However, some grew fast, including the standard-bearer of the early Five Year Plans, Magnitogorsk, with its huge integrated iron & steel works beside the magnetite ores of Mount Magnitnaya. By 1939, its official population was 146000 and, by 1959, 311000. Other places, if not wholly new foundations, had been merely villages and were now transformed into major cities. Thus, the settlement of Kuznetsk on the west Siberian coalfield had only 4000 people in 1926. It was renamed Stalinsk (today Novokuznetsk) and in 1929 construction of its great steelworks began; during the first three Five Year Plans to 1939, the town jumped to an official figure of 165666 and then to 376730 people in the more reliable census of 1959.

The appearance of so many new towns meant a rapid growth in the Asiatic part of the country, where urban development before the Revolution had been slight. For example, Kazakhstan had 44 urban places in 1926; by 1949 there were 151 (Gladysheva & Nazarevskiy 1950: 112). Nevertheless, in relative terms the eastern parts of the country did not gain much ground. Of the two hundred or so towns on greenfield sites, only about half were in eastern, Asiatic regions (Davidovich

1959: 58). In 1926 the eastern regions had contained only 20 per cent of the total urban population; 1939 their share had risen slightly to 24 per cent (Table 3.2). Nevertheless, in absolute terms the growth in the east was substantial, from 5 300 000 to 14 500 000.

Table 3.2   Urban population in the European and Asian USSR.

	West		East	
	Millions	%	Millions	%
1926*	21.0	80	5.3	20
1939†	45.9	76	14.5	24
1956*	54.2	67	26.3	33
1959†	68.6	68.6	31.4	31.4
1962‡	76.5	68.4	35.3	31.6

Sources: * Davidovich (1959: 40); † Davidovich (1965: 17); ‡ *Itogi Vsesoyunoy Perepisi Naseleniye 1959 goda: SSSR Svodniy Tom*, 20–29 (Moscow: Gosstatizdat).

Such a geographical spread of the urban network, especially to the east, accorded well with Marxist doctrine. It was creating a more even level of development, decreasing the colonial core–periphery nature of the country and assisting in the full exploitation of resources for society as a whole rather than for profit. In reality, however, the achievement in this direction was limited. The urban share of the east was still far out of line with its share in terms of area or natural resources. Notwithstanding the conversion of the small-scale antiquated Urals iron industry to a vast modern iron & steel and heavy engineering economy, despite the opening up of the Kuzbas coalfield around Novokuznetsk, and despite the foundation of many new mining towns, the bulk of industrial growth before the Second World War was concentrated in the older pre-revolutionary urban areas. The existing infrastructure of communications, established services and already-built housing meant that new factories could be brought on stream most rapidly in the older towns. The existing population provided at least the core of an industrially trained labour force, while the influx of labour from the countryside could be more quickly accommodated by overcrowding existing housing rather than by building new apartments. In 1931 the Central Committee Plenum passed a resolution that all further industrial development in Moscow be suspended, whereas in practice the following decade saw the fastest industrial growth in the city's history. By 1940 Moscow alone was producing 14.7 per cent of total national industrial output (Veselovskiy 1950: 105). In Khar'kov, the sixth largest town of the USSR in 1926, 57 new factories were established, of which 26 were wholly new and 31 were actually moved in from elsewhere (Novikov et al. 1934); in consequence its population doubled from 417 000 in 1926 to 833 000 in 1939.

War and the later Stalin period

The German invasion of 1941 abruptly terminated the Third Five Year Plan and brought its own set of consequences for the urban growth of the country. In the west, war damage to the urban fabric was colossal. Many towns were to all intents and purposes reduced to rubble, including such major cities as Stalingrad (Volgograd) and Minsk. In some instances, including that of besieged Leningrad (St Petersburg), the population had still not regained pre-war levels, even by the 1959 census, 14 years after the end of the war. Other towns, which had similarly not recovered from war losses by 1959, included Smolensk, Vitebsk, Kremenchug, Novorossiysk and Kerch. In all, 1710 towns were severely damaged (Dmitriyev et al. 1988: 46), but almost all towns within the war zone suffered damage to their fabric ranging up to severe, and loss of population by death either from the fighting or by rounding up and subsequent incarceration in German or Soviet forced-labour camps. Most of the pre-war Soviet Jewish population lived in towns within the area occupied by the Germans and suffered accordingly. Altogether, in town and country 25 million were left homeless (ibid.).

Thus, west of a line from Leningrad to Moscow to Stalingrad the war was a major setback to urban growth. East of that line it was a stimulus to even faster growth. Industries and the people to staff them were evacuated eastwards ahead of the advancing German army, especially to the Volga region, the Urals and Siberia. When the war ended, many of these industries (or branches thereof) and some of their personnel remained in the new locations. Novosibirsk more than doubled in size between 1939 and 1959, from 404000 to 886000, and in reality this growth was almost certainly from a lower 1939 base population and therefore greater even than these official figures indicate. Omsk and Krasnoyarsk also more than doubled and most of the Kuzbas towns grew still faster. By 1956 the share of urban population in eastern regions had risen to 33 per cent (Table 3.2) and in absolute numbers to 26300000 (Davidovich 1959: 40).

Although the war inflicted so much damage in the west, the rate of recovery was remarkable. In 1959, only 22 towns were still below 1939 population levels (although this figure includes only towns listed in the 1959 census, that is, those with over 15000 in the RSFSR and over 10000 in the Ukraine). Some regained and surpassed their pre-war size with astonishing speed. Stalingrad, officially 445312 in 1939 was a virtually empty waste of rubble by the end of the Battle of Stalingrad, yet by 1959 as Volgograd it had reached 592382. Minsk, which endured exceptionally heavy damage, nevertheless more than doubled over the intercensal period, from 237495 to 509489. The war was in fact no more than an interruption of phase two urban development and then only in the zone of fighting. What it did do, by reducing the already inadequate housing stock when the inflow of population was once more accelerating, was greatly to increase the severity of overcrowding.

Once the war and the recovery period in the Fourth Five Year Plan from 1946 to 1950 were over, the processes of urban development were resumed on the same lines as in the pre-war plans. Overriding priority still went to heavy producer-goods industries and new towns were generally founded in connection with exploiting new mineral discoveries. Over the whole country, the total number of urban places had by 1956 increased to 3989, of which 1566 were full towns. They contained over 80 million people in 1953 and 100 million at the 1959 census. Thus, despite the ravages of war, there were a further 1227 new urban places by the end of phase two. If in the pre-war period an average of 34.5 new urban places were established each year, in the 1939–56 period the rate reached 72.2 every year.

In the later Stalin years, new mineral finds were still giving rise to the foundation of new mining centres such as the diamond town of Mirnyy in Yakutiya (although this only achieved formal urban status in 1959). But increasingly the newly formed towns were developing as satellites and dormitories of existing towns. Emphasis in growth still rested heavily on the established cities. The recovery of western towns from the war meant a slight fallback in the urban population share of the east. By the 1959 census the proportion of urban dwellers in the Urals and Asiatic parts was 31.4 per cent, despite an absolute growth to 31.4 million (Table 3.2).

In east and west alike, in largest and smallest places, in old-established towns and the newest settlements of town type, the surging increase in industry and labour force was not matched by a corresponding increase in the provision of housing and services. Throughout the entire second phase, a large share of the extremely restricted resources available for construction of housing and services inevitably had to be concentrated in the wholly new, or virtually new, urban settlements. Even in these, the flood of in-migrants swamped the abilities of the building industry to keep pace. Thus, in Magnitogorsk by 1931, many of the 83 000 inhabitants were still living in tents and mud huts and the average amount of space per head was about $1.9 m^2$; a year later the 196 000 population had only $1.8 m^2$ per head (Kotkin 1993: 175). Balkhash in Kazakhstan, a town founded in 1931 as a centre of copper mining and smelting, was planned to have four-storey houses; but by 1941 the main accommodation was still "barracks". By 1951 there were 20 buildings of 4 or 5 storeys, 78 of 2 or 3 storeys but 587 of one storey, the last category housing 41.6 per cent of the population (Ivanova 1962: 11, 15–16).

Particularly in the pre-war period, but also after the war, much of what was built was in the form of privately erected, traditional wooden houses. By 1940 the share of private housing in the total urban stock was over one-third (36.8%) and by 1952 it was still as much as one-third (33.4%) (*Narodnoye Khozyaystvo* . . . 1963: 499). A decree of 1948, permitting the allocation of plots for private construction, speeded up the process of replacing wartime losses and markedly increased the private share in new construction (Andrusz 1984: 99). This dependence on the private sector was particularly seen in smaller towns, where private housing construction was often dominant until the end of the 1950s. Onega, for example, is described as having "whole microregions of private houses" (Kalinin 1980: 74). In Mariinskiy Posad, in the Chuvash ASSR, a survey about 1970 showed that even then 57 per cent of its population still lived in a private house or part of a private dwelling (Khorev 1972: 131).

The majority of the working population who were not in private accommoda-

56

tion were in communal flats built by either local authorities or enterprises. Each room in an apartment of up to four or five rooms housed a family, with the kitchen and bathroom shared between them all. Not surprisingly, conditions in the communal areas of such housing were generally appalling. This overcrowding of groups of family units was a far cry from the 1920s concepts of communal living.

Old and new accommodation alike became ever more crowded. From the start of the Five Year Plans, housing provision began to fall further and further behind the growth of urban population. In the three years up to 1931, the Donbas coalfield district increased its population by 38 per cent, but its housing stock grew by only 25 per cent (Lissitzky 1984: 184–5). In Moscow, between 1926 and 1931, 450000 people were put into new homes (Veselovskiy 1950: 96), but during those five years the population can be estimated to have increased by at least twice that figure. In the 1926 census some 150000 workers (0.58%) lived in communal dwellings; yet ten years later 11 per cent of urban dwellers were in such accommodation, the proportion rising to 25 per cent in Moscow (Sosnovy 1954: 224–5). By 1934 Moscow's population had reached 3663300, or 1662600 more than in 1926 (French 1984: 359). One of the reasons given at the 1931 Central Committee Plenum for ordering a master plan for Moscow to be drawn up, was that infrastructure was lagging behind population increase.

In Leningrad between 1913 and 1940 there was an increase in useful living space from $21800000\,m^2$ to $25700000\,m^2$ (Shaw 1978: 186). With over 2100000 people on 1 January 1914 (Lopatina 1959: 88) and taking the official and probably exaggerated 1939 figure of 3015100 (ibid.: 109) as an approximation for 1940, this represented a fall in useful living space per capita in Leningrad from about $10\,m^2$ to about $8.5\,m^2$.

Wartime damage and the diversion of housing construction resources to other more urgent needs made the situation still more critical. During the Fourth Five Year Plan of reconstruction after the war, the building industry was at full stretch making good wartime losses and giving first priority to rebuilding factories; there was no spare capacity wherewith to reduce the deficiencies of accommodation. As time went on, the disparity on a national scale became steadily worse. The amount of space per urban dweller grew steadily less (Table 3.3). Living space (i.e. excluding kitchen, bathroom and corridors), for which a norm of $9\,m^2$ had been established, had dropped to under $4\,m^2$; this included built-in cupboards if they opened into a room, although not if they opened into a corridor. In 1926 the national average of general (useful) living space per head (a figure including all rooms, kitchen, bathroom and corridors) was $8.2\,m^2$, higher than the pre-revolutionary figure of $7.2\,m^2$ as a result of redistribution of the housing of the wealthy. By the outbreak of the Second World War, at $6.9\,m^2$ it had fallen below the 1913 level and, by the time of Stalin's death, the figure was still below the 1926 level. The accommodation of a whole family in one room was the rule rather than the exception. For many, the best they could get was a "corner" (*ugol*), a curtained-off or partitioned-off part of a room. Of total capital investment in the

Table 3.3   Useful living space per urban dweller (m^2 per capita).

	Urban population (millions)	Total housing (million m^2)	Useful space
1913	28.1	180	6.4
1926	26.3	216	8.2
1940	60.6	421	6.9
1950	69.4	513	7.4
1955	86.3	640	7.4
1960	103.6	958	9.2
1965	120.7	1238	10.3
1970	136.0	1529	11.2

Sources: Narodnoye Khozyaystvo SSSR 1956, 163 (Moscow: Gosudarstvennoye Statisticheskoye Izdatel'stvo); *Narodnoye Khozyaystvo SSSR v 1970g*, 7, 68, 546 (Moscow: Statistika).

national economy between 1928 and 1954, only 17.9 per cent went to housing and of that half was allocated in only the last five years (French 1979: 79).

This overcrowding, resulting from the lack of capital, effort or concern devoted to housing, by the end of the Stalin era brought about some of the highest urban population densities found anywhere in the world. In the centre of Moscow within the Garden Ring road, population density by the mid-1930s was up to 100 000 per km^2 (*Istoriya Moskvy* **6** 1959: 44); even a decade after Stalin's death it was still 50 000 per km^2, which Saushkin (1964: 195) then claimed was one of the highest in the world. But in Leningrad's innermost area between the Neva and the Obvodnyy Canal, densities reached 180 000 to 250 000 per km^2 (Shvarikov 1945: 315). In Khar'kov even the newly constructed 6 ha *kvartaly*, or living units, contained 2400 inhabitants, a density of 400 persons per hectare, or 40 000 per km^2 (Novikov et al. 1934: 26).

In these appalling conditions, only the elite received any relief. The ending of Constructivist styles had been followed by a reversion to the classical, in a heavy, ponderous, over-ornate version. The classical revival, already foreshadowed in the Lenin Library building by Shchuko and Gel'freykh in 1927–9 (Fig. 3.1), was led initially by architects from pre-revolutionary times such as Zholtovskiy, who in 1934 designed the "House on the Mokhovaya" in Moscow, later the headquarters of Intourist. This ponderousness became even more pronounced in the late Stalinist period, after the war and the period of reconstruction. But however over-elaborate in style, these buildings were usually soundly constructed, with large rooms, stone-faced on the exterior and marble-lined in interior public spaces and with parquet floors. They were allocated to the elite of Soviet society – party leaders, senior officers of the armed forces and the KGB, the managerial class and certain leading figures in the academic, artistic and entertainment worlds.

Such buildings are found everywhere, but most commonly where such social groups are concentrated, in republican capitals and, above all, in Moscow. There they are found in greatest number along stretches of the Moskva embankments,

Figure 3.1   The Lenin Library, by V. Shchuko & V. Gel'freykh, 1927–9.

around the Garden Ring and along main radial avenues such as the Leningrad Prospect – all highly visible locations. Usually, the lines of Stalinist blocks formed a showy facade along such principal arteries. Behind them remained one- or two-storey pre-revolutionary houses, often of wood and even more often dilapidated. It was facadism, in a latter-day version of the Potemkin village.

The highly ornate appearance of the principal late Stalinist buildings is most vividly seen in the seven skyscrapers that today are still major features of the Moscow skyline. Of the seven, two are apartment blocks (Fig. 3.2); of the rest, one is the main university building, two are hotels and two office blocks (one the Foreign Office). Another example of the late Stalinist style, the Kaluga Gates building at the inner end of the southwestern radial, Lenin Prospect, was built by prison camp labour, including Solzhenitsyn (1975, *passim*), and on completion was allocated to KGB officers (Fig. 3.3).

Such grandiose buildings reflected the emergence of the USSR from the Second World War as one of the two superpowers and the consequent flourishing of the "imperial" principle in the later years of Stalin's rule. Moscow in particular was seen, not merely as capital of the Soviet Union, but as the focus of the bloc of CMEA/Warsaw Pact countries, and indeed as the centre for communism throughout the world – "the greatest international political and economic centre"

Figure 3.2 A Stalin period apartment block on Ploschad' Vostaniya, Moscow.

(Yevstratov & Matveyev 1967: 66). At a time when scores of millions of people had less than $5m^2$ of living space, ostentatious opera and ballet theatres and government offices were absorbing capital and the capacity of the construction industry. Similarly, the construction of a limited quantity of roomy, well built apartments for the elite reflected the parallel development of Djilas' "New Class", the *nomenklatura* or new aristocracy of Communist Party members.

The lack of emphasis on housing and urban fabric meant that very little urban renewal took place. Expansion of factories meant that a certain number of houses and older buildings were pulled down; it was usually poorer quality, working-class houses which lay in the immediate proximity of the expanding plants and which had to be removed. Elsewhere in existing towns, renewal was confined to clearance of limited sites to make room for individual buildings, often imposing office or apartment blocks as expressions of the "imperial principle".

Little enough happened in the country as a whole without the approval of Stalin, who kept a particularly close eye on new developments in his capital's appearance. "The plan for the general reconstruction of the capital was worked out on the direct orders of I. V. Stalin. Comrade Stalin personally took part in the resolution of all basic questions" (Veselovskiy 1950: 100). The closeness of his attention to detail and the weight of his influence are nowhere better expressed in

Figure 3.3   Stalin period apartments for KGB officers, Kaluzhskaya Zastava, Moscow.

architecture than by Moscow's Moskva Hotel beside the Kremlin; the differing right and left halves of its facade are the result of Stalin approving the architectural drawings without noticing that two alternative versions were being presented, an error no-one cared to correct (Fig. 3.4).

Figure 3.4   Moskva Hotel, Moscow: alternative facade designs.

That Stalin was personally responsible for much in urban and architectural design is evidenced not merely by the endlessly repeated attributions of sycophants in his day, but also by the speed with which extravagant architectural display came under attack after Stalin's death. As early as 1955, that is to say two years before Khrushchev's secret speech to the Plenum of the Central Committee of the Party attacking Stalin, a government resolution declared that "wholly unjustified towering superstructures, numerous decorative colonnades and porticoes and other excesses borrowed from the past, have become a general feature in the construction of housing and public buildings, in consequence of which in recent years vast public means have been over-expended on housing construction, with which could have been built millions of square metres of living space for the workers" (Il'in 1963: 364).

Planning in the second phase

During the second, Stalinist, phase of Soviet urban history, two principles of urban development remained absolute. First, it was taken as axiomatic that the urban environment provided the way forward for the progression to socialism and thereafter to communism. Thus, Gladysheva and Nazarevskiy (1950: 113), writing of urban growth in Kazakhstan in the context of its environmental rigours, declared, "of a series of ways of developing the desert, semi-desert and dry steppe, the opening up of land by the foundation of towns is one of the best. Towns are, as it were, the most organized troops in the attack on nature."

Secondly, belief in, and official commitment to, the necessity of planning to determine and control urban development was fundamental. In the general sense of *planirovaniye* (national economic developmental planning), the allocation of funds from the central government to local urban authorities, centrally taken decisions on the opening of new mines, location of new factories, expansion of existing industry and construction of lines of communication – all formed part of the national Five Year Plans; what happened to towns was therefore controlled by the plans of the central government, as converted to precise orders by Gosplan. The emphasis on industry before all else was not haphazard or by default; it was a conscious intention with a specific aim.

Concepts of organized urban layout remained fundamental to town planning. Kaganovich had told the Central Committee of the Party in 1931 that "we must provide for the widening and straightening of streets. Naturally we cannot permit the chaotic development prevailing in capitalist cities." Similarly, the functions of the city had to be systematically laid out: "We must so plan a city that the population is distributed evenly throughout its districts and, accordingly, equally distribute the cultural institutions, such as schools, hospitals, clubs, theatres, baths, shops, etc." (Kaganovich, n.d.: 90).

Construction of accommodation should be arranged in *kvartaly*, defined as plots of land, on average 6 ha in extent, with roads on all sides and built with facades facing the streets (Novikov et al. 1934: 23). The *kvartal* should contain a crèche, kindergarten, club and cafeteria and should form part of a living region (*zhilkom-pleks*), which would embrace shops, post office, primary medical point, savings bank, hairdresser, repair shops, sports facilities and some internal open space with gardens and lawns (ibid.: 25) – in other words, the *zhilkompleks* was the forerunner of the microregion of post-Stalin times. If the aims of setting up completed living complexes were rarely achieved in the Stalin period, new housing was regularly constructed in the square, four-sided *kvartal* blocks with interior courtyards.

The "greening" of towns was a basic belief of the planners. The 1930s Khar'kov plan laid down that half the built-up area should be occupied by greenery. But despite the attention paid in the plans to concepts worked up in the preceding phase, the emphasis in *planirovka* (the physical laying out) now shifted to economic, and especially industrial, objectives. "Under Soviet conditions it is not the market that is the main factor determining the growth of cities, but the planned development of industry, the growth of large-scale, socialist economy throughout the whole country and the systematic development and distribution of the productive forces of the country" (Kaganovich, n.d.: 91).

Thus, the imposition by *planirovaniye* (national economic planning) of a particular role on the urban areas of the Soviet Union and the enforcement of rigid priorities deeply affected the nature of physical urban planning (*planirovka*) during phase two, an influence that was largely negative. In theory, all towns were to have development plans drawn up and this requirement was spelt out in a decree of 1933. In practice, few towns had completed the drafting of plans and had them officially approved by the end of the Second World War, and not many more had done so by 1953. Nizhniy Novgorod (sometime Gor'kiy), one of the fastest growing Soviet cities, trebling in size between 1926 and 1939, had to cope without an overall plan (Andrusz 1984: 229).

The major exception was of course, Moscow, once more capital and now showcase of the socialist system. The 1931 Plenum, which so savaged the planners of phase one, also ordered a long-term master plan for the city to be drawn up, and laid down specifications for the plan. There was to be a maximum population of 4 million; no new industry was to be established; service and amenity provision was to be improved and distributed evenly throughout the city, and special attention was to be given to aspects of the city's transport network (Richardson 1991: 112–13). Seven teams submitted proposals, including those led by Ernst May, Kurt Meyer and Hannes Meyer from abroad. The scheme of the Swiss Hannes Meyer had some resemblance to the earlier plan of Shestakov, in that it included a major regional element with 19 new satellites forming an urban system; the first such satellites would be located to the east and south, the directions from which raw materials came to Moscow, and these would reach populations of 200000–350000. In Moscow itself, central axes would be lined by the buildings of government and administration at international, national and republican levels (ibid.: 114–17).

None of the seven "brigades" had their scheme accepted, largely because all

Figure 3.5   The 1935 General Plan for Moscow.

envisaged massive clearance of the past fabric and wholesale reconstruction. Instead, a further scheme was devised under the supervision of Kaganovich, and on 10 July 1935 the "General Plan for the Reconstruction of Moscow" was approved (Fig. 3.5). Its task was "to build and create high-quality structures for workers in order that the construction of the capital of the USSR and the architectural setting of the capital should fully reflect the grandeur and beauty of the socialist epoch" (*Istoriya Moskvy* **6**, 1959: 29).

The principles on which the plan was based were those outlined in the previous chapter, many of them reflecting some consensus of views expressed in the earlier phase of debate. One of these principles was the limitation of city size. Although Moscow was already far beyond the ideal size, measured in tens of thousands (indeed, it had reached some 3 700 000), the plan envisaged a ceiling of 5 million. In order not to exceed that limit, no new industry was to be introduced to the city. Housing was a prime target of the plan, with 15 million square metres to be built within ten years and inner-city population densities to be reduced to 40 000 per km². Around a city area enlarged from 28 500 ha to 60 000 ha there was to be a forest-park green belt some 10km wide (Yevstratov & Matveyev 1967: 63). The architecture of new buildings was to be neoclassical; Frank Lloyd Wright commented of the plan that it was "far ahead of any city planning I have seen elsewhere" (Richardson 1991: 121).

In the event, very little indeed of the 1935 General Plan was ever accomplished and those parts that were carried out were almost wholly related to improvement of the transport situation and therefore of the infrastructure for industry. The River Moskva and its tributary the Yauza were given 35km of granite embankments, improving river flow and navigation, and new northern and southern river ports were built. From the northern port, prison labour from the Gulag dug a canal capable of taking sea-going ships north to the Volga. Reservoirs built along the canal's route also served to improve the city's water supply. Finally, further work was done on Moscow's Metro underground system, although this had already been started and the first 11.6km of line were opened to traffic in the same year that the General Plan was approved. It is worth commenting that for none of the plan's aims, which were actually achieved, was a unified city-wide plan necessary.

Of all the other aspects of the plan, nothing was accomplished other than the creation of Manege Square (between 1967 and 1990 renamed Square of the Fiftieth Anniversary of the October Revolution), the widening of Red Square, the widening and straightening of Tverskaya (for a time Gor'kiy) Street and the widening of parts of the Garden (Sadovoye) Ring, which marked the line of Moscow's sixteenth-century walls. These alterations mostly adjoined the Kremlin and were primarily designed to enhance the setting and grandeur of the parades on May Day and the anniversary of the October Revolution; they can be seen as expressions of the "imperial principle". Apart from these isolated instances, nothing of the projected new layout of the city came about. Even the establishment of a surrounding green belt had to await Moscow's second master plan of the 1970s.

Not only was there failure to construct what the plan proposed, there was massive construction in defiance of the plan. New industry was established on a very large scale, especially to the southeast of the historic central core, near the southern river port, and to the northwest, around the northern port and the end of the Moscow–Volga Canal. It is true that many of the largest new plants had been started up before the plan was confirmed, such as the electrical equipment factory in 1928 and the car factory in 1929, but their expansion was not curtailed and further new plants were in fact built.

Much of the new industry was in very large plants, such as the Stalin (later Likhachev) Automobile Works; in 1932 the First Ball-bearing Factory was opened, today employing over 13000 workers. Much was environmentally thoroughly undesirable, such as the reconstruction and extension between 1929 and 1935 of the "Hammer and Sickle" steel works close to the city centre. By the 1959 census, out of 3938000 people in Moscow of working age, over 1200000 or 30 per cent were engaged in industry (Saushkin 1964: 86–7). Rarely if ever in the development of a major metropolis anywhere in the world, let alone a national capital, can the growth of heavy industry have played such a large part at such a late stage in its history.

Leningrad, the second city of the USSR, was one of the few other places to have a plan drawn up before the Second World War. On 10 August 1935 the Central Committee of the Party and the Council of People's Commissars ordered the drawing up of a general plan, under the guidance of the architects L. A. Il'in and V. A. Vitman. The plan was promulgated in 1936, just one year later than Moscow's. Among its objectives was the removal of the administrative heart of the city some 10km southwards to a new centre to be built at the intersection of a north–south axis from the old centre (the Moscow Chaussee) and a new curving east–west axis. This aspect of the plan did not get beyond the building of a large new House of Soviets, together with the enlarging of two squares along the Moscow Chaussee. The ring of industries in the southern region of the city was to be displaced to a ring still farther out (Shvarikov 1945: 314–17). In 1938, a scaled down revision of this plan was drawn up, which recognized that the transfer of the old city centre was not immediately possible (Ruble 1990: 45).

Unlike Moscow, where wartime damage was restricted to bombing raids and was considerably less than in London and other major British cities, Leningrad suffered severely from bombing and artillery fire during its 900-day siege, with over 10000 buildings totally destroyed. It might be supposed, therefore, that there was considerable opportunity to carry out radical reconstruction. Yet in the postwar rebuilding, no further effort was made to implement either the pre-war plan or its successor, which was drawn up in 1946–8 under the guidance of the architects N. V. Baranov and A. I. Naumov; by the time that it was replaced by a further general plan in 1966, even less had been carried out than in Moscow.

Other cities, such as war-ravaged Volgograd (Stalingrad), of necessity had plans drawn up for the reconstruction process, but their effective implementation was hindered by frequent changes and revisions. Volgograd got its first general plan in 1945, but in 1951 it was revised as being too wasteful of space through the use of low buildings; 25 per cent were three to five storeys, 30 per cent two storeys and 25 per cent one storey, together with a further 20 per cent of single-storey private housing (Lipyavkin 1971: 56). Even the revised plan was replaced by a wholly new one in 1962, under which 50 per cent of buildings were to be of five storeys, 45 per cent of nine storeys, and five per cent of 12 to 16 storeys (ibid.: 262–3).

Birobidzhan in the Far East was one of several cities for which a plan was conceived by Hannes Meyer (Richardson 1991: 117–18), but little seems to have been carried out. Throughout the period up to 1957, in other cities where plans were finalized they too remained on paper, while realities on the ground were wildly divergent. According to Davidovich (1956: 71), Karaganda, the new coalmining centre of Kazakhstan, was originally planned as a unitary (*yedinyy*) town with long lines of communication; clearly, this was meant as a linear city, although Davidovich, writing in 1956, was not going to call it so. He points out, fairly enough, that such a plan would have meant journeys to work of up to 1½ hours each way. Instead, what grew up was "a disorganized cluster of numerous towns and settlements". Clearly, from Davidovich's comments, some towns founded or rapidly expanded in the early Five Year Plans were originally designed as linear cities, including, as well as Karaganda, Novomoskovsk (then Stalinogorsk), Novyy Orsk and Malgobek in the North Caucasus. All in practice developed either as clusters or as a chain of separate settlements. As a result, Davidovich was rejecting the planning concept of linear cities as impracticable and advocating greater readiness to plan for a compact group of urban settlements (ibid.).

The disregard of plans, even in the most important cities, can be attributed almost wholly to one cause. The needs of industry and the wishes of industrial ministries were paramount, sweeping aside the aspirations and objectives of the planners whenever the two sets of objectives clashed. The key ministries for heavy industries and defence were directly represented by influential Party figures in the All-Union Council of Ministers, to which Gosplan was answerable. The town planner came at the bottom of a chain of command through town council, district council and republican government to central government. In a conflict of interest, it was "no contest". For industrial ministries, for the Council of Ministers, for the Politburo and above all for Stalin himself, industry came first.

Therefore, in planning a city, the basic principle in deciding its physical layout should be the requirements of its function, including the dimensions of the sources of employment. Following from this, it was vital to take into consideration the length of journey to work. On these two considerations would depend whether the planned city should be unitary or a group of settlements. To insist on a unitary plan was "dogmatism". In addition, both the physical constraints of the site and the existence of past developments had to be taken into account, although the latter did not mean that undesirable elements should not be replanned (Davidovich 1949: 72–7).

Obviously, achievement of the industrial plan targets could be fastest where there was already a good infrastructure in place, and especially transport lines. Moscow, for example, was the best connected city of the USSR, the focus of eleven trunk railways, with extensive marshalling yards, and possessing direct air links to every city of consequence in the country. The ready availability of an existing skilled labour force was another attraction for key industries to locate in the older cities; the larger the city, the more diverse the skills already in place. Once an industrial ministry decided to locate in a particular city, it seized a prime location to suit its needs, regardless of the land-use designated by the plan or the environmental suitability. This use of existing urban infrastructure and labour meant, of course, accelerated growth beyond "ideal" norms. Even before the end of the Stalin period, some writers were rejecting the principle of a maximum size: "The problem of 'optimal size' of towns cannot be resolved by setting 'limiting norms' of maximum and minimum population for all towns and in all circumstances" (Davidovich 1949: 15).

One can sum up the whole Stalin period, the second phase of Soviet urban development, as one in which the State paid only lip service to the concept of coherently planned cities designed to achieve the optimum form of living. In reality the State had other, conflicting objectives, which it pursued and in large measure attained, at the expense of the town plan and of the quality of life of the citizens.

CHAPTER 4

Khrushchev to Gorbachev:
the third phase of urban development

Urbanization 1957–85

The death of Stalin in March 1953 was followed by an interregnum while the Party leaders jockeyed for power. Meanwhile, all the State policies continued as they had done since the Second World War, including those affecting urban areas. By 1957, Khrushchev was firmly in control and he felt able to set the Soviet Union on a modified path of development. In that year he made his secret speech to the Central Committee attacking Stalin, and thus by implication the inviolability of his policies. Suddenly, for the first time since the 1920s, there was again a sense of new opportunities, of new hope in the USSR, as the speech triggered a series of relaxations of the worst rigours of Stalinism. It was the period known inside and outside the country as "The Thaw". Concepts, which had been discussed in the 1920s and then prudently ignored throughout the Stalin period, could once more be raised. Strumilin revived thoughts of communal living, although his was by then very much a lone voice. Contacts with the West, both academic and professional, became possible, were even encouraged. Town planners could safely make statements approving of ideas and theories deriving from Western sources, although with cautious caveats. Not least among the Western developments in which Soviet planners could now begin to show interest were the British post-war new towns, on which a paper (subsequently published) was given at a conference held in Moscow in 1960 (Varlamov 1961). The British new towns, of course, owed not a little to Ebenezer Howard's concepts; this interest on the part of the Soviet planners thus revived an influence that had been strong in the 1920s.

However, Khrushchev's freedom of action was still severely constrained by the consequences of the long years of the previous regime, by indurated patterns of thought and action among the elite and the bureaucracy, by their refusal to contemplate a diminution of their powers, by the slow-to-dissipate fears of long-terrorized ordinary working people, and above all by the previous lopsided economic developments. Such constraints notwithstanding, the desperate plight of the workers, and especially their chronic housing shortage, created an irresistible set of pressures for the new administration. These pressures resulted in such a major

69

change in the path of development of the Soviet city that 1957 marks a clear start to a new, third phase in that process.

The period after 1957 saw the urbanizing of the Soviet population completed. By the start of 1961 the balance between urban and rural dwellers was achieved, since when the urban share of an ever-larger total population has continued to grow steadily, to reach 66 per cent at the 1989 census. In absolute numbers this has meant an increase of over 100 million from 87 million in 1956 to 188 million in 1989. It has also meant a further huge increase in the number of urban places. From the 1566 full towns and 2393 settlements of town type that existed in 1956, the equivalent figures by 1989 had risen to 2190 towns and 4026 settlements of town type, making 6216 urban places in all (Table 4.1). As in the Stalin period, this growth included new "greenfield" foundations, often linked to mineral extraction. Other new towns resulted from expansion of villages and the growth of suburban dormitories and satellites around major centres.

Table 4.1 Urban places by size groups: number of towns (T) and settlements of town type (S), and percentage of total urban population in each size group.

000s	1959				1979				1989			
	T	%	S	%	T	%	S	%	T	%	S	%
>1000	3	9	–	–	18	20	–	–	23	22	–	–
500–1000	22	15	–	–	25	11	–	–	33	11	–	–
250–500	32	11	–	–	64	14	–	–	78	14	–	–
100–250	91	14	–	–	163	15	–	–	162	13	–	–
50–100	156	11	–	–	223	9	2	<1	275	10	3	<1
20–50	444	14	30	1	605	11	48	1	653	11	67	1
10–20	443	6	355	5	566	5	421	3	606	5	539	4
<10	488	3	2555	12	398	1	3381	9	360	1	3417	8
total	1679	83	2940	18	2062	87	3852	13	2190	87	4026	13

Source: Narodnoye Khozyaystvo SSSR v 1989g (1989: 25).

Urbanization in phase three was guided theoretically by the development of a planning structure of urbanization, the concept of a unified system of settlement. This was discussed and worked on by academics and design institutions throughout the 1960s. It was a pyramidal structure, with each town in the hierarchy of appropriate population size and function. Moscow, the all-Union capital, was the apex of the entire system. As might be imagined, such a scheme was heavily indebted to the central-place model of Christaller, although that acknowledgment was seldom made at the time.

The concept was officially adopted only in 1976, as the "General Scheme for the System of Settlement, 1976–90." By then the old 1920s concept of an optimum size of town had been abandoned *de facto*. The original proponents of the Unified Scheme had thought very much in terms of optimum sizes for each level of the hierarchy. Instead, the approved General Scheme made grouped settlements, or agglomerations, the basic unit, so unifying large, medium and small towns (Borisov et al. 1981: 8) within a radius of 100–150km. Nevertheless, the scheme still envisaged strong constraint on the growth of the largest towns, linked with intensified development both of small and medium towns and of towns generally in the under-urbanized Asiatic regions.

At the base of the General Scheme pyramid would be the replacement for the myriad rural settlements, the villages and hamlets. This replacement was the *agrogorod* or agricultural town, a concept dating from the Khrushchev period. At the time of the 1959 census, there were in the USSR some 720 000 villages and hamlets, ranging in size from the huge farming communities of the north Caucasus with up to 20 000 or more inhabitants, to the tiny two- or three-family hamlets of the European northwest and the *khutor,* or isolated farmstead, of the Baltic Republics and Belorussia. Although by the 1970 census the total number of rural settlements had been reduced to 469 000, in all but a few hundred cases this was only a paper change, as small hamlets and isolated farms that had been counted separately in 1959 were now lumped together.

The average population of a rural settlement was only 152 in 1959 and very little larger in 1970; the provision of services was extremely difficult and expensive and, in consequence, rarely adequate. The *agrogorod* scheme, by bringing the population scattered in many small places into a settlement of 10 000–20 000 or more, would permit the effective provision of health, educational and other services, would achieve the Marxist aim of abolishing the distinction between the countryside and the town, and would also create the lowest tier in the Unified Settlement hierarchy.

In reality the *agrogorod* was never more than a paper scheme. The cost of completely reconstructing the existing rural settlements, and the demands it would make on a building industry already at full stretch in the towns, made it quite impracticable. At the same time, each *agrogorod* would have to serve a huge surrounding area of farmland, involving massive wastage of man-hours in the journey to work and requiring the construction of an efficient network of all-weather roads to give access to the fields; to this day such a network is non-existent in almost all rural areas. In addition, there would have to be the build-up of a massive vehicle park to transport the workers.

The *agrogorod* was dropped. Instead, a policy was adopted of key "growth pole" villages, wherein would be concentrated all new investment in services and in the establishment of industries processing local agricultural produce. Smaller settlements would be phased out. The minimum population for a key village would be 1000, with 2000 as a preferred ideal.

Yet again, reality created problems unforeseen by the plan. In a number of areas, key villages were designated and expanded by attracting population from the surrounding villages and hamlets. However, the older age groups often formed a significant element in rural areas, as a result of the out-migration of young and qualified persons to the towns and the higher wages of industry. Many of the older people were unwilling to leave the family homes where they and their ancestors had always lived. So they remained in the face of growing abandonment, dereliction and a lack of the welfare services they increasingly needed. The intense reluctance

71

of the older generation to leave their natal villages was clearly demonstrated in the aftermath of the Chernobyl' nuclear explosion, when many refused to be evacuated or, when compelled to leave, later returned despite the contamination.

The problems at the base of the Unified Settlement pyramid were only one reason why the hierarchy and the network of towns and settlements of town type, which had come into being by the 1980s, were far from what was envisaged when the system was promulgated in the 1960s. In fact the network today displays a considerable measure of polarization, giving a pattern of a relatively limited number of very large cities and agglomerations, containing an ever larger share of the total urban population, standing in a sea of small, even tiny, urban places, the latter frequently characterized by stagnation or decline rather than growth.

Nine-tenths of all Soviet urban places fall into the category of small, that is, under 50000 population and three-fifths are very small indeed, under 10000 people (Table 4.1). The absolute number of places under 10000 slowly but steadily grew, by 4.8 per cent between 1970 when there were 3576, and 1987 when there were 3748. This increase has been caused by the creation of settlements of town type; the absolute number of full towns in the smallest size category fell over the 1970–87 period from 423 to 368. Small towns between 10000 and 50000 grew in number very much faster than the very small group; they have increased by 23 per cent since 1970. In this size group, the number of both towns and settlements of town type increased. The share of the total Soviet urban population in both very small towns and small towns has fallen. In many places the period saw an absolute decline in population. In the RSFSR since 1959, one small town in five has stabilized or decreased in population (Lyubovnyy et al. 1985: 110). As discussed in the next chapter, these are problem towns.

Table 4.1 indicates that although middle-size towns (50000–100000) increased substantially in number from 189 to 264, or by 40 per cent, over the 17-year period, their share of the total urban population, at under 10 per cent, has scarcely altered at all. Clearly obvious from the table is the growing role of the very largest cities in the pattern of urbanization. At the time of the 1959 census there were only three Soviet cities over the million mark – Moscow, Leningrad and Kiev – and the last of these had only recently reached the threshold. By 1970 there were nine and in 1989 no less than 23; the proportion of the total urban population they contained had risen from ten per cent in 1959 to 14 per cent in 1970 and 21.9 per cent in 1989. Now, nearly a quarter of urban inhabitants live in "million" cites and this share will certainly increase. In 1989, another 36 cities were between 500000 and a million and of these, at their rates of growth at the end of the Soviet period, one might have expected at least six to pass the million mark by the end of the century (Table 4.2).

Thus, approximately a third of the urban population and 22 per cent of the total Soviet population already live in these two largest categories of town. The effort to restrain the growth of most of the towns in these size classes by making it necessary to have a *propiska*, or permit to reside, has had only limited effect; with the advent of Gorbachev and *glasnost*, calls were made for the abolition of such

Table 4.2   Cities with populations over 500000, 1989 (thousands).

Over 1 million					
Moscow	8967	Novosibirsk	1436	Alma Ata	1128
St Petersburg	5020	Yekaterinburg	1367	Odessa	1115
Kiev	2587	Tbilisi	1260	Donetsk	1110
Tashkent	2073	Samara	1252	Kazan'	1094
Baku	1757	Yerevan	1199	Perm	1091
Khar'kov	1611	Dnepropetrovsk	1179	Ufa	1083
Minsk	1589	Omsk	1148	Rostov-na-Donu	1020
N. Novgorod	1438	Chelyabinsk	1143		
500000 to 1 million					
Volgograd	999	Tol'yatti	630	Orenburg	547
Riga	915	Irkutsk	626	Penza	543
Krasnoyarsk	912	Simbirsk	625	Tula	540
Saratov	905	Krasnodar	620	Kemerovo	520
Voronezh	887	Bishkek	616	Mariupol'	517
Zaporozh'ye	884	Karaganda	614	Ryazan'	515
L'vov	790	Barnaul	602	Astrakhan	509
Krivoy Rog	713	Khabarovsk	601	Nikolayev	503
Chisinau	665	Novokuznetsk	600	Tomsk	502
Vladivostok	648	Dushanbe	595	Nab. Chelni	501
Izhevsk	635	Vilnius	582	Gomel'	500
Yaroslavl'	633				

Source: Narodnoye Khozyaystvo SSSR v 1989g (1989: 22–3)

restrictions (CDSP 1986, 38 no. 36: 21). With the demise of the Soviet regime in 1991, the end of the *propiska* at first seemed likely, but at the time of writing in early 1995 there appears to be a continuation of the practice, although it is not clearly defined in law. Current developments on the political scene will surely make it harder in future to enforce restrictive regulations of this type.

Agglomeration, corridor and region

The concentration of an ever greater part of the population in a few urbanized areas is even more marked than these figures suggest. Few of the large cities stand in relative isolation and most are the foci of a group of satellite towns. These agglomerations, in some measure the equivalent of Standard Metropolitan Areas in the USA, are not at present treated statistically as units, but over the post-Stalin period there has been a growing recognition that they are the only meaningful basis for analysis and planning. Nevertheless, the USSR was extremely slow in adopting such units as a planning basis. In 1976 there were still only two integrated regional plans incorporating a major city with its surrounding oblast – those for Moscow and Leningrad (Kibal'chich & Lyubovnyy 1976: 244).

No longer was it sensible or even possible to speak of a maximum population size or an ideal size. Every such concept throughout the Soviet period was overtaken by the realities of growth almost as soon as it had been formulated. For so long megalopolis, the millionaire city, was seen in the USSR as one of the undesirable consequences of capitalism. Although there are still geographers with this view, such as Khorev, most workers in the field in recent years have praised the very large city as being cost-effective. In the face of the urban reality, geographers, economists and others have recognized that analysis of the Soviet city and effective planning for the city must comprehend both the city and its surrounding area. Such recognition was made official policy in the 1976 General Scheme for the System of Settlement. It was further suggested that the development of agglomerations would assist the process of abolishing the distinction between countryside and town. "Urbanization, and particularly such of its forms as agglomerations, urbanized regions and urbanized zones, will inevitably drag rural settlement into the orbit of urban forms of life-activity. So these new forms of settlement are also the way to resolve the problem of 'town-country'" (Dmitriyev & Mezhevich 1982: 23).

Considerable work by Soviet urban geographers since the 1960s has gone into the question of defining agglomerations. Ausmane (1980: 13) defines the Riga conurbation by the 1 hour 45 minutes isochrone and by the presence of at least two per cent of the employed population commuting to Riga. Others have examined and classified agglomerations or groupings of functionally interrelated towns. They can be monocentric, where a cluster of satellites surround a major focal city; the satellites may be industrial, residential or specialized as in the case of educational/research satellites. The best known of these last is Akademgorodok, outside Novosibirsk, where the university, many branches of the Academy of Sciences and a range of research and development institutions are located. Alternatively, the agglomeration may be multicentred, where a group of towns have grown up in close proximity, as in parts of the Donbas coalfield. At the time of the 1979 census there were 193 agglomerations, containing over 2000 urban settlements and 113 500 000 inhabitants (Lappo 1987: 123–4), that is to say, 69.4 per cent of the total urban population of the country and 43.3 per cent of all its inhabitants.

The idea that what might be termed in the West "standard metropolitan areas" should be the basis for study and planning was taken still further by certain Soviet urban geographers such as Lappo. They proposed the development of urban corridors along lines of communication linking the major agglomerations, the whole forming the "structural framework" (*opornyy karkas*) of the country's settlement pattern. Advocates of the agglomeration/corridor approach to settlement planning tended to be concentrated in the Institute of Geography of the Academy of Sciences, headed by Lappo, Pivovarov and Pol'yan. However, there was a no less vocal group who disapproved of their approach as neglecting the fundamental issue of social production as the basis for urban development and planning and referred to it scornfully as "agglocentrism" (Agafonov et al. 1983: 180). Not least of their objections was that it by-passed the concept of a Unified System of Settlement. This group was strongest in Leningrad and Moscow State Universities, and included, among others, Lavrov, Agafonov and Khorev.

74

The housing drive

The failure of the Stalin years to provide either housing or services even remotely to match the urban population explosion had brought about a shortage of accommodation and a poverty of urban living standards probably unequalled in the developed world since the worst slum conditions of west European cities in the earlier stages of the Industrial Revolution. Indeed, the nearest parallel to the Soviet city at Stalin's death was the early industrial city of the West; even the newly created towns with modern housing on at least partially planned layouts could be rather crudely equated with the planned industrial settlements built by the more enlightened mill and factory owners of nineteenth-century Britain.

But even in Soviet new towns population growth was uncontrollably out of phase with planned layouts and housing construction, let alone service provision. Even Moscow had privately erected shanty towns on its margins, generally out of sight of the Western visitor, where villages of grossly overcrowded and dilapidated wooden houses, along dirt roads, had been incorporated into the expanding town and remained as eyesores of appalling living conditions within the urban periphery.

Thus Khrushchev, in rejecting the reign of terror which allowed Stalin to enforce the acceptance of such conditions on the mass of the working population, had little option but to give his priority to a massive and very rapid programme of housing construction. At the same Plenum where he attacked Stalin, he launched the building drive that characterized the Soviet city for the rest of its period of existence. As part of the programme and in line with his high-level administrative reforms, Khrushchev established *Gosgrazhdanstroy*, the State Committee for Civic Construction, which was subordinate to the State Committee for Construction (*Gosstroy*), which in turn came directly under Gosplan. Its task was to oversee the crash programme and to bring about greater speed and economy in its achievement by standardization. The scale of the task was so formidable that by the time that Khrushchev fell from power in 1964, only a start had been made on improving the housing situation. Brezhnev was faced with the same compelling priority and the necessity to continue the crash programme. This third phase of development, where the needs of housing distorted and impeded the plan as industry had done in the previous phase, continued in effect to the end of the Soviet era. Even now, the end of the pressure is not in sight; indeed, recent developments have considerably set back the attainment of fully adequate accommodation for all.

The conditions of 1957 meant that initially there could be only very limited urban renewal; existing housing, however dreadful, had to be retained until sufficient new accommodation had been built to permit decanting of the inhabitants. Thus, the new blocks of flats were put up on the edges of the built-up area, where space was immediately available, but directly adjacent to established networks of services – water mains, sewers, gas pipes, electricity and telephone cables – to which the new housing could be quickly and cheaply hooked up. Intra-urban transport lines, particularly buses, could be relatively easily extended into nearby areas. In consequence, an outstanding feature of the building programme has been

75

urban sprawl and loss of amenity space. The employment of the microregion concept as the basic spatial unit of housing construction encouraged building on city margins. To renew old central areas by whole microregions at a time would have involved the effort, time and cost of clearing larger areas, with the consequent diminution of existing housing stock. Renewal in inner areas has consistently tended to be on limited point-sites in any one development.

Even before the end of the Khrushchev period, there were exceptions to this general locational rule. In Tashkent, for example, as in other Central Asian cities, extensive sections of the traditional central areas of the non-Russian period, consisting of narrow, winding alleys lined by mud-walled houses facing inwards around a courtyard, were swept away to make room for wide streets on geometric patterns, lined by apartment or office blocks. In the particular instance of Tashkent, considerable assistance in clearing old central areas was afforded by the 1966 earthquake.

As time progressed and the first inroads into the shortage were made, such urban renewal became more frequent. In west central Moscow during the later 1960s, an extensive area of old, pre-revolutionary buildings near the Arbat was razed to create the radial avenue, Kalinin Prospect (Fig. 4.1). This is lined by a two-storey podium of shops and restaurants, from which rise towering blocks of offices and flats. Muscovites described the hated street, which destroyed a large section of a much loved old quarter, as being "like a row of teeth with gaps", but it was undoubtedly urban renewal. The width of the street and the gigantism of its buildings can be regarded as a further expression of that "imperial principle", which was so evident in the late Stalin period. In general, however, despite such examples, the overwhelming bulk of new housing from 1957 to the present day

Figure 4.1 Kalinin Prospect, Moscow (now New Arbat).

76

Figure 4.2   Five-storey brick apartment block of the early Krushchev period, Zvenigorod.

has been located on the fringes of existing built-up areas.

In the early years of the housing drive, the normal building material was brick; a light ochre-coloured brick is a hallmark of the Khrushchev period (Fig. 4.2). Most of the blocks of flats were only five or even four storeys high. Anything higher was required by law to have a lift, and the manufacture of lifts was quite unable to meet demands. Four-storey blocks tend to be more common in smaller provincial towns; in larger cities the blocks generally were of five storeys and in the very largest even higher. In Moscow, along the main thoroughfares, ochre brick buildings of ten or twelve storeys from this era are common. For many provincial towns, however, even blocks five storeys high were a novelty. In Alma Ata (Almaty), the capital city of Kazakhstan, only after 1960 did any buildings of this height appear (Kozybayev et al. 1983).

Brick buildings were slow to complete, far too slow for the urgency. From the start of the Khrushchev programme, intensive research and development was undertaken on methods of prefabricated construction and standardization of manufacturing and assembling housing components. In the late 1950s and early 1960s, trucks could be seen trundling through Moscow, carrying complete room units, which were then stacked up and bolted together. However, the basic unit of standardized building relatively quickly became the large prefabricated panel of reinforced concrete (Fig. 4.3). By 1972 the panel was accounting for at least 50 per cent of housing construction (Il'in 1972: 165). By 1991 it was probably accounting for nearly all housing in the public sector. From one end of the USSR to the other, hundreds of thousands of five-storey blocks, made with prefabricated concrete panels, were erected (Fig. 4.4).

Figure 4.3
The standard prefabricated
concrete panel.

Each flat had one, two, or three rooms, together with kitchen and bathroom. Roughly a half had two rooms and a quarter each had either one or three rooms. Very few were ever built with more than three rooms, especially in local authority housing as opposed to the co-operative ventures. As a result, the elite tended to remain, as they have done to the present, in the larger Stalin-period flats of non-prefabricated construction, and with more and larger rooms. But by the ordinary citizens, who had suffered the crowding, inconvenience and squalor of communally shared flats with joint use of kitchen and bathroom, the new self-contained apartments were joyfully received, however few rooms there were.

Throughout the 1960s, as experience in prefabrication was gained and as the

Figure 4.4
Standard Krushchev period
five-storey housing of prefabricated concrete panels,
Khabarovsk.

Figure 4.5   Construction of high-rise blocks of prefabricated sections, Minsk.

number of lifts manufactured increased, so the average height of buildings also grew (Fig. 4.5). Nine-storey blocks tended to become the minimum by the end of the 1960s. Into the 1970s, blocks of nine storeys often formed long "curtain walls" between point blocks rising up to 16, 20 or even 25 storeys (Fig. 4.6). In 1974 a minimum of twelve storeys was laid down for large cities. This increase in height was justified, post hoc, as economizing on precious urban space. The social problems, which had emerged in such tower blocks in Western societies, were dismissed as the products of capitalist society rather than a consequence of the type of building. Indeed, the phenomena of graffiti and other forms of vandalism have until recently been seen relatively rarely in the Soviet Union. The housing shortage has meant that recipients of new flats have felt little to complain about;

Figure 4.6   High-rise blocks, Tepliy Stan, Moscow.

whether this honeymoon period will persist, once better housing is taken for granted, remains to be seen. Certainly, it is already the case that the inhabitants of five-storey flats of the earliest Khrushchev period are becoming increasingly vocal about their shortcomings.

In reality, it seems likely that the emphasis on high-rise construction – by the 1980s some planners were forecasting up to 30 or more storeys – has not been primarily concerned with the economics of urban land availability, which was nearly always a far less acute problem in the USSR than in west European countries. Rather, it has been a question of economy of time and costs of construction, by saving both on the length of infrastructure lines (water pipes, electricity cables, sewers, etc.) and on the length of transport routes.

With the assistance of the high-rise apartment block and with greater levels of capital investment, the tempo of provision of new dwellings has gone on rising. Every year from 1970 to 1991, over 100 million m^2 of housing was built throughout the country, in both urban and rural areas. In urban areas alone, over the three decades of the housing programme from 1956 to 1986 inclusive, over two thousand million square metres (2 092 60 000 m^2) of housing were erected. Perhaps rather surprisingly, private construction, although slowly declining both relatively and absolutely, still accounted for about an eighth (247 600 000 m^2) of the new building. Over that period, in town and countryside like, over 331 100 000 people received either new apartments or enlarged old ones; this figure includes, of course, many who moved into new or improved accommodation more than once over the three decades.

By any standards, the Soviet achievement in housing construction over the 30-odd years after 1957, when Khrushchev began the programme, has been truly colossal. The spread of new housing has been accompanied by the provision of services, which in the early 1950s had been seriously lacking. By 1990, 93 per cent of State and co-operative housing had mains water and 91.8 per cent had sewerage (*Narodnoye Khozyaystvo*. . . 1991: 193). In consequence, the desperate conditions, which formed Stalin's legacy to the Soviet city, have been enormously alleviated. Nationally, the planned sanitary norm of accommodation space, set at 9 m^2 per capita back in 1922, had been broadly attained by 1986 and in many major cities such as Moscow and in many areas of European Russia such as the Baltic Republics, it had been surpassed. In consequence, in the Russian Republic the norm was raised to 12 m^2 in the 1984 RSFSR Housing Codex, Clause 38. One level of rent was payable up to that norm; above it, higher rents were due for the extra space, but the norm was to be seen as a maximum, not a minimum (*Gorodskoye* . . . 1984, no. 1: 13–14). In practice, this norm is less used nowadays than the "useful living space" or "general living space" indicator, which includes corridors, kitchens and bathrooms and which is approximately 50 per cent larger than the "living space" figure.

The microregion

In the colossal effort of housing construction that characterized the whole period since 1957, the basic spatial unit of planning and building has all along been the microregion. In practice it has deviated not a little from the original concept envisaged in the 1920s debates and enlarged upon by Strumilin. Above all, the idea of communal living was never from the start taken seriously and, by the Second World War, the family was being lauded as the basic social unit of a stable socialist society. Thus, the designs for communal living, with separation of age groups and separation of domestic functions, were discarded in favour of separate family apartments in a group of blocks. Each group would have the necessary daily or weekly services, either in separate low-rise buildings within the group or dispersed on the ground-floor levels of the apartment blocks. The normal microregion would have pre-school facilities (crèches and kindergartens), shops selling basic food supplies, a laundry and dry cleaners, a polyclinic for all health care, and some form of entertainment or leisure centre – a club, cinema or library. The microregion is therefore an expression of planning and is one of the few ways, certainly the most significant way, in which the planning process has actually affected the development of Soviet towns. But the realities of each stage of urban growth have affected the nature of the microregion in ways not necessarily, or usually, desired by the planners.

In Stalin's lifetime, apart from a handful of experimental microregions, they had not been constructed at all. However, there had been a number of *kvartaly*, the apartment blocks that were to be the constituent units of the microregion. When the great housing programme was launched in 1957, the microregion became, as it has remained, the almost universal lowest level grouping of individual apartment blocks. The desperate need for haste, however, has meant that the reality of the microregion has not reflected much more than a simple geographical grouping; in a British comparison, most microregions are closer to a housing estate than to the neighbourhood unit of a planned new town such as Basildon or Crawley. The major shortcoming of the microregion resulting from the haste was that each block, as it was finished, was at once occupied, but provision of the basic services, intended as a fundamental feature of the scheme, lagged far behind, often by years.

Theoretically, any flat in a microregion should be within 100–300m of the nearest shops, with 80 per cent of the population not over 1000m away (Nikol' skiy 1982: 65). In reality, the vast majority of microregions did not and still do not meet the norms of service provision. Where shops have been provided, they are not in readily accessible precincts, but scattered through the microregion on the ground-floor level of the apartment blocks, thereby entailing much more effort and time in shopping. In particular, any given microregion is very unlikely to have the full range of shops selling daily and weekly necessities. Thus, journeys to neighbouring microregions are often necessary. In theory, this geographical dispersal of supply points is being drastically reduced as more and more *gastronomy* (supermarkets) are built, but the shortage of goods which characterized the late

1980s and early 1990s meant that prolonged searches over wide areas were still essential, while the greater availability of goods following the demise of the Soviet Union has done nothing to relieve the situation, as the hyperinflation of prices now causes citizens to hunt desperately for the cheapest goods.

A group of young Soviet architects at the end of the 1960s, in putting forward their view of the ideal communist city (Gutnov et al. 1970: 8), could say that "The microsector, however, as a basic structural unit for contemporary residential areas does not satisfy all the complex social, economic and technical needs involved. The result: bad conditions of health and sanitation, traffic frustration, a great waste of time, and the isolation of individuals in extremely confined spaces."

All along, the microregions have tended to be quite distinctly larger than the 2500 or so inhabitants postulated in early theory. The widespread use of ever-higher tower blocks has been combined with a general maintenance of the same surface area as the earliest microregions, with the result that the average population of the microregion has increased still further (Fig. 4.7). Populations between five and ten thousand are now common. The term "microregion" is also used rather loosely by the Soviet man in the street and may often refer to what the planners term "a living region", consisting in fact of up to half a dozen or more microregions. One residential district of Tashkent was described to the author as a "microregion", with a population of 150000!

At a higher level in the urban structure, plans group several microregions to form a "living region" (*zhiloy rayon*) of 30000–50000 people with higher levels of service provision, for example higher-level schools. In the largest cities of all, such as Moscow, general plans envisage groupings of "living regions" into a

Figure 4.7 The Olympic Village, Moscow, built for the 1980 Games and for subsequent use as a residential microregion.

"town region" (*gorodskoy rayon*) with a major service centre, which would obviate the need for journeys to the overall city centre, except on rare special occasions. The 1971 Moscow Genplan envisaged eight such "town regions", one of which was the old central district, the overall city focus (Fig. 4.8). In practice, the other seven surrounding "town regions" never even began to develop their foci; indeed such regional centres have not effectively emerged anywhere.

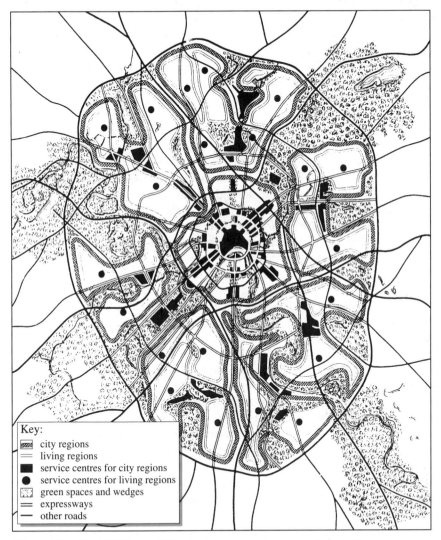

Key:
- city regions
- living regions
- service centres for city regions
- service centres for living regions
- green spaces and wedges
- expressways
- other roads

Figure 4.8 The 1971 General Plan for Moscow: main structural elements.

Urban densities

The rehousing of the bulk of the Soviet urban population since the 1960s has done much to reduce substantially the previously excessively high densities in inner city areas. Nevertheless, the continued presence of residential buildings in the most central districts has meant that population densities have remained high in comparison with Western cities. Certainly, there is no central business district with a "doughnut" hollow centre of minimal night-time population. At the same time, the housing of people in apartment blocks brings about higher densities in outer city areas than is found in British or American cities, where ever larger houses and gardens cause a fall-off in density towards the outer suburbs. On the contrary, the outer parts of Soviet towns usually have the highest apartment blocks and their densities may well exceed those in the intermediate zones of 1960s five-storey housing.

Very little study of changing urban densities has been carried out by Soviet geographers. For almost all cities, statistics have not been published to permit the calculation of densities of discrete areas within them. For many large cities, where the area within the city limits has been published, it is possible to calculate overall population density, but this figure has little significance. Boundaries have from time to time been extended, often far beyond the area then developed, thereby reducing the overall density. Rarely are figures for area and population of urban districts available. The one exception is Moscow, although even for the capital the population of individual districts has only been published at irregular and often lengthy intervals.

In 1970 the outer ring of Moscow's constituent districts, or boroughs, had very markedly lower densities than the inner ring (Fig. 4.9, Table 4.3; French 1979: 83–7). This reflected both the continuing excessively high densities of inner areas at that date and the presence of wide areas of still undeveloped land in the outer districts. Since then the intensive development of new microregions in these outer areas has left little land still available and the use of high-rise blocks everywhere has greatly increased outer borough densities. Meanwhile, the rehousing programme has steadily reduced the erstwhile overcrowding of the centre. As a result, the variation in density throughout the city has been greatly decreased, but the overall average is higher, in spite of increases in the area of Greater Moscow during the 1980s. In 1963 the overall average density of the city was 7000 persons per km^2; by 1974 it was 8385. By 1989, density was 8862 per km^2 within the city limits, excluding the overspill town of Zelenograd; within the orbital motorway the density was 10000 per km^2 and within the built-up area 16000 (Glushkova 1989: 67).

In consequence of boundary changes and the formation of new districts, it is not possible to make direct comparison of changing densities for more than a dozen or so of Moscow's districts, but it is clear that there has been a large fall in central densities and an equally prominent rise in outer densities (Fig. 4.10). In 1970 there were five districts with over 15000 per km^2, all in the centre, of which two were over 20000 per km^2; by 1989, there was only one over 15000 per km^2,

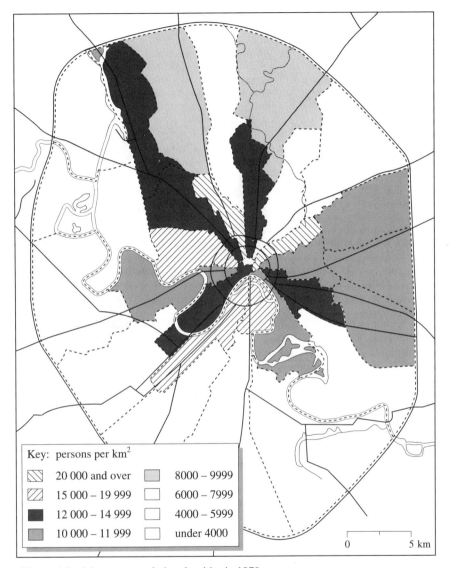

Figure 4.9   Moscow: population densities in 1970.

Sverdlovskiy District with 16 208 persons per km^2 (Table 4.3). Moreover, in 1989
there were 13 districts with densities between 10 000 and 15 000, as against only
ten two decades earlier; if in 1970 there were four outer boroughs with less than
5000 per km^2, in 1989 there were none. In 1970 the density varied from only 2489
per km^2 in Krasnogvardeyskiy District to 22 857 in Baumanskiy District, a range
of 20 368 per km^2; by 1989 the range had fallen to 11 065, between 5143 per km^2
in Sokol'nicheskiy District and 16 208 in Sverdlovskiy District.

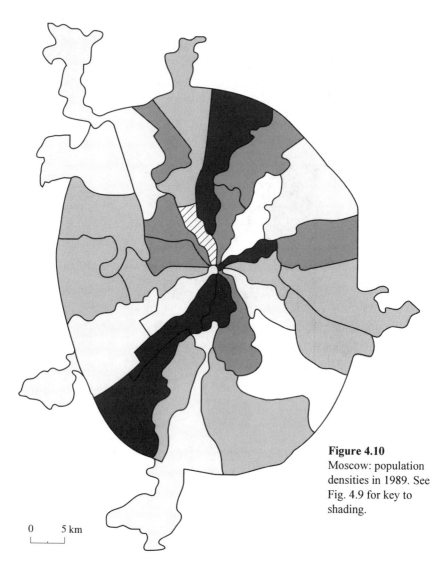

Figure 4.10
Moscow: population densities in 1989. See Fig. 4.9 for key to shading.

0   5 km

The concept of the green city

If population densities in the Soviet city are characteristically high, there has been throughout the planning era a compensatory factor in the emphasis given to providing green space and greenery in general. This process began in the 1920s and continued even in the desperate times of the Stalin era. Almost invariably, new streets were lined with trees; main traffic arteries, especially in Moscow, frequently have belts of trees between the central road and service roads on each side, thus reducing the sight and sound of traffic for pedestrians and dwellers in

Table 4.3 Population densities in Moscow (area: km^2; population: thousands; density: per km^2).

	1970			1989		
	Area	Population	Density	Area	Population	Density
Inner districts						
Bauman	6.3	144	22857	6.3	85.4	13556
Dzerzhinskiy	16.5	210	12727	13.4	148.7	11097
Zhdanov (Taganskiy)	14.2	173	12183	14.2	146.8	10338
Kalinin	12.0	142	11833	12.0	107.8	8983
Kiev	18.9	223	11799	18.9	164.1	8683
Krasnopresnenskiy	13.5	214	15852	13.5	136.7	10126
Lenin	13.8	182	13188	13.8	109.5	7935
Moskvoretskiy	9.3	168	18064	8.9	108.0	12135
Oktyabr'	16.1	303	18820	17.9	222.0	12402
Proletarskiy	22.2	258	11622	21.6	243.0	11250
Sverdlov	7.4	168	22703	7.2	116.7	16208
Sokol'niki	21.7	164	7558	21.7	111.6	5143
Frunze	15.6	222	14231	15.5	166.7	10755
Outer districts						
Babushkin	42.0	345	8214	32.4	343.0	10586
Volgograd	29.7	311	10471	34.7	332.4	9579
Voroshilov	42.8	231	5397	42.8	342.0	7991
Gagarin	49.3	204	4138	47.6	290.7	6107
Kirov	37.3	180	4826	40.5	58.3	14402
Krasnogvardeyskiy	67.9	169	2489	69.5	660.5	9504
Kuybyshev	49.6	306	6169	49.6	345.9	6974
Kuntsevo	44.3	304	6862	44.3	386.0	8713
Leningrad	27.3	342	12574	48.5	319.5	6588
Lyublino	56.0	167	2982	55.1	314.3	5704
Pervomayskiy	34.1	395	11584	34.1	369.5	10836
Perovo	32.2	259	8043	50.2	455.8	9080
Sovetskiy	60.9	317	5205	67.6	452.9	6700
Timiryazev	40.8	370	9069	47.3	417.3	8822
Tushino	30.2	209	6921	42.1	260.0	6176
Cheremushki	46.9	308	6567	38.8	509.1	13121
New districts						
Zeleznodorozhniy				15.0	157.2	10480
Sevastopol'				31.0	289.6	9342
Solntsevo				18.0	111.7	6206

Sources: Moskva v Tsifrakh (1972: 153–7); *Moskva v Tsifrakh 1989* (1989: 21–2).

the apartments along the route. New developments have included squares with trees and gardens (Mashinskiy 1951).

Every town, however small, was given its Park of Culture and Rest, even if this was little more than a patch of rather worn grass with a few seats and swings. Most were considerably more elaborate and would normally comprise, in addition to trees and bushes, lawns and flower beds, places of entertainment such as open-air theatres, cafes and possibly sporting facilities and funfairs. Moscow's 98 parks of

Figure 4.11
The River Moskva
near Zvenigorod in
Moscow's forest-
park green belt.

all types included 13 Parks of Culture and Rest, headed by the renowned Central Gor'kiy Park with a wide range of facilities; their area covered more than 2000 ha, with a further 6600 ha of forest-parks.

Largest cities, such as Moscow and Leningrad, were given surrounding green belts, Forest-Park Zones, where in intention at least, all further development of industry and housing was prohibited. Moscow's first Genplan in 1935 set up a forest-park protected zone 10 km wide around the city; the creation in 1960 of Greater Moscow was accompanied by a new zone covering some 180 000 km², of which 110 000 km² were woods and meadows (Fig. 4.11). In practice, reality rarely matched the goals and the sanctity of Forest-Park Zones was only too often ignored. There is no more vivid illustration of this than the expansion of Greater Moscow's boundaries in the mid-1980s to embrace six areas outside the ring motorway, where microregions had spilled out into the forest-park belt. The establishment of green belts within built-up areas to separate residence and workplace was achieved only in some of the wholly new urban foundations and even then frequently with but partial success.

One post-Stalin development could be seen as a distant descendant of the Disurbanist "Green City" view. This was the establishment of "overspill" decentralizing towns to take population, together with employment, out of Moscow. In 1958, Kryukovo, some 45 km northwest of Moscow beside the highway and railway to Leningrad, was designated as the site of the first such town. In fact, the concept and its embodiment in practice owed less to the Disurbanists than to the British experiment in overspill "New Towns" after the Second World War. The British experience aroused considerable interest in the USSR and was discussed at length – and favourably – at a conference on satellite towns held in Moscow early in 1960. As in Britain, such towns were intended to take population out of large cities together with employment, thus preventing the towns from becoming commuting suburbs; they would be located at a similar distance and would achieve similar target populations of 60 000–80 000; their constituent microregions with appropriate services resembled in plan the British neighbourhood units, except in the use of blocks of flats rather than individual houses. Kryukovo was planned with two industrial zones, to east and west, and seven microregions separated by preserved blocks of forest (Vilenberg & Loginov 1961: 55) and with a "traditional" style town centre.

Kryukovo was renamed Zelenograd, "Green Town", perhaps intentionally harking back to the 1920s concept and reflecting the 1950s revival of interest in the ideas of the pre-Stalin period. It developed successfully, but by no means achieved its ideals of providing better conditions than in the parent city. In 1978, the average useful living space per head in Zelenograd was $14m^2$, when the figure for Moscow as a whole was $16m^2$. Also, even more than the New Towns around London, it outstripped its original planned size of 65000. By 1989 its population had reached 158400. Unlike the British New Towns, Zelenograd has remained administratively subordinate to its parent city, to Moscow City Council.

A similar "new" town was designated in 1956 at Dubna, north of Moscow, where the Moscow–Volga Canal reaches the Volga. Unlike Zelenograd, Dubna was largely a single-function centre for nuclear research; consequently its employment and social profiles were very narrow. Yet it too showed points of similarity to the British New Towns, as Hausladen's study of the town has shown (Hausladen 1987a). Unlike the British towns and Zelenograd, which all outstripped their original population targets, Dubna was planned to be 100000 by 1991, but in fact its inhabitants then numbered only 67200. In a similar highly specialized functional category is the new town of Akademgorodok on the outskirts of Novosibirsk, referred to above. However, Zelenograd remained almost the only planned "overspill" town, not just for Moscow, but in the USSR. At the time that Zelenograd was launched, there were proposals to build three overspill satellites around Almaty (sometime Alma Ata), capital of the Kazakh Republic, two by expanding existing towns (Osborn & Reiner 1962: 245), but any such developments do not appear to have followed closely the "New Town" model.

If the moving out of populations from major urban areas into planned new towns has been, at best, a limited process, there was throughout the Soviet period a growing outward, greenery seeking trend on the part of individual town dwellers in their striving to acquire second homes in the surrounding countryside. Initially, in the 1960s, the second home, the "dacha", was one of the privileges of the highest elite. Increasingly, others began to seek this prime status symbol. Legally, dachas could be acquired only in defined dacha settlements to which access was controlled by particular bodies – ministries, Academies of Sciences, universities, and so on. The difficulties of acquiring second homes increased their desirability and many were obtained either illegally as by the purchase of agricultural land or in grey areas of transfer or "gift" from those properly entitled.

Numbers of dachas grew steadily during the Soviet period, but there were still many for whom the possibility of acquisition was restricted by lack of influence or money. For such people, one possibility was residence in a small town, where the normal accommodation was a single-storey individual house standing in a garden plot. In general, small towns were regarded as undesirable and were a source of heavy out-migration, but for people in the non-Russian republics the desire to have one's own garden plot was often strong and led to some actually preferring small towns as places to live. In Estonia the attraction of an individual house and garden in a small town was noted by Markov (1983: 13), while in his survey of the little town of Madneuli in Georgia, Vardosanidze (1986: 40) found that no less than 92.7 per cent of those asked wanted a garden and only 4 per cent wanted to live in a "pure" urban setting in a high-rise building.

In the larger cities, where the norm was the high-rise apartment house, there was often an alternative to both garden and dacha, and that was to join a garden co-operative. Many enterprises, institutions and ministries had their associated garden co-operatives. These provided members with allotments, plots of land usually on the immediate outskirts of a town, where apartment-dwelling citizens could cultivate their gardens, provide themselves with fresh fruit and vegetables, and find a green space of their own for relaxation. By 1987 there were 5 600 000 white-collar and blue-collar members of garden co-operatives (Rutkevich 1987: 94). Large cities are surrounded by extensive areas of garden co-operative allotments. The construction of a hut on the allotment was permissible, but it was not supposed to be a dwelling and heating was prohibited. In practice, this constraint was more honoured in the breach than the observance and many people in effect constructed their own "mini-dacha" on the town outskirts. Passengers flying into Moscow's international airport at Sheremet'yevo may see such an area of garden co-operatives as the plane makes its approach; they may also notice, at appropriate seasons of the year, that many of the huts on the allotments have chimneys with small plumes of smoke. These suburban second homes are indeed a classic example of the individual fulfilling for him or herself a need which the plan fails to meet.

Patterns of employment

Two of the fundamental principles of the Soviet planner ever since the 1920s have been, first, the maintenance of a close spatial relationship, preferably walking distance, between workplace and residence and secondly, their separation by amenity areas and greenery. In practice, neither of these goals has been achieved, save in the most exceptional circumstances. The very process of concentration of an ever larger share of urban dwellers in the very large cities, plus the outward sprawl of the microregions, have inevitably increased the average length of the journey to work. Moreover, the usual urban family unit has two employed members, sometimes more, and there is only a limited probability that both or all are employed in the same workplace; even if one person is well placed in relation to work, the chances are that the other family members are not and are therefore involved in tedious and time-consuming commuting.

Where the largest towns were concerned, the plans normally envisaged a halt on further new industry coming in and in most cases the shifting out of environmentally harmful industries. Once again, neither of these two objectives was achieved. Industrial ministries, intent on fulfilling and over-fulfilling their plan targets, were consistently unwilling to close down production while moves took place. Even when new plants were built outside the city (and, quite possibly, new technology made them less environmentally polluting), raised plan targets meant that the old factories within the town were kept operating. Of the 230 Moscow enterprises designated to move out during the 1970s, only 32 actually did so totally with another 7 moving partially (Glushkova 1986: 82). By 1989, still only 139 enterprises had gone (Trifonov & Makarova 1989: 38).

In fact, industry has continued to come into the largest cities, with their concentrations of skilled labour and markets. During the 1970s and 1980s, 20 new factories were set up in Moscow (ibid.). In 1987, the vice-chairman of Irkutsk Town Executive Committee was complaining that new industrial enterprises were still being brought in, to the point where the existing networks of roads, telephones, water and heating mains and the infrastructure of schools, pre-school institutions, polyclinics and hospitals had become inadequate (Kotsar' 1987: 96).

Under the 1971 Genplan for Moscow, the share of employment in central Moscow, defined as within the ring railway, was to be greatly reduced, thereby reducing commuting into the centre. In fact, since the plan began, the excess of workplaces over working population in the centre has increased by more than twice (Fedorov 1986: 8). In Frunzenskiy District, one of the inner ring of Moscow boroughs, in 1986 there was a population of 175000, but the district had 300000 workplaces (*Gorodskoye . . .*, 1986, no. 1: 14). In Zhdanovskiy District (total population 160000), the 47 industrial enterprises alone employ 190000 and the employment figure is rising; in the first half of the 1980s, 22 new service establishments were set up (*Gorodskoye . . .* 1985, no. 12: 19). Altogether in the first 15 years of the Genplan operation up to 1986, employment in Moscow in manufacturing alone "over-grew" by 700000 – the equivalent of a town of 1200000 people (Fedorov 1986: 4). Some Soviet authorities have even suggested that, for every new industrial job in Moscow, the total population grows by 25 (CDSP 1986, 38 no. 36: 21).

If the level of industry has not necessarily been what the planners sought, even less has industrial location within urban areas paid serious heed to the master plans. One writer in 1986 could say that Moscow's several dozen productive zones (i.e. manufacturing areas) had, in general, grown up spontaneously and that the role of territorial planning and management in the nation's capital had been diminished (Sokolova 1986: 15). In this matter of industrial location in urban areas, one sees more clearly than in any other issue the relatively weak position and powers of the town planner. Pressure from industrial ministries has systematically overruled the master plans of towns whenever any conflict has arisen.

Even where industrial zones have been defined, this has not always brought about rational use. In Leningrad in the 1950s, a number of large areas of 500–600ha were set aside as industrial zones, but lack of co-ordination in the planning and building of plants led to irrational use of space and duplicated engineering infrastructure (Litovka 1976: 73).

Problems have arisen in employment, not merely from locational issues, but from the structure of employment within a town. In a society where it was an expectation and a necessity for all adult members of a family to work, it was important that there should be equal job opportunities for both sexes. In theory, up to the 1960s, women were free to take on any work; even then, when certain jobs were closed to women on grounds of health and welfare, practice took little heed. There were, nevertheless, always certain forms of employment that were predominantly male or female. These tended to be much the same as in Western industrial societies – coalmining was male dominated, textiles were female dominated. Among ships' crews, about 90 per cent were male, in fishing 80 per cent of workers were male and in ship repair 65 per cent. Thus, in Far East ports such as Vladivostok, where unemployment was high (about 10%), 90 per cent of the unemployed were women (Sigov 1985: 120).

Planning concepts and their fulfilment since Stalin

Many Western writers have made effective critiques of the weaknesses of Soviet town planning, notably Bater (1977), Shaw (1983) and Andrusz (1984). In the USSR under Stalin, there could not be the faintest suggestion that what was done was not desirable. Even after the Khrushchev thaw, for a number of years criticism of what had been done could only be expressed indirectly, by making proposals for the future development of planning. Gradually, however, there grew up a considerable body of literature that made clear the shortcomings. Gutnov and his fellow architects in 1970 claimed that, "City planning to date has not given enough consideration to incessant growth as a continuing factor in the development of cities. This omission alone is ample proof that present theoretical thought in the field of building and planning is inadequate to direct a communist building program." (Gutnov et al. 1970: 6). By the 1980s many planners, sociologists, economists and geographers were calling for major changes in town planning approaches. Unfortunately, by then there was little enough time left for such calls to be heeded, adopted and put into practice.

Certainly, the third phase of urban development under the leadership of, first, Khrushchev, and then Brezhnev, saw the gradual compilation of town plans for almost all the larger cities and middle-size towns, as well as many smaller places. At the heart of planning theory over the post-Stalin period, as during it, a number of concepts survived from the earlier stage of debate. Indeed, after Stalin's death in 1953 there was a re-emphasis on some of the ideas of the 1920s by writers such as Strumilin, who advocated the microregion, and the Gutnov group, who favoured in many respects the principles of communal living. These efforts, like other half-hearted attempts to reopen the earlier total questioning of existing social structure, were short-lived.

The era of the massive housing drive made heavy use of the microregion as the planning basis for residence. However, practice fell considerably short of the integrated living unit of theory, usually in the failure to provide, or long delay in providing, the service infrastructure within the microregion. Nevertheless, the physical structure of the microregion has come to represent, perhaps, the most evident legacy of the planning era in the post-Soviet city. Not far behind in its present-day visual impact are the results of the stress on greenery and green space, which was always maintained, and which led to the general planting of trees along streets and the establishment of parks. The process of greening towns has perhaps been the most successfully implemented of all the 1920s concepts of the ideal city.

Other objectives of planning promulgated in the 1920s remained as unquestioned aims, but with little or no realization. One such purpose was the limitation of the journey to work, which in fact tended to become longer, especially in the latter stages of the period. Yet other principles continued to be cited as desirable, or important, or even essential, but with less and less confidence until they were abandoned entirely, as happened with the concept of optimum city size.

If some of the 1920s concepts were kept alive by town planners and some effort was made to put them into practice, little that was conceptually new emerged after the mid-1950s, other than perhaps the Unified Settlement System. Originally a rigid framework, as time went by and little was done to create it, the idea of such a system gradually became more flexible, until eventually it was little more than a recognition that any network of urban places has a set of hierarchical and functional relationships.

Khanin (1991), writing at the very end of the Soviet era, identified various approaches to settlement planning. One was the unified system of settlement, a second was that of the development of agglomerated settlement and a third the grouped system of settlement and the concept of the optimal (ideal?) city. But he comments drily of settlement theory that "we know many of its elements, laws and relationships, but forecasts based on knowledge of them are scarcely more accurate than weekly or other long-term weather forecasts," adding in a footnote that *their* accuracy is well known to be less than 60 per cent (ibid.: 129)!

Beyond these broad and highly generalized concepts, none of which ever formed any practical basis for planning, the period from 1957 up to the mid-1980s and the arrival in power of Gorbachev, saw little or no innovation in planning concepts and hardly any more development of a theoretical basis. For the greater part of that time, most of what was written on the subject was scarcely more than *post hoc* justifications, putting glosses of intention on processes that were at best only lightly under the control of plans. Explanations of what had been carried out were limited to the simplest, and nearly always assumed that resulting patterns were in accordance with planned objectives. The fundamental aims of creating an ideal place for people to live and work in remained and, in published work at all events, it was well nigh universally accepted that what the socialist system had done was, *ipso facto*, good and incomparably better than developments in the capitalist city. Nevertheless, if in the 1920s the community was seen as more important than either the individual or the family, by 1970 Gutnov and his fellows could write that "the communist system, in fact, focuses on the individual" (Gutnov et al. 1970: 26).

Certainly, as the post-Stalin years proceeded, the idea that "socialist city" was an instrument of social engineering and that a new urban environment would of itself create a new society, was gradually replaced by the general assumption that a new urban environment would have to develop, indeed was developing, in parallel with the development of society, which was of course towards communism. It was equally universally assumed, as Kaganovich had asserted at the opening of the Stalin period, that the existence of a different political system in itself meant that the city was different from its capitalist counterpart. In theory, urban development was controlled "by the people, for the people." That centralized control laid down standardized, and therefore egalitarian, norms for every aspect of the town. In practice, the inability of local soviets to exercise that power of control to any serious extent meant that norms, and thus planning ideals, were not achieved. Even the central power itself failed to bring about its stated aims for the town, for example its impotence in controlling the growth of the very large city. Such failures in practice, even more than the inadequate working out of sound and realistic planning theory, led to growing dissatisfaction with the operation of town plans. It was clear that divided responsibility for the running of a city and its constituent parts was a fundamental obstacle to the accomplishment of a unified city-wide plan. It was no less clear that, in a system where all resources were ultimately allocated from the top (by Gosplan, working on the orders of the Presidium), local authorities at the base of a long chain of command could not hope to receive the same share as the all-powerful industrial ministries, which were directly represented at Presidium level. In that respect the post-Stalin era was not significantly better than the Stalin period. The plans were drawn up in planning offices by architects who wanted to create their concepts of the ideal urban environment; these might receive lip-service blessing from those at the highest level of authority, but they rarely received priority. Khrushchev's effort to decentralize decision-taking to *sovnarkhozy* (regional economic councils) in 1957 was intended to increase the power of town soviets to take decisions, but this short-lived experiment never succeeded in getting off the ground and it died with his fall from power in 1964. Subsequently, from time to time half-hearted efforts were made to strengthen the hand of the local soviet, as in 1971 and again in 1979 and 1981 (Shaw 1983: 400), but in practice these had little effect.

The overriding of the plan by ministries was the principal reason why the plan had to be constantly revised. Almost as significant a cause, and frequently related to the first, was the failure of the planners to estimate accurately future developments, whether in economic or demographic growth. Having underestimated growth in population, say, it was a difficult and protracted process for local authorities to acquire additional resources to meet the larger figure, with consequent failure to achieve established norms of service provision. One might wonder if another factor in the inadequacy of the plan to provide the quality of life desired by the inhabitants was the classification of the detailed plan as secret, thereby preventing public discussion or constructive criticism. Matters were not helped either by the near-universal shortage of trained staff in the planning offices.

Further drawbacks arose from the rigidity of the Genplans; although far too frequently replaced by new plans, each plan as it was promulgated was regarded as definitive for the period of 20–30 years that it covered. Long before the plan period had expired, often in less than ten years, it was hopelessly out of date. Only towards the end of the Soviet period were voices raised to call for a flexible, rolling plan. Moreover, the long time-span of the Genplan meant little or no co-ordination with the five year plans for the economic development of the country, which were the principal tools for the allocation of resources. Perhaps not least among the weaknesses of the Soviet planning system was its heavy reliance, mostly total reliance, on architects to compose the plan. They tended to think in terms of architectural compositions rather than efficient functioning from the point of view of the citizen (Stepanenko 1981: 264). Grandiose streets more than a hundred metres wide were disagreeable to cross in winter blizzards, as one tracked from one empty shop to another, especially for the elderly and disabled. Only very late in the day did the planner wake up to the clearly manifest public preference for the old pre-revolutionary shopping streets, where the shops were close together and the human scale maintained. But by the time that the wishes of the urban population even began to be considered, the Soviet system was moving into its twilight.

CHAPTER 5

Problems of the Soviet city's legacy

As the previous chapters have indicated, the realities of the Soviet period as a whole failed to bring about the creation of the City of Socialist Man as conceived in the 1920s, or as expounded in literature and in the plans themselves over the following decades. The crisis state of the USSR by the 1980s, leading to its demise in 1991, highlighted a host of city problems, some arising from the same causes that have produced problems in the Western city, but others appearing as the product of the flaws in the Soviet system. All brought about serious deficiencies in the present quality of life of the urban dwellers. For all the achievements in bricks and concrete, city planners and local authorities today have been left facing a mountain of severe difficulties in making the city an even adequate place for a reasonable life, let alone an ideal setting for work, recreation and rest.

The abiding housing problem

Praiseworthy as was the colossal achievement of the USSR in housing construction after 1957, the task was far from being accomplished when the Soviet Union collapsed. Serious overcrowding still persisted. The massive building programme would have to continue through the foreseeable future and this was understood to be necessary long before the USSR collapsed. "For all the great scale of accomplished work in the social plan, the housing problem has not lost its sharpness" (Dmitriyev et al. 1987: 70). By the time of *perestroyka,* some four-fifths of the urban population lived in separate flats, but the remaining fifth – that is, some 37 750 000 people – occupied communal flats, with their shared kitchens and bathrooms, or hostels, or houses fit to be condemned (Grebennikov et al. 1987: 195). Even in Akademgorodok, the satellite town of Novosibirsk, which is devoted to teaching and research institutions and which has always been one of the showpieces of the Soviet Union, there were over 3000 more families than flats, with the result that 16 per cent of families lived in communal apartments (Timyashevskaya 1986: 117), a figure only marginally better than the national average.

Various reasons account for the abiding pressure on housing. In part, the initial shortage of the mid-1950s was so extreme that the process of catching up was not complete. The norm of housing space was far from being achieved everywhere. In general it was the smaller towns and towns in the Asiatic parts of the USSR, both Siberia and Central Asia, that had the poorest provision of living space per head. At Union Republic level, the disparity in urban living space per capita was very marked (Table 5.1). Out in front were the Baltic Republics with $16.8–19.7 \mathrm{m}^2$; trailing far behind were the Islamic republics of Central Asia and Azerbaydzhan with $9.1–10.4 \mathrm{m}^2$. As the table indicates, the gap between those worst and best supplied with housing has been steadily widening, from $5.8 \mathrm{m}^2$ in 1970 to 7.0 in 1980 and to 8.5 in 1990. Over each of those two decades, the urban dweller in Turkmenia gained on average 0.8 and $0.7 \mathrm{m}^2$ of additional useful space, $1.5 \mathrm{m}^2$ in all. His counterpart in Estonia over the same period gained 2.7 and $3.5 \mathrm{m}^2$, a total of $6.2 \mathrm{m}^2$ or more than four times as much. Within the Russian Federation, the eastern regions did significantly worse than those in Europe. In Rubtsovsk in the Altay Kray in 1972 (population then 158000), 73.4 per cent of workers had less than $9 \mathrm{m}^2$ per family member; in 1980, still 68.5 per cent, more than two-thirds, were below the old national norm (Artemov 1986: 72).

Table 5.1   Urban housing fund (m^2 per capita).

Republic	1970	Rank	Gain 1970–80	1980	Rank	Gain 1980–90	1990	Rank
USSR	10.8		2.0	12.8		2.5	15.3	
RSFSR	10.8	6	2.2	13.0	6	2.4	15.4	6
Ukraine	11.8	4	2.0	13.8	4	2.3	16.1	4
Belarus	10.5	7	2.4	12.9	7	2.1	15.0	7
Estonia	13.4	2	2.7	16.1	1	3.5	19.6	1
Latvia	13.7	1	1.9	15.6	2	1.8	17.4	2
Lithuania	11.0	5	2.4	13.4	5	3.2	16.6	3
Moldova	9.8	8	1.7	11.5	=8	2.4	13.9	9
Georgia	11.9	3	2.4	14.3	3	1.7	16.0	5
Armenia	9.4	11	1.4	10.8	10	2.6	13.4	10
Azerbaydzhan	9.3	12	0.5	9.8	13	2.3	12.1	11
Kazakhstan	9.6	=9	1.9	11.5	=8	2.8	14.3	8
Kyrgyzstan	8.7	=13	1.2	9.9	12	2.0	11.9	13
Uzbekistan	7.9	15	1.2	9.1	15	2.9	12.0	12
Turkmenistan	9.6	=9	0.8	10.4	11	0.7	11.1	15
Tadzhikistan	8.7	=13	1.0	9.7	14	1.9	11.6	14

Calculated from *Narodnoye Khozyaystvo SSSR* for 1969, 1979 and 1989.

In every republic, the smaller the town, the worse it tended to fare. But it is not only size and region of town which made a difference in housing provision; within towns there could be even more marked variation between one part of town and another. In the Tsentral'nyy (Central) District of Minsk, the Belorussian capital with 1543000 people, the living space per capita in the early 1980s was only $5.57 \mathrm{m}^2$ (*Minsk . . .*, 1983: 430). Moscow, despite its partial protection by the requirement of a residence permit, had in 1988 no less than 344800 families and single persons on the waiting lists of the local authorities (Andrusz 1990: 234).

There, a family had to have under $6 m^2$ per capita to qualify for a place on the hous-ing waiting list. At the national level there were 12 660 000 households on waiting lists, representing 22.3% of all households (ibid.: 239). What these figures mean is that a massive additional amount of building was and is still required, simply to give every urban dweller the old original Soviet minimum laid down in 1922.

A major contributory reason for the failure to catch up with the norm of living space was the continuing influx of population to the towns. Even the very largest, with restrictions imposed on in-migration by the requirement of the *propiska* per-mit to reside, went on growing. The continuing and unplanned extension of indus-try and employment in Moscow caused severe labour shortages, but also led to equally unplanned and undesired growth in population. Through the 1970s, Mos-cow grew by over 100 000 a year (Table 5.2), of which never more than 22 000 was by natural increase, the excess of births over deaths. Moscow has the one of the lowest rates of crude natural increase in the country. Thus the net balance of migration over that decade was an inward gain of 88 000–98 000 every year. In the early 1980s the rate of total growth fell somewhat to 60 000 in 1984. It then rose again to over 90 200 in 1986, of which 24 431 came from natural increase; the rest, 65 769, was by mechanical growth, that is to say, the excess of in-migration over out-migration. In 1988 natural increase accounted for only some 10 000 of the 72 800 growth of the city population. "For all intents and purposes, limits on resi-dence permits have been abolished for a substantial portion of those who wish to move to major cities" (CDSP 1986, 38 no. 36: 21).

As the capital, the show city and the best supplied and serviced city in the Soviet Union, the right of residence in Moscow was fervently sought. Those with

Table 5.2 The growth of Moscow.

April	1956	4 839 000	C	Jan. 1	1975	7 632 000	S
Jan. 15	1959	5 045 905	S	Jan. 1	1976	7 734 000	S
August	1960*	6 046 000	S	Jan. 1	1977	7 818 000	S
Jan. 1	1961	6 208 000	S	Jan. 1	1978	7 909 000	S
Jan. 1	1962	6 296 000	S	Jan. 17	1979	8 011 000	C
Jan. 1	1963	6 354 000	S	Jan. 1	1980	8 099 000	S
July 1	1964	6 408 000	S	July 1	1981	8 265 000	S
Jan. 1	1965	6 443 000	S	Jan. 1	1982	8 363 000	S
July 1	1966	6 463 000	S	Jan. 1	1983	8 457 000	S
Jan. 1	1966	6 482 000	S	Jan. 1	1984*	8 537 000	S
July 1	1967	6 507 000	S	Jan. 1	1985	8 655 900	S
Jan. 1	1968	6 590 000	S	Jan. 1	1986	8 727 900	S
Jan. 1	1969	6 642 000	C	Jan. 1	1987	8 818 000	S
Jan. 15	1970	7 061 008	S	Jan. 12	1988	8 894 300	S
Jan. 1	1971	7 188 000	S	Jan. 1	1989	8 967 100	C
Jan. 1	1972	7 229 000	S	Jan. 1	1990	9 000 100	S
Jan. 1	1973	7 410 000	S	Jan. 1	1991	9 003 000	S
Jan. 1	1974	7 528 000					

Sources: C = census of corresponding year; S = statistical publications of *Tsentral'noye Statisticheskoye Upravleniye* of corresponding year.
* Enlargement of city area.

influence, those whose particular skills and abilities caused departments and enterprises to obtain special permission, those who married Muscovites, all succeeded in gaining the coveted *propiska*. In the 1970s and 1980s on average 5000 people every year acquired residence rights in Moscow by marriage (Glushkova & Khorev 1990: 9). Cases were known of Muscovite girls marrying outsiders in a *"mariage de convenance"* for reward, just to get them into the city, whereafter they got divorced. "Graduates of Moscow higher schools are stricken every year by wedding fever! Remaining in the city is often the sole object of matrimony in such cases. It is no secret that sometimes laws are even broken and so-called 'fictitious' marriages concluded in pursuit of this goal, and all merely for the purpose of getting one's passport stamped 'permanent residence permitted'. Such marriages are not only to some degree or other fictive, but are almost 100 per cent 'defective'." (CDSP 1986, 38 no. 36: 22).

Many resided illegally and unregistered; by the nature of things their number cannot be guessed. The severe shortage of labour, especially unskilled and less skilled labour, resulting from these restrictions discouraged too rigorous pursuit of illegal in-migrants. During the 1980s, shop after shop, factory gate after factory gate in Moscow displayed "Help wanted" notices. Once ensconced in Moscow, people rarely and unwillingly left. For certain labour-deficient occupations, notably in the construction industry, a system was developed whereby several tens of thousands of workers were allowed to reside in Moscow on a temporary basis, the so-called *limitchiki*. In practice, once in the city, they completed their contract period, then moved to more prestigious jobs. During the 1970s, industry took up 44 per cent of the limit and brought in a total of 250000 workers, but the number employed in industry rose in all by only 2000; similarly, construction trades brought in 180000 but the workforce grew over the decade by only 73000 (Glushkova & Khorev 1990: 6). Mostly of low skills, the *limitchiki* were regarded with considerable suspicion and dislike by the permanent residents. They were held responsible for the high crime rates; worst of all, they were accused, with a good deal of reason, of illegally absorbing themselves into the city's population.

Those brought in for particular employment numbered 700000 over the 15 years 1970–85; about half of them promptly abandoned the enterprise that had brought them in (ibid.: 6–8). Trifonov & Makarova (1989: 45–6) analyzed the structure of Moscow's in-migrants over the period 1971–85 and found that, of the annual increment, about 35000 were *limitchiki*, another 30000–35000 were out-of-towners marrying Muscovites, 5000–6000 were specialists brought in, together with their families, and 4000–5000 were family members, especially the elderly, reunited with their families.

The situation in Moscow, although surely the most intense in the USSR, was repeated in the other large cities with controlled in-migration. Leningrad (St Petersburg), also a restricted city, was envisaged in its 1966 Genplan as reaching a ceiling of 3500000 in 1990; in fact it passed that figure after only four years (Litovka 1976: 51). By the 1989 census, with a year still to go, it had reached 5020000, no less than 43 per cent over target. Similarly, Pityurenko (1983: 39) has

100

shown in the case of Kiev that consistently, from the 1959 census to 1976, inmigration accounted for roughly three-quarters of the city's growth.

In other, non-controlled, towns, the rate of influx was at times extremely rapid, especially where new growth industries had been set up or new mineral deposits were exploited. Bratsk on the Angara, beside the giant hydroelectric station providing power for aluminium smelting and cellulose industries, grew from 51 455 in 1959 to 255 000 in 1989. Even more spectacular was the growth of the Volga-side town of Tol'yatti (the former Stavropol, renamed after the Italian Communist Party secretary, Togliatti). Only 61 281 at the time of the 1959 census (or 72 441 within its present extended boundaries), by the 1970 census it had attained 250 853 and by 1989 it had left the half-million mark far behind with its 630 000 inhabitants. There was a ninefold increase in under three decades. This surging growth was principally the result of the huge Fiat-built car factory and associated industries. In "boom" cities of this type, the difficulties of the construction industry in keeping up with demand for housing were often at their most severe.

Yet a third reason why the task of housing construction remained as formidable at the close of the Soviet era as it had been 30 years earlier, was the growing urgency to replace older housing, which perforce had continued in use as a result of the acute shortage. Equally, there was increasing need to replace much of the housing put up in the early years of the crash programme. For example, in the towns of the Moscow region in 1984, 19.6 per cent of the housing stock still consisted of single-storey houses, 10.1 per cent of two, 5.2 per cent of three and 9.8 per cent of four-storey buildings; thus 44.7 per cent comprised what almost certainly was old housing, probably pre-Khrushchev and often pre-revolutionary. Another 40.9 per cent was in five-storey housing, almost certainly therefore in Khrushchev-period prefabricated apartment blocks (Ogarkov 1984: 82). That left only 14.4 per cent of housing stock, which might be expected not to need major repair or replacement, either immediately or in the near future.

The five-storey, prefabricated panelled blocks of flats put up in their scores of thousands during the 1960s were urgently required at the time and had to be built fast. Unfortunately, this has meant that they have not worn well. Their finish was always very poor and, at the time, experience with prefabrication and standardization in housing was limited. Even in the 1960s, a study of 609 blocks of flats (intended to last 30 years) showed that 64 per cent needed roof repair within four years of construction, 90 per cent within eight years and all in ten years (Cattell 1976: 275). Such blocks became known throughout the Soviet Union as *Khrush-choby*, a derogatory term conflating the words Khrushchev and *trushchoba*, a slum. By the 1990s they were all reaching, indeed often had reached, the end of their envisaged useful life and needed to be replaced. A few were pulled down, but the burden of total replacement, or anything remotely like it, on the already over-stretched construction industry would be so great as to be quite unthinkable, at least any time this century. Still older housing frequently had to come ahead of the *Khrushchoby* in the queue for renewal. In the Eleventh Five Year Plan, from 1981 to 1985, some 50 million m^2 of dilapidated housing were pulled down (Dmitriyev et al. 1987: 74). The 1986 target for housing repair in Moscow alone was $4\,800\,000\,\text{m}^2$, most of which was in the centre and thus might be expected to concern older buildings (*Gorodskoye* . . . 1986, no. x: 6).

A survey of Donetsk from the end of the 1970s showed considerable variation throughout the city in the proportion of housing that came up to standard (*etalon*), from only 54.5 per cent in Proletarskiy District to 83.4 per cent in Voroshilovskiy District. Worse still, under the plan for 1980 the gap between the worst- and best-provided urban districts would widen, from 55.3 per cent in Proletarskiy to 85.6 per cent in Voroshilovskiy District (Senchenko 1980: 143).

One result of all the pressures causing a continuing housing shortage was that all towns and districts within towns had long waiting lists of people wanting accommodation. Young couples getting married commonly had to continue living with one or other family. A survey of nearly 50000 couples in 1984, where at least one partner was under 35, showed that 43.8 per cent of those in urban areas were living with relatives; about three-quarters of these families had been married for less than five years (*Vestnik Statistiki* 1986, no. 4: 58). The situation has not been made better by undeserving people using corruption to secure preference on the list. A "new broom" council in Taldy Kurgan Oblast of Kazakhstan vetted its housing list and removed no less than 4000 names that were improperly on it (CDSP 1987, 39 no. 2: 11).

The huge tasks facing housing construction would be still harder to fulfil if the post-Soviet regimes were to attempt to meet the legacy of goals set by the Twenty-seventh Party Congress in 1987. These required that every family should have its own apartment by the year 2000. To achieve this would mean building not less than 2000 million m^2 of housing in 13 years, a 50 per cent increase over existing stock, or twice the already remarkable rate of construction over the previous 30 years (Grebennikov et al. 1987: 194). Even more would be needed to meet the second goal of giving every family member his or her own room. In Akademgorodok, for example, over 60 per cent of one-roomed flats are occupied by families of three, four or even five persons (Timyashevskaya 1986: 117). Although the end of the Soviet Union may have invalidated the resolutions taken at the Twenty-seventh Party Congress, the human need remains in the cities of the independent republics; the deepening economic crisis makes it almost certain that the targets are impossible to achieve and, for a large proportion of the population, perhaps the most burdensome problem bequeathed by the Soviet regime may well be that of inadequate housing.

The strain on the economy in general and on the building industry in particular in attempting to achieve these aims has been greatly increased by the raising of the established norm of housing space per capita. Fomin (1989: 110) assumed that by the mid-1990s the allocation would be $21-23\,\text{m}^2$ per head, although one must have grave doubts over his blithe assumption that this is realistically attainable by the first decade of the next century. Especially in the light of the current economic crises, one must have the most serious reservations whether the successor States of the USSR will even approach achieving any of these vastly ambitious targets.

Indeed, the end of the Soviet Union has already caused a severe worsening of the housing situation in the Russian Republic. First there are the large numbers of soldiers and their families previously stationed in East Germany and other parts of eastern Europe. The lack of accommodation to house the returning troops has made the military evacuation of eastern Europe a prolonged process. In the case of Estonia, the lack of housing was cited by President Yeltsin in January 1993 as reason for halting the removal of Russian troops, although the second reason given, of protecting the rights of the large Russian minority, was in all likelihood the stronger. This additional pressure on housing has been increased still more by the large-scale migration of Russians out of the non-Russian republics back to Russia. In 1991, the net in-migration to Russia from the other former Soviet republics was 139 800; the estimated immigration in 1992 was 198 600 (*Uchet migratsionnykh protsessov . . .,* 1993: 3). By the end of 1992 the official figure for refugees in Russia had reached 500 000, many of whom had not found homes or even jobs, but it has been suggested that the true figure may be around two million.

Urban sprawl, high-rise housing and the evaluation of land

The huge extent of new housing on city margins has caused considerable urban sprawl. In the decade 1974–84, 600 ha of Moscow, designated under the 1971 Genplan as green space, were built over (Glushkova 1986: 90). In 1960, Moscow's city boundaries were fixed at the Orbital Motorway, completed in that year. Outside this, the city was surrounded by an amenity green belt known as the Forest-park Zone, where all further development of industry and housing was to cease. In 1984 two immediately adjacent areas of the supposedly protected Forest-park Zone were incorporated into the city, having been heavily built over. A year later a further five incursions into the amenity zone were incorporated (Fig. 5.1). Out of one of these extensions of the city has been created a whole city district, Solntsevskiy District, with a population of 90 000; by the year 2010, when the next Genplan period was to have been complete, its population is expected to reach 235 800 (*Gorodskoye . . .* 1986, no. 8: 16).

The massive additional building needed for the future, examined in the preceding section, will cause further outward sprawl of cities into their surrounding amenity areas, and all the more so as increasingly numerous tracts of the old historic inner areas are being protected from redevelopment by conservation orders.

The problem of urban sprawl was at the heart of one of the sharpest debates among Soviet planners. Except in the largest cities, the share of high-rise buildings was for long astonishingly low. In Genplans compiled to 1965, one-storey buildings comprised 55–78 per cent (Ivanova 1972: 7). Karaganda, a town founded in 1934 and therefore wholly created in the Soviet period, in 1976 had 94.5 per cent of its built-up area covered by one-storey buildings; only two per cent had buildings over four storeys. In Volgograd, in effect an entirely post-1945 creation, the

103

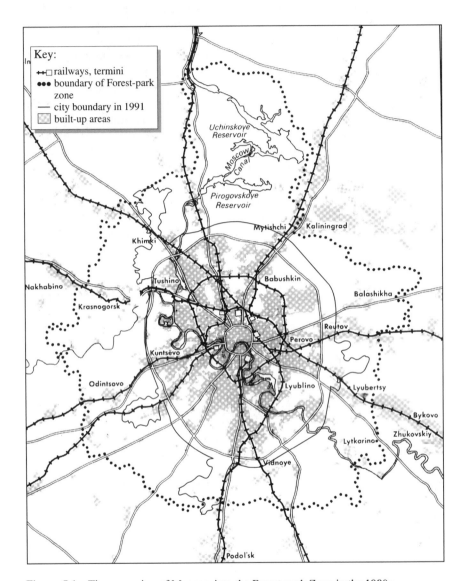

Figure 5.1   The expansion of Moscow into the Forest-park Zone in the 1980s.

equivalent figures were 84 per cent covered by one-storey buildings and 4 per cent with more than four-storey houses; for Dnepropetrovsk the figures were 86.2 per cent and 5.1 per cent respectively (Litovka 1976: 67).

This extensive use of urban land caused a number of planners and economists to advocate high-rise housing as most cost-effective. Such accommodation uses less land for a given number of people and reduces the cost of providing the serv-

Table 5.3 Housing in Moscow, by height of building (% of all housing).

Storeys	1966	1970	1980	1988
1	6.8	3.1	0.4	0.4
2	11.5	6.4	1.2	0.5
3	4.5	3.3	1.6	1.0
4	5.6	4.1	2.6	2.0
Total under 5	28.4	16.9	5.8	3.9
5	43.9	39.3	28.7	24.4
6	4.2	3.3	2.3	1.8
7	3.2	2.4	1.8	1.5
8	9.0	7.2	5.3	1.5
Total 6–8	16.4	12.9	9.4	4.8
9	7.0	19.6	27.7	24.3
10		1.8	1.4	1.3
11		0.5	0.4	0.4
12		6.1	14.4	15.3
13	4.3	0.3	0.3	0.4
14		1.8	4.0	5.1
Total 10–14	4.3	10.5	20.5	22.5
15 and over		0.8	7.9	17.0

Sources: Moskva v Tsifrakh (1966–1970gg.), Statistika, Moscow, p. 104; *Moskva v Tsifrakh 1989,* Finansy i Statistika, Moscow, p. 96.

ice infrastructure. One of the most visible developments in Soviet towns of every size over the last 30 years has been the upward shift of the urban skyline, and nowhere more so than in the largest cities. As Table 5.3 makes very clear, in Moscow the share of very high blocks (curtain-wall blocks of 9 or 12 storeys and point towers of 15 or more storeys) has risen sharply. However, this move to high-rise building has been very largely confined to the largest cities. Blocks of 12–16 storeys were restricted to Moscow and Leningrad and other towns over 250000 people or,as an exception, to towns with severe space restriction or where there were large clusters of nine-storey buildings. Smaller places should be limited to five-storey buildings, with 9 as an exception (Sarkisyan 1983: 183).

This development reflected, *inter alia,* the growing sense in the twilight of the USSR that it was economically essential to give a calculable value to land. There was a widely spreading recognition of the errors and dangers implicit in the Marxist doctrine that only labour adds value and that therefore land, as a natural good, has no monetary price. This is scarcely a new recognition. As far back as the early 1960s, some economists and geographers had been indicating that pricing of natural goods was vital, more especially in the context of water supply. Equally, if land is not priced, there is no incentive for land users to economise in their space requirements and many of them, especially in industry and construction, have been notoriously bad at doing so. Enterprises held on to unused land, against "a rainy day."

Reluctance to suggest that land should be priced led to various proposed alternative methods of assessing land worth, but the outcome was essentially the same – the creation of a "surface of land value", that is to say a map of the varying desirability of different areas. One of the pioneering attempts to construct this "surface of land value" was made by Kabakova (1973, 1981; outlined in Bater 1980: 126–9). Her evaluation of urban land worth was calculated on the basis of accessibility, engineering construction suitability and other factors, including social considerations such as service provision. The resulting pattern of land value, largely because of the weight given to the centre by the accessibility and service provision factors, looks remarkably like the pattern derived for Western cities in the 1960s on the basis of rents by W. Alonzo; from highest values at the centre, ratings descend outwards in concentric rings.

If Kabakova's 1973 model was purely theoretical, by 1986 Gosstroy's own Scientific Research Institute of Construction Economics, under her leadership, was accepting that land should be priced. Urban land was allotted values in money terms, ranging from 2 million roubles per hectare in central Moscow to 700 000 roubles per hectare on the periphery; the Institute calculated that, by the end of the next Genplan period in the year 2010, the equivalent values would be respectively 3 million and over 1 million roubles per hectare, while in areas of new construction values would then be 700 000 roubles, although with the rising inflation in the USSR and post-USSR, these figures have since become meaningless.

From there, Kabakova went on to urge that there should be payment for land in order to encourage economic use of space in towns, and even that construction enterprises should have to pay for the construction site, to prevent them from using more space than was absolutely necessary for the building process. Similarly, sanitary and protection zones and technical/engineering zones should be given cost assessments to encourage efficiency and thus reduce the amount of land needed for such purposes (Kabakova 1986: 12–13). As Sokolova (1986: 14–15) pointed out to Soviet readers of *Gorodskoye Khozyaystvo Moskvy* (*The urban economy of Moscow*), in Poland and Hungary payments for land were already exacted, in the case of Hungary since the 1960s, and however complex the process of costing land might be, without it there was little hope of ever providing the necessary standards of living or of intensifying urban land use. As the post-Soviet republics move to a market economy, with the gradual termination of the command economy, land markets must emerge, but as yet it is far from clear how this process will take place.

Meanwhile, the lack of anything better than a theoretical model of urban land values has frequently meant a quite astonishingly low intensity of land use in central city areas. For example, in the very heart of Yekaterinburg (Sverdlovsk) there are whole city blocks either of derelict land or of land with only an occasional pre-revolutionary wooden house (Fig. 5.2).

Service provision

If neither the quantity of housing nor its spatial expression in the microregion were what the planners and their Genplans hoped to achieve, even less success can be

Figure 5.2 Semi-derelict wasteland in the central downtown area of Yekaterinburg (Sverdlovsk).

attributed to the provision of infrastructure and services of every description. In part this reflected the lack of priority and investment given to infrastructure. For example, in 1987 there was not a single town in the Crimea with a water supply or sewerage system that accorded with the approved general plans (*Gorodskoye Khozyaystvo Ukrainy* 1987, no. 4: 27). This was also a reflection of the urgency of the housing programme, which far outstripped the services that were intended to accompany it, as an integral part of the microregion concept. It has been the normal situation that the incoming inhabitants of a newly constructed microregion have had to wait a year or two, occasionally longer, before the surrounding disturbed surface is landscaped and grassed over and paths made, or before services arrive.

An entirely typical instance is that of Microregion 15 of Babushkin District of Moscow where it was reported in 1986 that the housing had been completed and occupied but that the school, polyclinic, two kindergartens and a department store planned as part of it had not been built, although the microregion was intended as a district centre (*Gorodskoye* . . . 1986, no. 9: 13). In Zheleznodorozhniy District, where much new building took place, the lack of pre-school and school places, and lack of space for more, meant that children had to be bussed to neighbouring districts (*Gorodskoye* . . . 1986, no. 11: 7). In Moscow about 75 per cent of children under school age make use of pre-school facilities, a great improvement over the 40 per cent of 1961 (Glushkova 1986: 84), but that still leaves a quarter of the city's children below school age with nowhere to go, when very nearly all mothers are working.

At Kazan' it was reported that "the development of the social infrastructure in the town significantly lags behind demand" (Vorontsov 1984: 91). Nor are Moscow and Kazan' alone. "In almost all large cities, the forecast population size, on which the development of the social infrastructure was calculated, proved to be below the actual size" (Stepanenko 1981: 265). Plans have failed hopelessly to cope with the situation. The plan for service provision in Sovetskiy District of Novosibirsk (which includes Akademgorodok) for 1991 was to fall short of the established norm level by more than 20 per cent (Sevast'yanov 1986: 97). If the situation is very bad in the largest cities, which are often the show-places and are always the best provided for, the case of the small town and settlement of town type, examined later, is far more serious.

Not the least cause for the failure of the town plans to meet their goals, where housing and all forms of service infrastructure are concerned, has been the divided responsibility for these matters. Local town authorities, industrial ministries and other government departments all play a part in the provision of accommodation and services. This began in the early Five Year Plans when new factories were set up and, desperate for labour, built the necessary housing. By the early 1960s, for example, the housing in Novokuznetsk was operated by no less than 155 separate enterprises, headed by the giant iron and steel works, which had 40 per cent of all housing in the town (Osborn & Reiner 1962: 24). In the mid-1970s, ministries and boards still accounted for 70 per cent of all investment in housing construction, 65 per cent in kindergarten and day-care centres and 30 per cent in hospitals and polyclinics (Morton & Stuart 1984: 16). From the beginning, the enterprises took on responsibility for building and managing various aspects of the physical infrastructure (electricity, mains water, sewerage and transport) of towns.

Thereafter, the situation did not change significantly. In 1987 the vice-chairman of the Irkutsk Town Executive Committee was lamenting that 50 per cent of all water, sewerage, heating and electricity systems in the city were the responsibility of different departments, other than the city council. In consequence, Irkutsk was in crucial need of 21 km of new heating mains, 77 km of water mains and 70 km of sewers (Kotsar' 1987: 97–8).

This division of responsibility for what should so obviously be unified in planning, execution and operation has been one of the most common and most serious complaints of Soviet local authorities and planners. In the words of one author, "In all the many plans, scarcely is one town seen as a single, whole organism" (Stepanenko 1981: 265). Considerable disparities between one part of a town and another result from different rates of expenditure by various ministries and departments. In Bratsk the cellulose-paper industry spent about twice as much as the non-ferrous industry, although the latter employed twice the labour force (Bocharov & Lyubovnyy 1979: 53).

To try to combat the ill effects of this divided responsibility, in the 1980s some towns attempted to introduce what was called the "single-client" principle of "a unified designer, a unified customer, a unified contractor." But this was only an experiment in a handful of towns and in any case it only covered social infrastructure. There was not a comparable unified basis for mains services. Now, with the shift to a free market it is hard to see any future for such experiments.

The divided responsibility inevitably has meant, sooner or later, conflict of interest, usually between the plan, seeking to optimize living conditions for the inhabitants, and industries, seeking sites that can be most quickly developed and most economically exploited. In resolving such conflicts, the town planner is always at a disadvantage, operating as he does at the lower end of a chain of authority running through all the levels of administration.

Where housing, as opposed to services, is concerned, the situation improved somewhat into the 1980s, as the building, renting and managing of accommodation by the individual enterprise was intended to cease and the housing stock in enterprise management gradually began to be passed over to the local authorities. However, Andrusz (1984: 48) has pointed out the frequent reluctance of local councils to take over the additional responsibility. This was especially the case where the housing concerned had a large backlog of repairs waiting. As a result, the process of acquiring unified control of housing within a city went slowly. In Minsk in 1982 the local city authority controlled 54.3 per cent of housing stock, ministries and boards 23.6 per cent, co-operatives 16.7 per cent and private persons 5.7 per cent (*Minsk . . .* 1983: 168). In Donetsk in 1983 the local Soviet controlled little over a third of the housing stock (35.6%), almost exactly the same as the ministries and departments (35.8%); the remainder was either private (25.0%) or co-operative (3.6%) (Belenko 1983: 17).

Ministerial and enterprise ownership of housing and responsibility for services have not always necessarily meant lower standards than in local authority areas. Tolokontsev's study of towns in Moscow Oblast found that in 85 per cent of them enterprise housing made up more than 50 per cent of all housing and in 37 per cent of towns the share was over 80 per cent, making them in effect "company towns". Generally, such housing was average in terms of space provision. The worst instances were found in some of the towns run by the local authorities (Tolokontsev 1988: 13–15). In Leningrad, where the share of housing and services under municipal control was one of the highest in the USSR, housing was constructed on council-owned land on the outskirts, well away from services (Ruble 1990: 82).

Retailing and supply to the consumer

Among the services that have failed to meet the demands of the Soviet urban population, shopping facilities stand out for their level of inadequacy. This is no new characteristic of the Soviet city. Throughout the Stalin era very little was provided in the way of new shops for the rapidly growing urban population. The lack of attention paid to consumer goods industries or to the distribution system meant that a severe shortage of almost all goods was a constant of Soviet life. For the ordinary citizen most foods and clothing were rationed and most consumer durables were simply unobtainable; one could argue not unreasonably that there was very little for a shop to do.

During the Stalin period, for such shopping as was possible, the consumer had largely to rely on the shops already established before the Revolution. This involved, for the most part, journeys into the traditional city centres and prolonged queuing once there. Perhaps what is slightly surprising is the degree of continuity, by which shops set up under private enterprise before the Revolution succeeded in maintaining not only their retail specialism, but also much of their qualitative evaluation in the eyes of the public. On Kirov Street in Moscow, the late nineteenth-century shop specializing in tea and built in an agreeably romantic "Chinoiserie" style, continues to the present as a specialist tea emporium. The most fashionable grocer of pre-revolutionary Moscow on Tver' Street (sometime Gor'kiy Street) not only remained as one of the better-supplied *gastronomy* (supermarkets) of the city, *Gastronom* No. 1, but was all along universally referred to by the name of its erstwhile private owner as "Yeliseyev's".

Continuity of shops is perhaps one reason why streets that were prime shopping foci in Tsarist times tend to remain in favour even now, whether in St Petersburg's Nevskiy Prospekt or Moscow's Arbat. Undoubtedly a major cause of their popularity is that these streets are among the rare concentrations of shops in close proximity. Another reason may well be that they retain the human scale and create an atmosphere of "cosiness" in cities which rarely display that characteristic. The Arbat was the first street in the Soviet Union to be pedestrianized (Fig. 5.3). This adaptation has in fact modified its role to the supply of the tourist and leisure shop-

Figure 5.3   The Arbat, Moscow: a pre-revolutionary shopping street, pedestrianized in the 1980s.

Figure 5.4 A shop on the ground floor of an apartment block, Chilanzar, Tashkent.

per, with cafés, art shops and second-hand bookshops, but its popularity as a place of resort is evident in the crowds which throng it every day of the week.

As Soviet towns expanded in size and outward spread in the third phase of development after 1957, the need for vastly greater provision of retailing services became ever more pressing. In theory, the comprehensive design of the micro-region would make the daily and weekly necessities immediately available with minimum effort, journeying or time-loss. In reality, few microregions have ever enjoyed full provision of services at the prescribed norms.

Equally significant for the shopper has been the universal practice of distributing new shops, not in concentrated shopping precincts, but on the ground floors of the apartment blocks (Fig. 5.4). The blocks are large and often spaced out at some distance from each other. From one shop to its immediate neighbour may easily be 50m or more and, if a major road has to be crossed, 100m or more. In consequence, the ordinary citizen has to walk very considerable distances to meet daily and weekly shopping needs, especially for food. The customer normally has to tramp around extensively, visiting a number of shops scattered through the home microregion and its adjacent fellows. When to this is added the very high failure rate in obtaining goods in the first place tried (or even the second), together with the triple queuing system inside shops, this all makes shopping an extremely time-consuming and physically exhausting process. In Gachechiladze's questionnaire survey of nearly 2000 people in the Tbilisi Metropolitan Region, he found that retailing (the supply and quality of goods) ranked first among social problems perceived by the inhabitants (Gachechiladze 1990a: 479).

Figure 5.5   Central department store, Irkutsk.

Journeys for food purchases may also be made to the centre, but for more occasional major purchases it is nearly always necessary to make a trip to the city centre and to the principal department store or stores (Fig. 5.5); a highly specialized retail outlet, likely to be the only one in a city, may be located anywhere and visiting it may involve lengthy cross-town journeys. It has been calculated that, in the USSR, shopping simply for food took the average family 7.6 hours a week, adding up nationally to 35 000 million man-hours a year; a saving of only ten minutes per day per worker would save the country 7000 million man-hours a year (Nikol'skiy 1982: 62). It was not uncommon practice for workers to do shopping in working hours, with consequent loss of production.

This tedium of visiting a large number of specialist shops to buy weekly requirements was eased by the growing number of food supermarkets (*gastronomy*), together with the collective markets, although it was not until 1960 that the Soviet Union opened its first self-service food shop. Even today only a minority of supermarkets, or of any kind of shop, are self-service. Many of the new *gastronomy* are located towards the outer areas of towns, often between a group of microregions. The very largest cities are beginning to establish department stores outside the inner city core. Thus, in Zhdanovskiy District of Moscow, a new department store was built in the Grayvoronovo microregion, at the outer limit of the district (*Gorodskoye . . .* 1985, no. 12: 19). In Krasnogvardeyskiy District, an area of recent fast development on the southeastern outskirts, where the population has grown from 170 000 in 1968 to 603 000 in 1987 and was expected to reach 700 000 by 1990, three self-service department stores, a department store for children's goods, and a specialist electrical goods shop all have been built (*Gorod-*

skoye . . . 1987, no. 7: 26). In southwest Moscow, in the Teplyy Stan region, the Yardan department store has been opened on Profsoyuznaya Street, less than three-quarters of a mile from the Orbital Motorway.

For the overwhelming majority of Soviet urban dwellers, the chore of shopping is carried out on foot or with the help of public transport. Most commonly, since almost all able-bodied adults are employed, people do their shopping on the way home from work. Retail and service outlets nearest to public transport stops are the most heavily patronized, with two to three times the turnover of establishments in off-route locations, and their income per square metre of trading space is five or six times as high (Il'in 1982a: 96).

To date, there has been almost no development of shopping precincts or malls, with local concentrations of shops permitting greater choice and speedier accomplishment of a range of purchases. Some Soviet planners were advocating such precincts in the late 1960s, although to no effect. The call for precincts was renewed during the 1980s in proposals for Trading and Service Centres (*Torgovo-bytovyy Tsentr*, or TBTs), which would even have facilities for car parking. They were to be designed on two scales, to serve populations of 6000–10000 or 15000–20000 (Borisov et al. 1981: 127). The problem has been to get such Trading Centres built. In his study of Latvian small towns, Puchin (1977: 41) remarked of Tukums that housing blocks totalling some 8000 m^2 had been built, but that not one building of the TBTs, intended to be an integral part of the development, was built; instead of a complex, it was "a disorganized heap of buildings."

If the planners have so far failed to incorporate shopping precincts as urgently needed integral parts of development plans, then, as one might perhaps expect, the ordinary people with the backing of their local authorities have taken matters into their own hands. In a rather remarkable way Moscow has seen the emergence of what might be termed quasi-spontaneous shopping precincts. They are located at the crucial break-of-journey sites beside Metro stations. For long these locations have seen a little row of three to half-a-dozen kiosks selling tobacco, newspapers and stationery, ice-cream and lottery tickets (Fig. 5.6), joined by mobile trolleys and tanks for pies and other hot take-away foods, ice-cream and *kvass* (bread beer). Such operations were normally carried out by employees of a district retailing organization.

The next stage saw the appearance of entirely unofficial kerbside vendors, either representatives of collective farms or freelance individuals who sold flowers, sunflower seeds and fresh fruit and vegetables in season, either from trestle tables or even from bags and boxes (Fig. 5.7). In Central Asia *non* bread is sold regularly from the kerbside. In the final stage the number and size of stalls increase and the range of goods on sale widens. Nowadays, clothing stalls may well be included. The stalls are set up on a permanent basis around a small precinct, sometimes with a large sign proclaiming "Fair" (*yarmarka*), as at Belyayevo Metro in southern Moscow (Fig. 5.8) or at Babushkin Metro in the north. Private persons with goods to sell, such as second-hand clothing, appear at these fairs. So too do fortune-tellers, palmists and other entertainers. The largest and most

Figure 5.6 Street kiosks selling papers, ice-cream and tobacco, near October Square, Moscow.

bustling fairs are where Metro and a collective market are side by side, as at Riga Metro on Mir Prospect. This also has a main line terminus alongside, giving easy access for out-of-towners.

One might very well see this informal Metro precinct, with its air of semi-

Figure 5.7 Flower sellers outside Medvedkovo Metro Station, Moscow.

Figure 5.8   "Fair" of kiosks at Belyayevo Metro station, Moscow.

spontaneity and impermanence, as a latter-day expression of the traditional Russian fair, the principal retail outlet for most Russians before the Revolution. It is certainly the focus for much of the burgeoning private trading in the post-Soviet era. This type of precinct reflects the triumph of popular demand for services and for convenience of location over the inadequacies of provision by formal planning. Indeed, one is perhaps beginning to detect the influence of this development on the planners, pushing them into providing concentrated shopping facilities at break-of-journey locations. Beside the Teplyy Stan Metro in southwest Moscow, one of the more recent additions to the network, a row of some half-dozen shops has been built, including a supermarket.

Related to the Metro fairs in their spontaneous popular origins were the wholly unofficial and sometimes illegal markets, although many were long tolerated by the authorities. These were specialist markets, for example for pets of all kinds, or motor car spares. They usually took place on the city outskirts on certain days of the week (especially Sunday). *Izvestiya* (5 August 1987: 6) described unavailing police efforts to raid and disrupt the unofficial car spare part market on the Moscow ring motorway; it interviewed some of the desperate seekers of spares and ended its article by demanding that "relevant organizations" do something about meeting the need so obviously expressed. Some previously unofficial markets, such as the art market, were made legal under the provisions of the 1986 law on private enterprise; the art fair was enabled to come in from the cold of its previously peripatetic locations in fields beyond the orbital motorway. In Izmaylovo Park on the eastern side of Moscow, every Sunday there is a large "collectors" fair for private sellers of souvenirs, antiques and other collectibles.

The direct sale of foodstuffs to the consumer has of course been a major element of supply since Khrushchev allowed the establishment of collective markets in the towns. To these markets, collectives, state farms and individuals bring produce from their fields and private plots. In the small towns, most markets are open-air, with roofed stalls and trestle tables (Fig. 5.9). More important markets will have roofed-over areas to shelter the stalls, and in the largest cities, special enclosed halls have been built by the local authorities to house the markets, as in the Baumanskiy and Rizhskiy Districts of Moscow. Moscow has no less than 45 markets, with some half-dozen in enclosed halls.

In the 1960s and 1970s the collective market was for most urban dwellers the principal and most reliable source of fresh food. In 1979 the collective markets of Moscow sold 99100 tonnes of potatoes, 117500 tonnes of vegetables, 74300 tonnes of fruit and 3200 tonnes of meat and poultry (Nikol'skiy 1982: 64), in all averaging over 35 kg of produce per capita. Prices tended to be somewhat higher than in the State shops, but so was quality and availability.

By the opening of the 1990s the cost gap between State prices (although in largely empty shops) and collective market prices had widened to between three and ten times. The soaring prices meant that food in the market often sold only very slowly, despite the general shortages and interminable queues, and it was quite possible to see stalls with plenty of meat but few buyers. By 1988, despite an increase in population of over half a million, sales of produce in Moscow's collective markets had fallen to 59100 tonnes of potatoes, 72100 tonnes of vegetables and 42600 tonnes of fruit. Only meat sales held up, with 2900 tonnes of meat and 87700 poultry carcasses (*Moskva v Tsifrakh 1989* 1989: 72).

Figure 5.9 A collective market, Irkutsk.

In consequence, when the State shops receive deliveries, they sell out very rapidly. Very commonly, when a delivery lorry arrives with fresh supplies, it is not considered worth carrying its cargo into the shop: the goods are sold on the pavement directly from their containers and, as a result, shelves remain permanently empty. In the autumn of 1990, the author saw a large Moscow shop closed, with the bleak notice "There are no goods." In the prevailing shortages, it was for long the practice for goods to be bought on sight – for the purchaser's immediate needs, for possible future needs, or for family, friends or neighbours who might need them. Almost every Soviet town-dweller carried an *avoska*, a "serendipity bag", comprising anything from a string bag to a briefcase, in which to put whatever happened to be on sale.

The steady deterioration in supply in the last years of the Soviet period meant that people made ever longer journeys to the larger towns where the availability of goods was always better, with Moscow the best supplied of all. Since the late 1950s it has been commonplace to see on Moscow's streets countrywomen heading for the capital's railway stations, burdened with huge loads of salami sausage, or oranges, or other delicacies rarely seen in small towns and villages, which they have bought acting as emissaries for groups of families or even for the whole village. Glushkova (1986: 84) calculated that 30–34 per cent of shoppers in Moscow stores were from out of town.

As the shortages intensified in the later 1980s and more and more people moved ever further up the urban hierarchy in search of scarce goods, so resentment grew among city inhabitants at such "raiding" of the town. At government level, attempts were made at rationing, but, as Soviet citizens grimly commented, rationing works only when there are things to be rationed. At the level of the shop, proof of local residence began to be demanded. Above all, the practice developed of selling supplies of all kinds, from foodstuffs to motor cars, through the place of work. In the science town of Dubna, north of Moscow, in the mid-1980s some 40 per cent of foodstuffs were sold through the place of work; shops left their shelves empty until late in the day to discourage non-locals (Hausladen 1987a: 113).

The result of the shortages and the malfunctioning distribution system was, in effect, a diminished role, if not complete loss of function, for the formally established shop. Shelves were commonly bare except for totally unwanted goods. In one sense there was always a bypassing of the shop in the special distribution system for the *nomenklatura* (the Party elite) with distribution points of strictly and narrowly limited access, and with all the goods, home produced and imported, that were quite unobtainable by the population at large. The Gorbachev regime made it declared policy to abolish this major privilege of the elite, but by the start of the 1990s there was the growth of an alternative system of supply, accessible only to the favoured. That was provided by the hard-currency-only shops such as "Rifle" on Kuznetskiy Most in Moscow, selling high quality Western-made clothes and patronized by only a handful of customers. If the old special shops were behind closed unmarked doors in absolute discretion, the new moneyed group now enjoyed a greatly increased visibility. The collapse of the Soviet Union initially saw the further development of the hard-currency shop, as foreign venture capital was invested in shops selling Western products for *valuta*, such as the Irish Shop on Kalinin Prospect. Attempts by the Yel'tsin administration to check hard-currency sales and to introduce tills to the private street stalls have so far had only limited impact on either the usurpation of the rouble by the dollar or on street trading.

The deteriorating environment

Throughout the world, the growth of the industrial city has seen a corresponding increase in the range and severity of incidents of environmental pollution. The Soviet city did not escape this damage and in many respects suffered worse harm than its Western counterparts. During the twentieth century, growing concern about the dangers to health of urban dwellers in Western developed countries gradually led to enactments to control pollution through factory acts, clean air acts, smokeless zones and the like. In the USSR the overriding priority given for most of the Soviet period to extremely rapid industrialization for long meant that little enough serious consideration and almost no practical measures were devoted to these issues. Moreover, the emphasis throughout the Stalin period on heavy industry and manufacture for military purposes meant that a high proportion of the factories that were constructed – ferrous and non-ferrous metallurgical, chemical and cement production – were highly pollutant. Worse still, their relationship to defence requirements permitted no questioning or discussion whatsoever of the need for such plants or of their location and functioning.

As a result, by the beginning of the 1960s, many Soviet cities were suffering levels of air and water pollution rarely equalled in twentieth-century Western towns, and the post-Stalin era did little enough to improve matters. In 1988, Tolokontsev (1988: 21) could write, "The low quality of the natural environment (water, air, vegetation) is the most negative side of urban life." In hundreds of towns, emissions into the atmosphere exceeded maximum permissible concentrations (MPC). In 1987 over a hundred large cities had emissions exceeding the norms by ten times or more; total emissions from stationary sources in that year came to 64 100 000 tonnes, of which 15 600 000 were solids and 48 500 000 were gases and water (*Soviet Geography* 1989, 30 no. 6: 512). In some instances air pollution was at frightening levels. The non-ferrous metallurgical town of Leninogorsk in Kazakhstan has lead and zinc concentration and enrichment plants; in 1989, lead emissions there were on average 30 to 40 times MPC, but had occasionally reached 440 times MPC (*Soviet Geography* 1990, 31 no. 6: 431).

The worst offenders in industrial air pollution were – and still are – the metallurgical and power-generating enterprises, responsible for 26.2 and 24.8 per cent respectively of all air emissions; they are followed at some distance by the oil and gas (8.9%) and chemical (7.1%) industries (*State of Natural Environment* . . . 1990: 6). As a result, the towns most seriously affected include the steel towns of

Magnitogorsk, Novokuznetsk, Mariupol' (sometime Zhdanov) and Chelyabinsk and, together with Leninogorsk, non-ferrous metallurgical towns such as Bratsk and Ust-Kamennogorsk. Air emissions at Magnitogorsk surpassed 2 000 000 kg per capita and were about 1 500 000 kg per capita at Novokuznetsk and Mariupol' (*Soviet Geography* 1989, 30 no. 6: 514–15). Kotkin's (1991: 135) description of Magnitogorsk quoted a 1989 Komsomol survey, which found that every year each hectare of residential land in the city received on average 6.6 tonnes of pollutants, with only a third of dangerous gases removed by cleansing; frequently, cleansing devices were inoperative. The official country-wide report compiled by the committee set up by Gorbachev (*Goskompriroda*) identified the Kuzbas coalfield and its associated heavy industrial region as "one of the ecologically troublesome regions of the country" (*State of Natural Environment . . .* 1990: 38–9). In industrial areas and especially around energy, metallurgical and petrochemical plants, annual deposition of sulphur surpasses two tonnes per km^2 (ibid.: 14). Asbest in the Urals, the principal asbestos-producing centre in the USSR, in 1990 emitted 503 000 tons of pollutants into the atmosphere, an increase of 6.4 per cent over the five years since 1985 (*Sverdlovskaya Oblast v Tsifrakh . . .* 1991: 76); this represents nearly 6000 kg per capita, but it is not known what percentage of the emissions is asbestos. As this is largely a one-industry town, one must assume that asbestos forms the major part of the pollutants.

Even in Moscow, so frequently referred to as the show city, some 2500 tonnes of SO$_2$ are emitted during the heating season, while, over the year as a whole, industry puts out more than a million tonnes of oxides (Trifonov & Makarova 1989: 38), in consequence putting the capital high up on the list of offending cities. In towns of the central industrial region around Moscow, emissions of nitrogen dioxide in Voskresensk are six times MPC and in Klin six to seven times MPC; emissions of sulphur gases are five times MPC in Podol'sk and three times MPC in Klin (ibid.: 39).

Appalling as such figures are, they represent an improvement over earlier situations, as levels of trapping and cleansing wastes have improved. Between 1981 and 1985, total industrial air emissions rose by some 6 per cent; in the second half of the decade they fell by about 7 per cent (Table 5.4). Meanwhile, there was a slow increase in the proportion of wastes trapped and treated, so that the total of escaped emissions fell over the decade by about 14 per cent.

This amelioration was unfortunately offset by the increased pollution of urban air by road transport emissions as overall numbers of vehicles rose. In Moscow, road traffic now accounts for two-thirds of total air pollution, including 70 per cent of all carbon monoxide and 90 per cent of hydroxides (Trifonov & Makarova 1989: 39). In Yerevan too, motor vehicles are the principal source of air pollution, producing 170 000 tonnes of gross discharges (Valesyan 1990: 575). In Yerevan the altitude increases the problem by causing incomplete oxidization and higher fuel use, but, in general, Soviet petrol is of lower octane rating than in Western countries and is therefore more polluting; Soviet car engines have a low efficiency. In 1986, 42 per cent of cars tested in Moscow were above norms for toxic discharge;

Table 5.4   Emissions into the air from stationary sources (million tonnes).

Date	Total emissions	Trapped or cleansed	% trapped	Escaped
1981	260.8	195.6	75	65.2
1982	262.8	197.1	75	65.7
1983	267.7	200.8	75	66.9
1984	270.9	205.9	76	65.0
1985	275.4	209.3	76	66.1
1986	273.3	207.7	76	65.6
1987	275.7	212.3	77	63.4
1988	271.6	209.1	77	62.5
1989	268.2	209.2	78	59.0
1990	255.6	199.4	78	56.2

Sources: Columns 1 and 4 calculated from the figures for Columns 2 and 3 given in *Narodnoye Khozyaystvo SSSR* for corresponding years.

although this proportion had fallen by half in 1988, 70 000 out of 400 000 new cars coming onto the city's roads still had unfit engines (*Gorodskoye Khozyaystvo Moskvy* 1989 no. 9: 7). It is hardly surprising that, in 1987, emissions from vehicles in the city totalled 36 200 000 tonnes (*Soviet Geography* 1990 31 no. 3: 234).

The situation in the air is matched by the pollution of urban watercourses. Until the 1960s, it was rare for towns to have sewage treatment plants, and raw sewage was pumped straight into rivers, while the overwhelming majority of factories did the same with untreated effluent. Traumatic events, such as the catching fire of the River Iset in Sverdlovsk (Yekaterinburg) in 1965 and of the Volga at Kuybyshev (Samara) in 1970, led to major efforts to clean up the country's rivers. Sewage and wastewater treatment plants have been built but they are far from consistently effective. In 1989, only 32 per cent of wastewater treatment achieved the required standard. In that year the discharge of contaminated waste water came to 32.2 km^3, of which 14.2 km^3 were municipal waste and 14.3 km^3 industrial, the remainder coming from farms. The chief offenders were wood pulp and paper works, petroleum refineries and petrochemical, metallurgical, coal and mineral fertilizer plants (*State of Natural Environment . . .* 1990: 16). All over the country, rivers with factories on their banks regularly exceeded MPCs, often by ten or more times, especially in the aftermath of catastrophic spillages or accidents.

Where sewage was concerned, large cities tended to do particularly badly. By the late 1980s only 58 per cent of sewage in Leningrad was treated (Pryde 1991: 77). In the Crimea in 1987, not a single town had a sewerage system that accorded with its approved Genplan (*Gorodskoye Khozyaystvo Ukrainy* 1987 no. 4: 27). Recycling of water gradually increased in the 1970s and 1980s, but in Moscow only 43 per cent of water was recycled (Khorev & Glushkova 1991: 184).

The *Goskompriroda* report in 1990 (*State of Natural Environment . . .* 1990: 3) stated that Soviet cities produced annually some 3 million m^3 of solid domestic waste, of which 96.7 per cent was dumped, only 2.2 per cent incinerated and 1.3 per cent recycled. At that time the RSFSR had only seven incinerators and two garbage treatment plants, and events of the past few years make it extremely unlikely that any progress has been made in the plans to establish some 78 waste treatment and handling plants and 85 waste burial grounds by the end of the century. Even in Moscow only 15 per cent of waste was processed by industrial methods and the other 85 per cent was in suburban dumps (Khorev & Glushkova 1991: 183). Much toxic and inflammable waste was dumped in the grounds of enterprises (Bobylev & Korotkova 1984: 21).

Mining towns frequently suffer from both dumps of slag and waste and from subsidence problems. Exploitation of a coal seam under Karaganda in Kazakhstan commenced in the late 1970s amid claims that it was 350 m deep and entirely safe. Within four years, problems began. Some 430 ha are now under threat of total or partial destruction, including $600000 m^2$ of living space, 58 service, cultural and social facilities, and 17 industrial enterprises. The local council refused to order the Karagandaugol coalmining trust to stop the operation, because of the significance of coalmining to the city economy (CDSP 1986 38 no. 24: 25).

The poor environmental conditions of the Soviet city had inevitable consequences for the health of the citizens. Direct correlations were found between the size of a town and the frequency of lung cancer; on the other hand, correlation was also found between the per capita area of greenery and life expectancy (Tolokontsev 1988: 25, 28). In Yerevan a link was established between chemical industry discharges and birth disorders (Valesyan 1990: 576).

The rise of crime

For long, all statistics and most information relating to crime in the USSR were most strictly controlled; indeed in the period up to the late 1950s they were almost wholly absent. *Glasnost* began to make a certain number of statistics publicly available, but only at the all-Union level. Total figures for all crimes show an overall upward trend in the second half of the 1980s, from 2080000 in 1985 to 2461700 in 1989 (*Narodnoye Khozyaystvo* SSSR *v 1989g*: 255). There was a further rise of 20 per cent in overall crime in 1990 (CDSP 1991 43 no. 14: 29). Unfortunately, published figures do not allow one to distinguish which of these crimes were committed in urban areas as a whole, still less in individual towns. However, articles in *Izvestiya* have reported that street crime rose from 1987 to 1988 in all republics other than Georgia, with a further very sharp increase in the first six months of 1989 (Ryan 1990: 159, 163). Thin as the material is, pioneer efforts have already been made to analyze the geographical distribution of crime within the former USSR through the work of Gobiani and Gachechiladze in Georgia, and from outside the country by Louise Shelley in Washington.

What is clear is that there is a strong correlation between rates of in-migration and rates of crime (Shelley 1980: 116; 1981: 78). The new arrivals, often from rural areas or from very small towns, may well have trouble adjusting to a very different lifestyle, which may include different ethnic–cultural values. They are separated from their families and familiar, stabilizing environments. Many have problems finding somewhere to live and many spend considerable periods living in *baraki* (dormitories or hostel-type accommodation). In consequence, towns showing fastest population growth show correspondingly fast growth in the rate of crime. Such new and rapidly expanding towns tend to have more serious crime figures, not only because recent migrants form a high proportion of the total population, but also because such places frequently have very poorly developed services of all types, including places of entertainment. They also have high rates of alcoholism, itself conducive to crime. Above all, new towns frequently have poor accommodation. Siberia, with its high rate of population turnover and low-quality housing, has a poor record. In Surgut, the West Siberian oil centre, 36.8 per cent of the population live in dormitories and a further 12.5 per cent in temporary housing. Similarly, towns with large transient populations show high crime figures. For example, seaports such as Vladivostok, where sailors comprise over a tenth of the total population, or nearby Nakhodka where they form over 20 per cent, have bad crime records (Dienes 1988: 800).

Although in general, as elsewhere in the world, the larger the urban place the higher the crime rate, the very largest Soviet cities, notably Moscow and Leningrad, had lower crime rates than those in the next size category. The rate of conviction per 100000 population in cities with over 1500000 inhabitants was 442; in cities with under 500000 it was 500 per 100000 (Shelley 1980: 120). The reason for this apparent anomaly was primarily the requirement for the *propiska* (residence permit), which cut down on the number of in-migrants and thus on one of the most unstable elements of Soviet urban society. Allied to this was the practice of deporting so-called "parasites", unemployed persons, from Moscow and Leningrad (Shelley 1981: 80–84). Correspondingly of course, this tended to put up the crime rates in the towns receiving these undesirable elements. The *propiska* requirement meant that many would-be migrants settled in the area surrounding the destination city and commuted to work. Studies in Leningrad showed that in the 15–18 year-old age group, crime rates were higher among those who commuted to work or school than among those who did not (ibid.: 81).

Within a town the most usual receiving areas for new in-migrants are the outermost suburbs, the most recently built microregions, which therefore tend to have the highest crime levels (Shelley 1980: 120). Other areas of towns tending to have high crime rates are some of the older inner parts, where traditionally living conditions and crime have been worst.

For most of the Soviet period the levels of crime were not reported and the deterioration in the later part of the period was little grasped in Western literature. What is now evident is that crime had reached such a point that the collapse of the political system and the parallel collapse of the economy in the post-Soviet period permitted the rapid rise of organized crime.

Problems of the small and company town

The centralized nature of the Soviet command economy resulted in a high degree of uniformity between the cities of the country, more especially between cities of comparable size. At least up to the late 1980s, the national economic situation and the overall government policy towards urban affairs at any given time produced much the same consequences in all the republics. From the Baltic to the Pacific and from the Arctic Ocean to the Caspian Sea, differences in the appearance of Soviet cities reflect different periods of construction rather than different areas. The *Khrushchoba* is identical in each of several thousand urban settlements; so is the Stalinist block of flats or the Brezhnev high-rise block. Occasionally in non-Russian areas a nod has been given towards local traditional styles of architecture in the form of decorative motifs on the facades of buildings of both the Stalinist and subsequent periods. Although these may be a refreshing slight modification of the otherwise endless uniformity, they are only facades that do not hide the standardized form of the building. Only the older towns, pre-dating the Revolution, display clear regional characteristics in their inner city areas. Inner Russian Moscow is as distinct from inner European St Petersburg as the core of Estonian Tallin is from the core of Uzbek Bukhara, yet in all these cities the suburban microregions of the 1960s and 1970s are to all intents and purposes interchangeable. Lukhmanov (1989: 150) acknowledged this in saying that there are extremely few regions in the USSR that have developed their own "local" type of towns; he cites two exceptions: the Baltic Republics and the Far North.

If the physical fabric of different towns shows a high level of similarity, the social fabric also tends to be uniform, again in towns of comparable size. Similar accommodation, similar types and conditions of employment, and similar levels of provision of services and goods of all kinds, naturally tend to have a consistent effect. It is most commonly the smallest towns, local centres of agricultural regions, where the link with the countryside and with regional ethnic and cultural traits is strongest, which display the greatest variation in mode of living. This is equally true of "old town" areas surviving within large modern cities, especially in Central Asia; the populations of such "traditional" areas are usually heavily if not exclusively dominated by indigenous ethnic groups.

There were, however, certain broad categories of Soviet towns which could be distinguished by their own characteristic sets of urban problems. Each group required and requires its own set of solutions. But even these differentiating problems can, for the most part, be linked to a single national situation. The planner may have sought the same or similar objectives across the Soviet Union, the industrial ministries may everywhere have imposed their requirements in the same high-handed way, but the people have exerted their influence against the plans, not infrequently in different responses to differing manifestations of national problems.

One category of town with problems sufficiently severe to have drawn considerable attention from Soviet authorities and researchers is the small town. There was some difference of opinion among Soviet authorities about the definition of a small town, whether this should be of under 50 000 or under 20 000 people. Khorev (1972), one of the leading writers on Soviet urban affairs in general and the small town in particular, takes both figures. Between 20 000 and 50 000 people defines a transitional type of small town with some traits of both smaller and larger places. The second group comprehends the very small town with less than 20 000 population. In these smallest settlements the problems of the category as a whole are seen at their most intense. The small and especially the very small categories comprise the great majority of all urban places, 5642 out of a total of 6216, or 90.8 per cent in 1989; no less than 4922 of these (79.2 per cent of all towns) were in the smallest category.

Many places classified as urban in the 1989 census were so small as to be well below the legal population minima established in the 1920s – that is to say, in the case of the RSFSR, 12 000 for town status and 3000 for settlement of town type; many, even in the Russian Republic, were well below the minimum threshold set by the least demanding republic, a mere thousand inhabitants for a Tadzhik settlement of town type. According to the census (*Gorodskoye Poseleniye* . . . 1991: 168–243) in the RSFSR alone, there were 161 towns under 12 000 and no less than 593 settlements of town type under 3000 (Table 5.5); that is, they should not legally be accorded urban status. Even more inappropriate was the status of the seven full towns that had less than 3000 inhabitants. The smallest of these, Vysotsk in Leningrad Oblast, had merely 929 people. Altogether there were 102 urban settlements in the Russian Republic numbering their populations only in hundreds. Smallest of all was the urban settlement of Leninskaya Sloboda in Nizhniy Novgorod Oblast, which had just 73 people, only 26 per cent of its population at the previous 1979 census. Such places can only be considered as "phantom" towns, ghosts of places that have lost their *raison d'être*.

Table 5.5 Declining towns in the RSFSR, 1979–89.

	Towns			Settlements of town type		
Size (000)	No.	No. in decline	%	No.	No. in decline	%
All	1037	147	14.2	2193	908	41.4
Under 3	7	3	42.1	593	422	71.2
3–4.9	17	5	29.4	524	248	47.3
5–9.9	82	20	24.4	713	194	27.2
10–19.9	243	62	25.5	321	41	12.8
20–49.9	360	46	12.8	38	3	7.9
50–74.9	118	7	5.9	2	0	
75–99.9	45	1	2.2			
100–249.9	87	3	3.4			
250–499.9	44	0				
500–749.9	18	0				
750–999.9	4	0				
Million plus	12	0				

Source: Gorodskoye Poseleniye RSFSR po dannym Vsesoyuznoy Perepisi Naseleniya 1989 goda (1991), Goskomstat, Moscow, pp. 168–243.

Figure 5.10 Chimbay, a small town of the Kara Kalpak Autonomous Republic, Uzbekistan.

Some of the small towns of the former USSR were long-established local centres, which never developed any significant function beyond some district administration or organizing focus for agriculture in the vicinity (Fig. 5.10). Not a few emerged as industrial or residential satellites in the neighbourhood of major towns. Some owed their origin to the lines of communication on which they stand. Very commonly, small urban settlements were founded as mining centres or as centres for exploiting other natural resources such as timber. Of the new towns that were created in the Soviet period, the great majority were for industrial purposes, but nevertheless have remained in the "small" category. Thus, in Sverdlovsk Oblast in the Urals industrial region, the number of towns increased between 1913 and 1966 from 7 to 40 and the number of urban settlements from 44 to 98. Of the 133 places in 1966, 30 towns were under 50000 and 72 urban settlements were under 10000 people (Animitsa 1969: 11). By 1 January 1991, of the 144 urban places in the oblast there were still 30 towns under 50000 (11 of which were under 20000) and 87 settlements of town type below 10000 inhabitants, including 62 under 5000 (*Chislennost'* . . . 1991: 221–9).

Such industrial foundations in particular, but a high proportion of small towns in general, tend to have only one significant source of employment. They are in effect company towns. Snytko (1971), in his study of towns in the Central Black Earth Region, found that half the places with populations between 10000 and 20000 had single industries, mostly food processing. In the Urals the single source of employment was usually mining or primary processing of raw materials (Animitsa 1969). Although the two categories – small town and company town – overlap considerably, not every small town has a narrow employment base and some single-industry towns can be at least in the middle size rank.

As elsewhere in the world, a single-employer situation creates a set of imbalances and difficulties. Frequently there are only single-sex employment opportunities. In the context of the USSR with the general economic need for two breadwinners in a family, lack of jobs for one sex (most frequently, although not invariably, for women rather than for men) discourages the development of stable, permanently resident families. The limited employment opportunities mean that in small towns there is a higher proportion of people working in jobs below their qualification level (Aitov et al. 1988: 238). In general both the age level and the skill level of the workforce are low. Job turnover and out-migration are high. Liiber's (1988) study of the small towns of Estonia showed that, over the period 1959–86, the healthiest demographic situation in terms of natural increase and a positive in-migration balance was enjoyed by polyfunctional centres. Indeed, Estonia, where few towns are other than small, demonstrates that such places can be popular, with a pleasant environment and over half the population living in individual houses with gardens (Markov 1983: 13). This is perhaps a special case, related to the particular ethos of Estonian society.

In the newly founded small town especially, the population is mostly under 30 years old. The common inadequacy of pre-school places in crèches and kindergartens causes mothers, or even both parents, to leave, continuing the social instability and the young age profile of the town. The situation is exemplified by Kachkanar in the Urals, an iron-mining and ore-concentrating town of 33048 in the 1970 census and still under 50000 in 1979. Over a ten-year period 58000 in-migrants arrived and 40000 left and the average age remained at 26 (Petrov 1981: 105–6). On 1 January 1991, the population of Kachkanar was 48900, suggesting that the migration pattern can have changed but little. The instability and lack of work give further cause for women to leave, bringing rises in divorce rates and in the numbers of single-parent families, which in turn creates stress for children and culminates eventually in rising crime rates (Aitov et al. 1982: 22).

Where the small town owes its origin to the location of minerals or other resources, further instability arises from the potential exhaustion of the resources concerned. A majority of the larger towns that displayed absolute population decreases over the intercensal periods since 1959 were single-industry mining towns, and coalmining towns in particular, such as Anzhero–Sudzhensk and Prokop'yevsk in the Kuzbas, Kopeysk in the Urals and Yenakiyevo in the Donbas region. This is a very common situation in the small towns, which usually have a much narrower industrial profile. Nor is it only mining towns that suffer from employment redundancy; Khorev (1972: 81) cites the case of the small railway settlement of Shakhun'ya in Gor'kiy Oblast, where the change-over to electrification led to a sharp fall in railway employment.

A very common type of small town is the local centre of an agricultural region; over 70 per cent of small and medium-size towns serve as the centre of a *rayon* (district) (Lyubovnyy et al. 1984: 109). There is a low-level administrative function and in almost all cases an industrial profile concerned with processing local farm produce. This may well be represented by a single factory. In some cases there is a more diversified industrial profile, which might include the manufacture of goods for agricultural use, but a narrow industrial base is the norm for such places. Not least among the causes of problems in this group of small towns has been the appalling state of Soviet agriculture. Twenty years ago, Khorev (1972: 19) pointed out that a rise in agricultural production would be a major stimulus for the small regional centre; although that is a stimulus for which such centres are still vainly waiting, the privatization of farming in the post-Soviet era may ultimately prove to be a boost to this type of small town. A further problem of this type of small local centre is that the services it should provide have been located in the central settlements of the large collective farms, which have thus usurped the town's functions (Markov 1983: 31). Not least among functions largely bypassing the Soviet small centre of an agricultural region was that of a market, exchanging agricultural produce from the farms and manufactured goods from larger towns. Farms supplied produce directly to State purchasing organs or transported it themselves to collective markets in the larger towns for direct sale to the populace.

Many small towns face serious problems of isolation and not just those established to work remote mineral deposits. In the Russian Republic, 22.2 per cent of all small towns are more than 20 km from a railway station and 10.5 per cent have no external road connection with a hard surface (Lyubovnyy et al. 1984: 112).

Not surprisingly, in the face of such problems a high proportion of small urban areas are in decline (Table 5.5). Between the 1979 and 1989 censuses, 25.8 per cent of towns and 42.2 per cent of settlements of town type in the RSFSR with fewer than 20000 people declined in size. Rates of decline were greatest in the smallest categories; of urban districts under 3000, 71.2 per cent declined between the two censuses, some by considerable amounts. Only five towns in the RSFSR fell by more than 20 per cent, the largest fall being recorded by Artemovsk in Krasnoyarsk Kray, which decreased by 40 per cent over the decade. Artemovsk is a goldmining centre, with a plant enriching the copper and silver found in the same mines; one must deduce that the mining is coming to an end. But no less than 211 settlements of town type in that Republic dropped by over a fifth, 45 of them by more than two-fifths. The greatest percentage fall was experienced in Derbeshkinskiy in the Tatar Republic, which decreased by 85 per cent from 1109 to 168 people (*Gorodskoye Poseleniye . . .* 1991: 206).

A consequence of the smallness of so many urban places and the proportionately large-scale haemorrhaging of population is that such settlements share closely the problems of villages. Usually, it is the young, best-educated and most skilled who leave for better opportunities in larger towns. As a result, the demographic structure is distorted, with few women of child-bearing age. In Estonia about a third of the small towns showed rapid population growth over the period 1959–86; these were mostly the satellite towns of Tallin. Another third showed declining populations; in these there was rapid ageing of the population structure (Marksoo 1988: 114; Liiber 1988: 127–9).

The out-migration of the young and skilled means that labour resources are impoverished and there is little incentive for locating new industry. The infrastructure is allowed to deteriorate, with resultant decline in the amenities and quality of life. The great majority of houses in small towns, other than those built wholly in Soviet times, are old, wooden and lacking in modern conveniences; small towns have the highest proportion of privately owned accommodation. Those newer towns constructed in the Soviet period often have little better to offer, sometimes consisting of no more than a desolate cluster of *Khrushchoby*, with no amenities or services other than the most basic. It is hardly surprising that, for so many of the young, the bright lights of larger cities are very attractive.

A further category of town with particular problems frequently coincides with the small and single-industry town. That is, the place located in the far north or far east, in conditions of remoteness and usually climatic severity. In the far north over half of the urban places have less than 5000 inhabitants (Lukhmanov 1989: 150). Some were founded as centres for reindeer herding activities, but many were set up as centres for scientific research, military defence operations or regional transport. A high proportion of the population are transport workers or are involved in servicing scientific work. Costs of establishing and maintaining such towns in the extreme regions are high. In the late 1980s, the cost of providing $1 m^2$ of living space and its backup of infrastructure and service needs in Moscow was 200 roubles. In Bratsk in southern Siberia the cost, even without such back-up, was 300 roubles, but in Magadan Oblast in the far northeast it was over 1000 roubles per m^2 of living space. To transfer a worker to certain parts of the north could cost more than 29000 roubles. (Alekseyeva 1987: 46, 49).

Such places are not usually linked, either economically or socially, with their regions (Lukhmanov 1989: 153–4), thereby increasing the sense of isolation. Commodities are not obtained from the locality, but are sent from the centre; indeed, what links there are tend to be by air with major centres such as St Petersburg (Leningrad), Murmansk or Vladivostok. The remoteness and difficulty of access to the rest of the country reduces the level of initial provision of infrastructure and the continuing supply of consumer goods. This, plus the distances involved, puts up the price of commodities and exacerbates the problems of living found elsewhere. The long and exceptionally cold winters, which may be up to nine or ten months of the year below freezing and dropping to –40°C and below, raise the cost of living, especially for families, owing to the additional requirements of heavy clothing and higher necessary calorie intake. The atmospheric conditions of winter include deep temperature inversions, which trap emissions from factories and create serious health hazards (Bond 1984d).

The majority of towns are founded for a single purpose, most usually mineral extraction, and the unfavourable living conditions therefore reinforce the same social disfunctions and out-migration found in company towns in other parts of the former Soviet Union. Young unmarried persons form a high percentage of the population; for them, costs are low, as they generally live in subsidized company hostels (*baraki*), eat in subsidized company cafeterias and find their limited opportunities for entertainment in the free clubs and cinemas run by the enterprises. With the high regional wage bonuses, savings can be quickly accumulated; then after only a few years at most, the worker, now trained, leaves and the place is taken by a newly arrived, unskilled youngster. Populations are therefore exceptionally unstable; the high rate of turnover means a constant shortage, not merely of labour, but particularly of skilled labour.

Some of the small towns have been growing in size, some even moving out of the category of small. Such places are usually satellites of major cities, increasing as their dormitory function grows or as industries linked to those of the conurbation centre are established. However, the vast majority of small places and almost all of the very small ones cannot but be considered as problem towns in the new age of a market economy. One must expect a significant number to disappear altogether from the map. All will pose questions to the new States, questions which will surely have expensive answers.

CHAPTER 6

The changing
social geography of the city

The change in society

The relaxation in the rigidity of controlled thought, which was commenced by Khrushchev, by the later 1960s was affecting many aspects of Soviet life, including both concepts of the Soviet city and its role in society, and methods of studying these. Liyber & Roozve (1984: 266) commented in 1984 that "Only ten to 15 years ago in the USSR, practically no-one studied problems of social-spatial differentiation." But then, "At the end of the 1960s and early 1970s, there was a breakthrough in ways of looking at urbanization and in attitudes to this process" (Kogan 1986: 5). No small part in this breakthrough was played by the growing discipline of social geography, escaping from the bonds of an "economic geography" that was largely taxonomic, non-analytical and sterile; the new direction in geography paralleled and was surely inspired by the growth in sociological studies of the town by researchers such as L. A. Gordon and E. V. Klopov, N. A. Aitov and others.

The new subdiscipline was aware of the social realities of the Soviet Union. "By social geography we understand the uneven distribution of one or another social group by area of the town" (Aitov et al. 1982: 15). Moreover, there was a recognition of the role of the individual: "Every urban dweller, every part of urban space follows its own, particular road, unrepeatable in all its details and particularities" (Kogan 1986: 10). The consequence of the recognition that needs, desires and perceptions of the individual exist was the introduction of questionnaire surveys to discover what they were. One of the outstanding pioneers in this type of research was the sociologist T. Zaslavskaya, then in Novosibirsk. The appearance of publications containing the results of such surveys, even in the relatively limited quantities to date, has cast much new light on all aspects of Soviet urban social geography.

Social geographers and sociologists were concerned that the town plan had been almost exclusively the preserve of the architects, who too often did not look beyond the appearance and spatial relations of buildings and who failed to reflect fully the complexities of economic and social questions (Stepanenko 1981: 264). Above all, although there remained until very recently a belief in the integrative

131

role of the town in creating a socialist society, the conviction that the urban plan could be an effective tool of social engineering, at all events in any short run, was greatly modified. As early as 1973, L. B. Kogan was writing, "it has been discovered that social behaviour (in the wide sense of the word) plays a decisive role in the development and formation of the planning organization of settlements and their system, that the character of life of people in the urban environment cannot be rigidly determined by the type of building, by the distribution of service establishments, etc." (Kogan 1973: 201).

At the same time, the sociologists were becoming increasingly dissatisfied with the simplistic classifications of social groups that were used throughout the Soviet era, as deriving from Marx. Instead, it was felt that it was a key task to evaluate "the integration and differentiation of the urban population, to define its groups, their developmental tendencies and factors stimulating their convergence" (Dmitriyev & Mezhevich 1982: 60). In earlier Soviet literature, Marxist doctrine, defining class by relationship to the means of production, allowed only two classes to be identified in the USSR – the working class and collective farmers – the latter still regularly referred to in the later Soviet years as "peasantry" (*krest'yanstvo*).

The obvious inadequacy of this naïve division of a large and socially very complex society has meant that other groups have had to be recognized – for instance, the intelligentsia – but without terming them classes. Instead, in accordance with stratification theory, they were designated as *sloya*, "layers", in effect classes in all but the strictest Marxist interpretation of the word. For the necessary social developments of the late Soviet period, a far more sophisticated and realistic subdivision of society was needed. "The concept of the social structure of our society, which in practice town authorities and workers in planning organs use, does not go beyond the level of acquaintance with basic social-class groups. That is obviously not enough" (Shkaratan & Rukavishnikov 1974: 36). So wrote two leading Soviet sociologists 20 years ago. They went on to draw up their own division of urban society into "layers" (Table 6.1). The word "layer" is in itself significant, with its connotations of a vertical sequence or hierarchy. Even more significantly, the need for such a division, they claimed, was that the different layers had different requirements of their urban environment and that these had to be taken into account by town planners. An even more detailed, if narrowly occupation-based, subdivision of society was worked out by Petrov (1981: 140–50) on the criteria of nature of work, rhythm and conditions of work, stress factors and the like; this classification resulted in a total of 67 "social–professional" groups.

These developments in approach not only gave much greater freedom to examine all aspects of Soviet society, but also put greater emphasis on the need to study the urban environment as it actually exists and its attractive or repellent qualities as influencing the choices of individuals, and also on the need to discover what in reality motivates the different groups of urban dwellers in all aspects of their activity – where they live, work, satisfy their domestic requirements or employ their leisure time. It was recognized that in exercising choice in where to live, the indi-

Table 6.1 Urban population by type of occupation.

	% of urban employed pop'n
Working class	
Unqualified physical labourers	12–14
Qualified, mainly physical work with machinery	22–24
Qualified, mostly physical, manual	22–24
Highly qualified, mental and physical functions in servicing complex technology	1–2
Mental workers	
Highly qualified, managerial, mental	2
Highly qualified, scientific–technical, mental	2–3
Artistic intelligentsia	0.5–1
Qualified mental	16–17
Non-physical, primarily mental, in service and management spheres – officials	12–14

Source: Shkaratan & Rukavishnikov 1974: 36.

vidual is motivated, consciously and subconsciously, by a complex of factors and perceptions (Vasil'yev et al. 1988: 42–3). The earlier approaches, which sought to establish "laws" of urbanization, were replaced in the 1980s by efforts to discover *how* various types of urban environment have come about and how changes take place (Kogan 1986: 13). The freedom under *glasnost* to discuss previously forbidden topics, and the belated start during the 1980s in the use of the computer for such work, began to transform the quality of social geographical examination of the Soviet city and our understanding of how it works. The more such studies were done, the more planners would have the essential information, on which to base realistic and acceptable plans. It was even suggested that a new, interdisciplinary study – "urbanology" – was needed to carry out the task (ibid.: 14).

Certainly, the late 1980s saw something of an explosion in this field of investigation. Perhaps little was more indicative of the changing times than the series of studies in political geography that appeared after the first multi-party elections and which analyzed the spatial patterns of voting and the factors causing variations. Thus, for example, in Moscow's spring 1989 election, Brakov, a hard-liner who stood against Yeltsin, was soundly defeated, receiving only 6.9 per cent of the vote, but in certain wards, including Kutuzov Prospect and the Frunze Embankment, his share rose to 18 per cent; these are streets with concentrations of the Stalin-period better-quality apartments allocated to the elite. In the central area where the highest-rank party members lived, the area known as "The Tsars village", Brakov's share of the vote rose to 30 per cent (Kolosov et al. 1990: 218–20).

Change in social structure

The greater quantity and depth of sociological studies indicated a number of clearly marked changes in Soviet social structure as a whole and in urban social structure in particular. These changes arose perhaps most markedly as people moved from the countryside to the town and as education levels changed. They also occurred with changes in the employment structure of a town. Thus, as trade and service sectors slowly developed, so too did the share of white-collar workers without specialist education (Dmitriyev & Mezhevich 1982: 65). This occurred first and foremost in towns that had a strong regional centre function, including administration.

Soviet sociologists have made numerous studies of mobility in their society and it is abundantly clear that social mobility and urban development were closely related and that they reacted intimately on each other. The most widespread factor in social mobility was undoubtedly education, including technical training. In the first place, those with higher levels of education tended to leave agricultural employment and the villages for the towns and for the higher-paid jobs in industry and the tertiary sector. Within urban society, education assisted upward social mobility. Less widespread throughout the population, but a more powerful factor for upward mobility, was always membership of, and rise within, the Communist Party, and this situation persisted right to very end of the Party in 1991. Rise to the upper layers of society was very difficult outside the Party structure and was usually only achieved by those with exceptional talents in the performing arts, sciences and sport.

The Soviet Union in its closing stages still had a high proportion of its population in lower paid, less well regarded forms of employment such as agriculture and unskilled manual labour. There was therefore considerable scope for mobility and, usually, that mobility was upward. Nevertheless, downward mobility did occur, even if as a self-inflicted condition, for example through alcoholism. Mervyn Matthews has demonstrated the existence and lifestyle of a layer of the poor in Soviet society in both rural and urban areas and concluded that upward mobility out of the ranks of the poor had become more difficult in the latter years of Soviet society (Matthews 1986: 151). What is certain is that the growing economic chaos under the Gorbachev regime increased the number of people near and below the poverty line, most particularly among pensioners. This process of impoverishment was further accelerated in the aftermath of the end of the Soviet Union; Dmitriyeva and her St Petersburg team of economists calculated that, by the beginning of 1993, up to 90 per cent of the population was below the poverty line (pers. comm.).

Mobility in the social sense was and is frequently accompanied by geographical mobility, as people change jobs and especially as they migrate from the countryside into the town or from a small town into a larger town. Size of town is a significant factor in the pace of social change among in-migrants. Of collective and agricultural workers moving into towns, 48 per cent move up to become skilled workers in small towns, but in the categories of large, very large and millionaire cities, the proportion rises to 57–59 per cent (Aitov et al. 1988: 240). The largest towns, with strong development of higher educational facilities, cultural organizations and high-level government operations have the highest proportions of intelligentsia with higher education. "One can say that all the social variations between towns of different size can be related to differences in the opportunities they offer for the all-round development of the personality" (ibid.: 237).

In smaller urban places, farmworkers still make up a measurable share of the population. Even as late as 1979, collective farm workers and their families constituted 2.1 per cent of the national urban population, the vast majority living in settlements of town type. Nationally, 8.4 per cent of *kolkhozniki* lived in such settlements, a proportion rising to 9.1 per cent in the Ukraine, 10.2 per cent in the RSFSR and 11.1 per cent in Latvia (Rutkevich 1987: 91). This situation might be seen as a faint echo of the medieval Russian town, where often a high proportion of its inhabitants derived their livelihood principally from agriculture.

The overall share of employment in unqualified work has fallen, as one would expect with the increasing sophistication of the economy, but the share of women in unqualified work has grown. This latter change reflects the greater constraints imposed on women by the need for nearness to workplace and by the times of working hours (Dmitriyev & Mezhevich 1982: 65); this in turn is a result of the additional burden expected of women in coping with the delivery and collection of children to and from day-care centres, and in doing the shopping on the journey between work and home.

These brief instances show how the widening both of the scope of Soviet urban studies and of their methods of approach, including quantified analyses, had by the opening of the 1980s already begun to transform the quality and quantity of social geographical examination of the Soviet city. Although one may expect considerably more in this field of investigation in the near future, the work during the late Soviet period laid the foundations.

Class and housing

Among the realities recognized in Soviet work by the end of the 1980s, although long clearly discernible to Western observers, was the differentiation of housing types occupied by the various social groups. Theoretically, in a pure communist society, the quality of housing should be uniform and the size of accommodation should be related only to need. These principles underlay most of the thinking of the 1920s and the concepts of communal living. In practice, from the very start there were differences in the amount of housing allocated and, indeed, it was recognized that this was so and should be so. Certain persons have always been accorded the right to larger flats. In some such cases perceived need has indeed been the reason for allocating larger flats, for example to architects, artists and others engaged in the creative arts. Other such privileged persons included those rewarded for contributions rather than need: Heroes of the Soviet Union, Heroes of Socialist Labour and various other award holders, senior officers of the armed forces and the KGB and senior members of the party.

Moreover, the differences in housing allocated to various groups has not been solely in terms of space. Over the years a hierarchy of housing has grown up in terms of quality, with, as one might expect, the best housing going to the privileged and powerful. This process became very visible in the latter years of the Stalin period after the Second World War. The large apartment blocks, in heavy and over-ornate vaguely neoclassical styles, may have been ostentatious in outward appearance, but they were well built, and usually stone faced, and the rooms inside were large. Apartments were frequently of three, four or even five rooms. These flats were primarily allocated to the *nomenklatura* – the Party elite and leaders in each walk of life. Indeed, many of them were designed with such future tenants in mind. The allocation of the Kaluzhskaya Zastava (Kaluga Gates) apartment blocks to KGB officers, described in Chapter 3, is a classic example, but the same was true of the two Stalin skyscrapers in Moscow (Fig. 3.2) devoted to residence, with their marble entrance halls and underground car parks. Other blocks of that period were built along the Moskva River embankments and lining the Leningrad, Kutuzov and Lenin Prospects, leading respectively northwest, west and southwest out of the city. Flats in the blocks on the Lenin Prospect in the southwest, near the Academy of Sciences, were often given to senior academicians. Because these buildings were spacious and well constructed of good quality materials (features by no means common in housing of later construction) they have to the present day tended to remain as the residences of the elite and powerful in all Soviet towns. Some were under the control of the Central Committee of the Communist Party or of individual ministries and other bodies. The rents of these more luxurious flats were extremely low, especially in comparison to income, an obvious reason why their privileged tenants should have little wish to find other accommodation. In the new era following the collapse of the Party, with its concentration of power in the hands of this relatively small group, it appears that they have organized a continuation of privilege for themselves. Privatization of flats is being achieved, in effect, by giving them to their present occupiers. All that is necessary is to register one's claim, for a purely nominal sum. This, of course, gives huge benefits to the best off members of the previous regime and prolongs the deprivation of the homeless and of inhabitants of communal flats.

For those whose incomes were still high, but who lacked the special privileges of the *nomenklatura*, those whom one might loosely describe in Western terms as upper middle class, a common type of accommodation was the co-operative flat, a form of property occupation which was first permitted in 1962. Each member of the co-operative put up a capital sum, to raise which State mortgages were available. The need for ready capital or the ability to repay the mortgage restricted co-operative participation to the better off townsfolk. A building site was allocated and the member acquired one of the completed flats, with the right to dispose of it or to pass it on to inheritors. It was quite usual for the members of a co-operative to have some common link, such as place of employment, although it was also usual to invite in other outside persons. The direct personal interest of the members ensured greater supervision of the construction, greater subsequent care of the building and its surroundings, and therefore higher quality of the living environment, often quite visibly higher. Co-operative flats also tended to be rather larger than the ordinary flats built by local authorities and enterprises. In 1986 the average size of State-built flat was 55.4m^2 and the average co-operative flat was 56.2m^2 (*Narodnoye* . . . 1987: 513). In Alma Ata (Almaty) in 1981 the average amount of living space for the population as a whole was 12.7m^2; for those in co-operative flats it was approximately 18m^2 (Kozybayev et al. 1983).

For the vast majority of urban dwellers the basic type of accommodation was a flat in an apartment block constructed either by the local soviet or by an enterprise. Within this broad category there was a wide range of quality of construction, from the recent, tolerably well built high-rise blocks, down through the older *Khrushchoby* to the even earlier communal flats. Various factors controlled the kind of accommodation which an individual or family received. Number in the family and size of existing accommodation were prime considerations in determining one's position in the housing list. In Moscow, only people with less than 6m^2 of living space, or under half the norm, qualified for rehousing. But even large and poorly accommodated families often found themselves pushed back down the list by the less scrupulous. At this level, social position was less significant than knowing the right person in the allocating authority, or being in a position to offer a bribe. The result was that, in this most frequently found type of housing, the social structure tended to be mixed, but with a distinct trend for status to be linked to quality. Those who could used any means in their power to improve their standard of housing. So many *Khrushchoby* were built in the 1957–65 period that they are the home for a very significant share of the Soviet population, not just the poorest, but only rarely are they occupied by any of the upper layers. Their poor present state means that many occupiers wish to leave for newer accommodation. The Moscow Town Exchange Office reported that 34 per cent of would-be movers wished to leave buildings without lifts – the characteristic feature of the *Khrushchoba* (*Gorodskoye* . . . 1986, no. 7: 24).

The other form of housing is private accommodation, which persisted throughout the Soviet era and which in 1986 made up 22.3 per cent of the total urban housing stock (*Narodnoye* . . . 1987: 519). Some of this private stock was a survival of the pre-revolutionary period; some represented rural settlements engulfed by the outward spread of towns. The majority of private dwellings were wooden, one- or two-storeys, often in a poor condition, lacking modern conveniences. Unlike the private accommodation of the Western city, this type of housing in the Soviet Union was usually low-grade and therefore the home of the poorest members of society. This was by no means invariable, however, and private housing was still being constructed right up to the end of the Soviet period. From 1971 to 1986 inclusive, $309\,900\,000 \text{m}^2$ of housing was built with private capital or with the help of government loans, representing some 18 per cent of total housing construction in both urban and rural areas over that period; the share of the private sector was rather less in the towns than in the countryside. But even the newly constructed private housing tended to be of lower quality. Nevertheless, since these dwellings were usually houses rather than flats, the average space in private accommodation was higher than in State-built housing. In the 1989 census only 11 per cent of families in individual houses lived in one room; 60.3 per cent had three or more rooms. The equivalent figures for separate flats were 16.1 per cent in one room and 34.1 per cent in three or more rooms; in both cases the remainder were in two-roomed accommodation (*Narodnoye . . .* 1991: 186).

At the very bottom of accommodation quality were the communal flats, where several families lived in one flat, sharing a common kitchen and bathroom. In such quarters, 61.1 per cent of families occupied just one room and 30.9 per cent two rooms (ibid.). Many communal flats were in old buildings, frequently of pre-revolutionary construction, but equally often communal flats were, and are, to be found in towns entirely constructed in the Soviet period and even in such show towns as Akademgorodok. Not surprisingly, conditions of living in communal flats nearly always leave much to be desired and not infrequently are atrocious; cleaning of the shared kitchens and bathrooms is only too often seen to be nobody's responsibility; quarrels between whole families in such close and over-crowded conditions are commonplace.

Just as there should in theory be no distinctions in quality of housing in a class-less society, equally there should be no locational differentiation between groups of society, whether called classes, layers or any other term, least of all on grounds of the comparative advantage of one group over another. In practice there has always been some spatial distinction of various groups within the Soviet city. It is true that such variation has usually been relatively weak as compared with most Western cities. The reasons for this are, however, historical rather than conscious sociopolitical planning. Even before the Revolution it was not uncommon for the different social layers to be closely juxtaposed in the town. Partly, this reflected the aristocrat–serf and rural estate-based structure of society, which meant that the town houses of the nobility and wealthy merchants had large retinues of servants; often social distinction was by different floor of the same building, with basements and attics occupied by the lower orders and the main floors by the middle or upper classes (Bater 1976: 373–80). Although this naturally was swept away by the Revolution, it meant that no particularly strong tradition of spatial segregation of social groups had developed by 1917.

Much more influential in preventing social differentiation by areas of a town from developing after 1917 was the appalling housing shortage described in Chapter 3. As the hordes poured in from the countryside in the post-collectivization, early Five Year Plan era of industrialization, all possible space was at a premium. Indeed, throughout the Soviet period other than the war years, the overriding concern of the Soviet citizen has been simply to obtain a home, if possible a self-contained one, but if not, any home. Families got a whole room to themselves if they could, a "corner" if they could not, but where it was located was rarely a matter of choice. Even the elite were for the most part thankful for what they were given, regardless of the convenience or desirability of its location. The power of picking and choosing between alternative sites did not exist, except perhaps for the handful at the summit of the power structure. The only limited possibility of choice for everyone else was private housing and this, where available, was almost invariably among the poorest quality accommodation. The exigencies of the time meant that the new housing tended to be dispersed, where sites for construction were immediately available. Thus, although new housing went chiefly to the emerging privileged classes (except of course in the case of wholly new towns), socially distinct areas did not emerge. The normal differentiation of social groups was by the building rather than the part of the town (French 1979: 97–8).

Exceptions to this general characteristic of segregation by building rather than by district have always existed. The new elite have always had their special enclave in Moscow, lying close to and west of the Kremlin, and described below in more detail. Other areas in towns are seen, sometimes have always been seen, as undesirable and left to the least influential members of society. In many multi-ethnic towns there are clearly distinct spatial groupings of different nationalities. Andrusz (1984: 220) has commented that it is impossible to identify ghettos in Soviet cities, only tendencies to social groupings. This is certainly true in broad terms, but one might feel that these tendencies are on occasion really quite strong. What is also very evident is that the tendency to segregate was becoming far greater as social, economic and political conditions changed in the USSR.

Perceptions of quality and changing social patterns

Over the past 15–20 years, the progress of the housing programme and the easing of the pressure of demand, even if slight, made it somewhat easier for people to exchange their apartments, the process that throughout the Soviet period was the normal recognized way of making a move. As a result, people began to seek out their preferred place of residence: "In line with the satisfaction of housing demands of the population arise a series of demands, relating not only directly to accommodation, but also to place of residence" (Dmitriyev & Mezhevich 1982: 113).

One of the principal difficulties in effecting a move has always been the heavy imbalance between numbers of people wanting more space and those wanting less (*Gorodskoye* . . . 1984 no. 7: 24). This difficulty caused Soviet citizens immeasurable effort and often despair. It added to the problems of newly married couples, unable to obtain a home of their own and forced to live with in-laws; it caused agonies to divorcing couples unable to find separate accommodation and forced to continue living in the same flat and sometimes the same room. Such problems have been the theme of more than one play, received with grimly humorous recognition by Soviet audiences. But from the later 1970s on, there was a far higher proportion of the population with that precious commodity of barter, a self-contained flat to exchange.

Frequently, the motive for moving was to obtain better accommodation. The Moscow City Exchange Office (*Mosgorobmen*) found that 34 per cent of those wanting to move wished to leave a building without a lift, 24 per cent to leave an unsuitable ground- or first-floor flat, and only 8 per cent to acquire more space.

But 26 per cent wished to move to another district (*Gorodskoye* . . . 1986 no. 7: 24).

Increasing numbers, therefore, sought to shift to a part of the city that seemed desirable to them, whether for convenience to work or service provision, or for perceived social or environmental amenity. This desire to move on the part of Soviet city dwellers created a geographical pattern of differing evaluations of the various districts within a town. In a Western city this variation in assessment is reflected in land and accommodation prices. To some extent this was true also in the Soviet city, where "social evaluation . . . is analogous to differential rent" (Vasil'yev & Privalova 1982: 9). In point of fact the resemblance to the Western housing market was still closer, because very often money payments were made to compensate for inequalities in the exchange of accommodation (Vasil'yev 1985: 63). Such "key money" payments could be considerable; a news report (*The Independent*, 23 December 1988: 11) cited a case where 1500 roubles were offered, representing at that time between seven and eight months' average earnings. Such unofficial transactions often took place at illegal open-air rendezvous for the exchange or letting of flats, rooms and beds. A thriving black market in property exchanges grew up, as also in the private renting out of space, usually individual rooms, by apartment holders. Although this was illegal, the intense shortage induced authorities to tolerate private renting for cash. In Moscow at the end of the 1980s this could be up to 100 roubles a month per room.

But just as commonly, space was used as a tradable commodity, instead of money, to even-out inequalities of exchange; people wishing to get into a sought-after area accepted less space than they yielded in the transaction (Vasil'yev et al. 1988: 43). Thus, the announcements of desire to move and exchange flats, known as *zayavki*, published in the weekly bulletins of exchange, provided evidence of this housing "market" and information on intra-urban population movements. In specifying the area or areas where accommodation was sought, these declarations were more useful in defining people's evaluations of desirability than records of completed moves, which may show only what had to be settled for. Moreover, unsatisfied applications were an indication of excess of demand over supply (Vasil'yev & Privalova 1982: 12).

Several Soviet geographers have made use of these *zayavki* (over 15000 were examined by Vasil'yev and Privalova) to throw valuable light on intra-urban movements and especially on evaluations of urban areas (Baklanova 1977, Vasil'yev & Privalova 1982, Barbash 1984a). Results vary, as one might expect. Each district of a town may have its attractions for different individuals or classes (layers) of individuals. Since, as Dmitriyev & Mezhevich (1982: 113) point out, there was no area with all good qualities and services, each person selected where to live on the basis of his or her own balance of perceived advantages. Studies in Moscow and Leningrad both found opposed streams of people wishing to move farther in towards the centre and farther out towards the periphery (Barbash 1986: 141). "Being used to an area" is a powerful force for many; surveys have found a strong sense of "*patriotisme du clocher*" among residents of all districts. Of respondents in a Moscow survey, 80–90 per cent admitted an attraction to the district where they resided (Barbash 1984a: 82). Many found the endless blocks of new flats, with few services, lacking in character and attraction. It was not uncommon for a set of parallel streets of identical buildings to be distinguished by number rather than by name, or by the same name and a number – "First Factory Street", "Second Factory Street" and so on. Surveys indicated that about a third of urban families were dissatisfied even with new accommodation, because of its "addresslessness" (Ruzhzhe 1974: 38).

For blue-collar workers in particular, proximity to place of work is often the attraction; thus some of the environmentally less desirable parts of eastern and southeastern Moscow were the objectives of large numbers of applications in Barbash's survey (Barbash 1984a: 85). Equally, the wish for convenient access to the workplace causes proximity to good transport facilities, especially to the Metro, to be an extremely strong attractive force. Tomsen's work on Moscow indicated that 80 per cent of respondents in outer parts of the city wished to live beside a Metro station (Barbash 1986: 140).

For most people, perceptions of desirability are based on a complex of factors, as Portnov (1991) found in his investigation of "prestige" areas in Krasnoyarsk and as Gachechiladze & Gudzhabidzhe (1979) found in their study of the Tbilisi agglomeration. Portnov's work, based on 2602 questionnaire responses, found that the historical centre and parts of the periphery, where recent building had been set in the best landscape environment, were most highly valued; these areas were rated six out of ten and higher. Lowest ratings, of three or less, were given to the remotest areas and worst environmental conditions, regardless of period of construction. Highest ranking factors of prestige were accessibility, technical quality of housing, and level of development of the social infrastructure. Density of housing and architectural aesthetic quality came lower in importance. In the case of Tbilisi, the key considerations were the quality of the natural environment (air quality and forms of pollution and degradation), the level of technical infrastructure provision (public transport and mains services), social infrastructure (educational and health services, shopping) and housing conditions. On this basis, areas such as Vake and parts of Saburtalo were rated good, while the bad included much of southeast Tbilisi and parts of Rustavi, where industry and transport functions went hand in hand with heavy pollution, remoteness from cultural provision and low grades of housing and communal services.

In the USSR, as in all social systems, it was the richer and more influential members of society who were usually the first to take advantage of developing possibilities of choice. A selective survey carried out in Leningrad in 1978 showed that 52 per cent of those questioned preferred to live farther out towards the city margins, but that the preference was more marked among those with above-average incomes of 210–270 roubles a month (ibid.: 82); the national average in that year was 160 roubles per month. Whereas, until the era of *glasnost*, researchers (as in the 1979 Gachechiladze & Gudzhabidze survey cited above) related people's evaluations of urban areas to environmental conditions, closeness to work, or cul-

141

tural facilities, after 1985 they were openly recognizing that in addition to these influences there was the less tangible or measurable, yet powerful, influence of "social microclimate, rhythm of life and prestige" (Vasil'yev et al. 1988: 44).

In particular, the steadily growing Soviet "upper middle class" of professional people seized the opportunity to develop their own "socially good" areas, comparable to the long-established habitat of the upper class *nomenklatura*, the wedge in west central Moscow. Vanagas, in his work on Vil'nyus and Kaunas, used the residence of professional–intelligentsia groups, including artists, writers, composers, architects and journalists, to define areas of social prestige (Vanagas 1984: 176–7). In Al'met'yevsk in the Tatar Autonomous Republic, Rukavishnikov found that the intelligentsia and white-collar workers tended to concentrate in particular small districts, in both the city centre and on the outskirts (Rukavishnikov 1978: 85). "Changes in the professional structure of society, the development of education and cultural enquiry – all this strengthens the urge to active choice of preferred places of residence" (Baklanova 1977: 55).

Areas of Moscow clearly identified as desirable in the Vasil'yev & Privalova (1982) survey included the west centre and a sector to the northwest along the Leningrad Prospect and Leningrad Chaussee. A third particularly favoured area, especially to the rising professional–managerial class, was the southwestern sector, a long wedge from Oktyabr'skaya Square past Gor'kiy Park and the University, all the way out along the axes of Lenin Prospect and Profsoyuznaya Street to the Orbital Motorway at Tropar'yevo and Teplyy Stan (Fig. 6.1).

Not all these socially "good" areas were newly perceived as desirable. The west centre was already a fashionable area of Moscow, even before the Revolution, and still has a number of the Art Nouveau, or "*Style Moderne*" detached mansions built in the two decades preceding the First World War for the gradually growing class of wealthy merchants, industrialists and businessmen. It forms a wedge lying due west of the Kremlin, with its central axis along the new Kalinin Prospect (now New Arbat), which was driven through the area in the 1960s, to the dismay of many Muscovites. Its limits are roughly defined by Gertsen and Kachalov Streets on the north and Kropotkin Street on the south. The inner point of the wedge, nearest the Kremlin on Granovskiy Street, is the building known throughout Moscow as "The Nest of the Gentry", where members of the Politburo and Presidium had their apartments and the walls of which are lined with commemorative plaques. The adjoining area was similarly given the soubriquet of *Tsarskoye Selo*, "The Tsar's Village."

This zone has not only a very high concentration of housing for the elite of the *nomenklatura*, but also the greatest concentration of foreign embassies, a well-nigh infallible sign of the socially acceptable areas of any capital. It also contains two of Moscow's nine conservation areas, Kropotkin Street and the Arbat (see Ch. 8); the latter is also Moscow's first pedestrianized shopping street. Among the numerous cultural assets of this "upper-class" section of the city are the Vakhtangov and Mayakovskiy theatres and the Tchaikovsky conservatoire; in fact, the central location puts all of Moscow's major cultural attractions within easy walking distance. A number of ministries are located in the huge high-rise blocks along

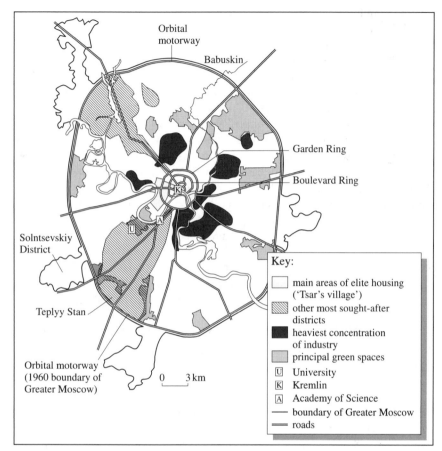

Figure 6.1 Social areas in Moscow.

Kalinin Prospect, and at its outer end are the former offices of the CMEA (Comecon) and the Council of Ministers of the RSFSR (the "White House", made internationally famous in the abortive coup of August 1991 and again in the violent events of 1993). The Foreign Ministry occupies a Stalinist skyscraper on Smolensk Square, near the junction of the Arbat and the Garden Ring. Across the Moskva River the wedge has a newer westward extension, past the Ukraina Hotel along the line of Kutuzov Prospect, at least as far as the former privileged hardcurrency shop for foreign diplomats.

Next in social desirability to the west centre was surely the southwest sector. Almost wholly without industry, its position on the southwest permits prevailing winds to keep the atmosphere cleaner than anywhere else in the city. The sector is well endowed with green space and has been almost wholly developed since the start of the housing drive in 1957. It has a high concentration of higher educational, research and development establishments including Moscow State Univer-

143

sity, the Lumumba University, the headquarters of the Academy of Sciences, the Social Sciences Library (INION), the Lebedev Physics Institute, the Lomonosov Chemical Institute, the Pirogov Medical Institute and the Institutes of Space Research, Russian Language and Geological Prospecting, among others.

Hardly surprisingly, this sector was and is sought after by those with higher educational qualifications, combining as it does proximity to work with above-average environmental conditions. It does in fact have an enhanced proportion of "specialists in non-material production", as well as of students (Barbash 1984b: 59). The professional employees of the R&D institutions live in the same sector and extend it outwards in a development rather resembling the classic sectoral pattern of Hoyt's seminal work (Barbash 1984a: 90). As, perhaps, a sign of its rise to challenge the established social heights of the west-central wedge, the southwest sector has its own cluster of 15 embassies lying just west of Moscow University; all have appeared there since the late 1950s.

The pattern of perceived desirability produced by study of apartment changes is also reflected by other surveys. Zaslavskiy's (1984) examination of subscriptions to journals shows that the highest rates of subscription to scientific and artistic–cultural journals occur in the centre and in the northwest and southwest sectors. His survey, being based on the 400-odd postal districts, has a greater precision of detail than most such analyses.

In contrast, Veshninskiy's 1988 questionnaire survey, to discover Muscovites' perceptions of the relative attractiveness of city districts, suffers from the restriction of its scope to residents in only four new outer regions of the city: Ivanovskoye in the northeast, Lianozovo in the northwest, Orekhovo–Borisovo in the southeast and Yasenovo in the southwest. There is a noticeable element of local pride in responses to the questions, "How do you like the external appearance of your living region, compared with where you lived previously?", "If you had to choose a new area to live in, which would you choose?" and "Of Moscow's living regions which you have seen, which is to you the most beautiful?" But despite bias in favour of respondents' own regions, a clear overall pattern emerged of preference for the west of the city, with the northeast neutral (balanced likes and dislikes) and the southeast evoking negative responses. When asked to name favourite streets, about 90 per cent of those questioned named streets in the centre within the Garden Ring, and the majority of those were in the west in the elite wedge (Veshninskiy 1988: 98).

Further emphasis on the social pre-eminence of the favoured sectors to west, southwest and northwest is given by Natasha Barbash's study of the spatial variation in the birthweight of children as an indicator of environmental conditions. She chose infants for her investigation, as mothers in late pregnancy are among the less mobile members of urban society and therefore reflect best the impact of their home environment. Density of employment and of transport routes, both related to the degree of industrialization, were found to have significant impact. In particular, a contrast was found between the Yugo–Zapadnaya district in the favoured southwest and the Avtozavodskaya district in the heavily industrialized southeast (Barbash 1982: 83–92).

Although Moscow, with the most elaborate class stratification of Soviet society, has provided some of the best examples of sectors seen as socially distinct and therefore sought after in moves by the socially aspiring, similar perceptions of "the uneven distribution of one or another social group by area of the town" (Aitov et al. 1982: 15) are found in other cities. In Vake and Saburtalo, the favoured districts of the Tbilisi agglomeration, environmental quality is high, with close access to unspoilt nature on the one hand and to workplaces and sociocultural features on the other; housing and infrastructure are good (Gachechiladze & Gudzhabidze 1979: 95).

Studies in a number of towns indicate that people with higher educational levels tend to prefer residence in the city centre, where cultural facilities are most concentrated. Work in Kaluga discovered that one of the features of the centre which respondents claimed to find attractive was the concentration of architectural monuments (Bakshteyn et al. 1986: 92–3). In Ufa in 1968 a high proportion of the intelligentsia lived in the historic city centre, where over half the population were engaged in mental (i.e. white-collar) work (Rukavishnikov 1980: 195). A decade and a half later, Ufa's central Kirov District still contained nearly all the city's higher educational establishments, many of its research institutes and most of the administrative offices and, in consequence, the majority of its population were intelligentsia or white-collar office workers. A study of Leningrad in the late 1960s showed that it was most commonly those with higher educational levels who wished to live close to the centre and who were ready to accept less living space, up to 17 to 22 per cent less, in order to do so (Dmitriyev & Mezhevich 1982: 117). Portnov (1991) in Krasnoyarsk also found the historic centre to rank high in prestige.

These conclusions are supported by Kogan's (1989) survey of 25 000 respondents, which found that, for those who lived in central areas, cultural institutions were more important than "nearness to nature", that is to green space. For those living in suburbs, nearness to food and service shops was important to 80–90 per cent of respondents. In the centre the equivalent figure was only 20 per cent; there 40–50 per cent professed the importance of cafes, restaurants, theatres and bookshops.

If Soviet cities had areas which were seen as "good" on grounds of centrality and access to cultural amenities or of environmental pleasantness and which were therefore sought after by the better off, the more intelligent and the more ambitious, equally there were parts of towns which were seen as less desirable or even positively undesirable. In Vasil'yev & Privalova's 1982 study of Moscow, the northern and southern peripheries came out lowest for availability of the benefits used in their model. The southeast, east and northeast are generally regarded as poor, largely as a consequence of the concentration of industries, especially heavy industry, in these sectors (Fig. 6.2). In Kalinin District two-thirds of the land is taken up by 50 factories and commercial establishments (including the "Hammer and Sickle" steel works), as against only 23 per cent of the land under housing (*Gorodskoye* . . . 1987 no. 1: 18). Mar'ina Roshcha in north Moscow is seen as an

Figure 6.2   Bauman District in east-central Moscow, an area of old housing and industry.

undesirable area with a high crime rate. Such areas are dominated by manual, semi-skilled and skilled blue-collar workers. In part this is because the factories, such as the huge car plant, originally built the housing for their workers. In part also, it is a result of moves by exchange into the area by those wishing to minimize the journey to work (Barbash 1984b: 58–9).

A parallel case occurs in Ufa, where the Kirov District, as cited above, had a concentration of the intelligentsia and mental workers; in contrast the Ordzhoni-kidze and Kalinin Districts contained large factories and the homes of blue-collar workers (Aitov et al. 1982: 15). In Tbilisi, Gachechiladze (1990b: 43–4) found what he termed "depressed" areas, such as Gldani, which is 15–20 km from the city centre (and originally linked by a single, overcrowded bus route) and suffers from several major air polluting sources.

Even today, after three decades of the housing programme, enormous differen-tials in housing quality, population density and overcrowding exist within Soviet cities. In Alma Ata (Almaty) the amount of living space per capita in Alatauskiy Rayon in the southwest of the city was 10.96 m^2, over twice that in Frunzenskiy Rayon in the east centre, with an appalling 5.19 m^2 (Kozybayev et al. 1983). Even greater variation was found in Minsk, where in 1982 the amount of useful space per capita varied from 19.16 m^2 in the southwestern Oktyabr'skiy District to an equally dreadful 5.57 m^2 in Tsentral'nyy (Central) District (calculations from *Minsk: Entsiklopedicheskiy Spravochnik* 1983). Population densities in the dis-tricts of Minsk ranged from 51 to 138 per hectare.

New in-migrants to a town have frequently had to take accommodation in those districts that were evaluated as less desirable. The new arrivals often found rented rooms or even "corners" (just as in pre-revolutionary and Stalinist times) in these areas, which were often on the city outskirts or in surviving engulfed villages with old wooden private houses and poor service provision (Aitov et al. 1982: 16). Shvedov's investigations showed that, in central parts of Moscow, between 50 and 62 per cent of the inhabitants had lived there for over ten years; in Babushkin, an area of industry in the northeastern outskirts, only 12.6 per cent had resided for more than ten years (Shvedov 1976: 28). About a quarter of all new in-migrants to Babushkin found difficulty in adapting; the equivalent figure in the desirable southwest research and development sector was 2.3 per cent (Vardosanidze 1977: 9). Other groups which are more frequently represented on the outskirts are those with lower educational qualifications and those with large families (Table 6.2); Zaslavskiy's (1984) study of journal subscriptions found the greatest numbers of subscribers to children's journals in the outer microregions.

Table 6.2   Average family size in Moscow.

Zone	1959	1966	1975	1979
Inner ↓				
I (within Garden Ring)	2.3	2.2	1.8	2.1
II equal widths	3.3	3.2	2.6	3.0
III } of the rest	3.4	3.4	3.2	3.5
IV of Moscow	3.6–3.5	3.5	3.3	3.8
Outer ↑				

Sources: Glushkova (1981: 39), Saushkin & Glushkova (1983: 89).

Often these outer districts are not only perceived as less desirable and therefore left to the less well informed new arrivals, they are in fact poorly provided with the necessary infrastructure. This is of course largely attributable to the recentness of housing construction and the well nigh invariable long lag in service provision. Lyublinskiy District in the outer southeast sector of Moscow, where there is considerable recent development, has a heavy concentration of hostels for young people, 123 in all; it fails to match this with adequate provision of pre-school facilities (*Gorodskoye . . .* 1985 no. 11: 18). As examined in the previous chapter, there is a clear correlation between areas of high concentrations of in-migrants and high crime rates; such areas include newly developing suburbs.

Certainly, Soviet citizens perceived these qualitative differences between one part of the town and another. Mervyn Matthews, in his study of poverty in the USSR based on questionnaire surveys of emigrants, found that over two-thirds of those asked thought that areas of poverty existed, at least to some extent; they included 11 per cent who believed that such areas were clearly detectable. The characteristics which the respondents considered indicated poverty included housing (66% of replies), services (61%), physical safety (51%), shopping facilities (45%), street condition (39%), transport (31%) and air quality (24%) (Matthews 1986: 72). That such perceptions, however subjective, are not without foundation is indicated by studies such as that of Vanagas in the two largest Lithuanian cities,

Vil'nyus and Kaunas. Parts of these cities that had high concentrations of crime, alcoholism and disease were those with high population densities, shabby housing, small and overcrowded flats and lack of services (Vanagas 1984: 176). Such conditions and the perceptions of such conditions have provided motives for moving within a city. A survey taken in Leningrad in 1978 found that the commonest reason for wishing to move, given in 40 per cent of replies, was the state of the environment; other reasons came far behind (Table 6.3).

Table 6.3 Reasons for moving within Leningrad (%).

Conditions of the environment	39.9
"Being used to the area"	16.1
Proximity to work or study	13.1
Level of services and transport	8.0
Proximity to relatives	5.8
Proximity to centre	5.4
Aesthetic perceptions	4.7

Source: Dmitriyev & Mezhevich (1982: 114)

Just as preferences cause people to make moves within a city to areas of greater perceived satisfaction, so they lead people to make selections between towns and between regions. While the Soviet Union remained a unified State and people moved without hindrance between republics, both size of town and climate played a major role. Greater size meant better provision, not only of infrastructure and cultural facilities, but also of consumer goods (and food in particular). Moscow was outstandingly the ranking city (*etalonnyy gorod*), followed after a long gap by Leningrad and Kiev (second and third cities by size) and then by Minsk, Odessa and the capitals of the Baltic and Transcaucasian Republics (Vasil'yev et al. 1988: 45). In these latter cases, the quality and level of sophistication of the urban environment played a significant part and, in the case of the Transcaucasus, so did the milder climate. Among smaller categories of towns, the southern Ukraine and the Baltic Republics led the way as most sought-after areas, with a fall-off in popularity to east and north. The least desired areas were the Urals, Siberia and Central Asia (ibid.).

Such perceptions of regional desirability have been confirmed by Kostinskiy's study of the regional preferences of Soviet youth in selected towns. Muscovite children and those from Murom, a small town in the central region of European Russia, put their own region first; those from Omsk and Chita in Siberia ranked their home region third and sixth respectively (Kostinskiy 1990: 735). It is hardly surprising that the young of Tbilisi put their native Georgia first, but it is perhaps significant that the next three preferences were given to the Baltic Republics, followed in fifth and sixth places by the Ukraine and Moldavia. Moscow University students and adult intellectuals also ranked the central region around Moscow in first place, with the next group of preferences going to the Baltic Republics, the Ukraine and the south of European Russia, although with some difference in ordering between these two groups (ibid.: 742–3).

That there is a real difference between towns, both in the existing quality of life and in the speed with which it is improving, has been emphasized by recent studies made by the Laboratory of Regional Economic Studies of the N. Voznesenskiy Finance–Economics Institute in Leningrad, which compared 71 towns with their situation in 1979 in terms of 58 indices (*Argumenty i Fakty* 1991 no. 21: 1). On most of these indices, Moscow took first place for degree of improvement. Thus, for improved level of food demand per inhabitant for meat, milk, fish, cheese, eggs, vegetables and so on, if Moscow is taken as 100 the next best were Leningrad (84.6%), Murmansk (81.7%) and Kaliningrad (79.9%). It is worth commenting that the latter three places are all major seaports and naval bases, with very high proportions of service personnel and party members. Least favourably placed in relation to Moscow were Groznyy, oil town and capital of the then Chechen–Ingush ASSR (45.3%), Elista, capital of the Kalmytskaya ASSR (47.6%), and Kyzyl, capital of the Tuva Autonomous Republic (46.5%). Where consumer durables were concerned, the dominance of naval bases was even more pronounced, with Petropavlovsk–Kamchatskiy at 113.1 per cent of Moscow, Magadan 109.4 and Murmansk 107.0; once again the north Caucasus area fared worst, with Elista at 50.0, Groznyy 48.9 and Makhachkala 46.9 per cent.

Other parameters, including health, living conditions (space, central heating, baths, sewerage, etc.), street conditions, transport, communications, retailing and restaurants, domestic services, education, culture, medical supplies, crime and ecological cleanliness showed a fair range of alternative places between the best and worst. In terms of health, the north Caucasus towns of Makhachkala and Groznyy outdid Moscow for improvement, whereas the worst were the Siberian towns of Kemerovo (75.5% of Moscow) and Yakutsk (73.2%). Yakutsk ranked lowest under "living conditions", with a level of improvement only 17.6 per cent of that in Moscow. Overall, the highest parameters of improvement, other than in Moscow and Leningrad, were attained by Murmansk, Magadan, Yuzhno–Sakhalinsk (another naval base), Tyumen', Syktyvkar and Petrozavodsk, while those at the foot of the table were Elista, Makhachkala, Groznyy, Chita, Ulan–Ude, Tambov and Kyzyl. Obviously, too much weight cannot be placed on the relative speeds at which improvements were taking place over so short a time period as a dozen or so years, but very definite regional patterns emerged in the survey and these must surely have influenced people's perceptions of where it was pleasant to live.

Perceptions of the relative desirability of different towns were studied, with fascinating results, by Vasil'yev et al. (1988). In some cases the amount of space surrendered in interurban exchange was very large indeed. For example, in 1990, people from Leningrad wishing to move to Moscow were losing 15 per cent of their living space, but those from Novosibirsk and Omsk in Siberia had to yield 50 per cent and those from Ashkhabad, capital of the Turkmen Republic, no less than 75 per cent (Sidorov 1990). The crisis outflow of Russian population from the republics of Central Asia in the post-Soviet period has gravely exacerbated this trend.

Moscow was always the ranking city, with all other towns seen as less desirable in differing degrees. Clearly, distance from Moscow was one negative factor; even more strongly negative was a town's heavy industrial function, while on the contrary, republican capital functions were usually an asset. Thus, Nizhniy Novgorod (Gor'kiy), only 439km from Moscow, ranked far below Tbilisi, the Georgian capital at 2390km from Moscow, or even Dushanbe, the Tadzhik capital at a remote 4637km. Of the ten best placed cities in the ranking of people's perceptions with regard to housing exchange with Moscow (i.e. surrendering least space, absolutely and proportionately to previously occupied size), only Leningrad and Odessa were not republican capitals. Interestingly, comparison of the rankings in 1986 with those of 1990 shows Kiev falling back from first to third place in the aftermath of Chernobyl (Sidorov 1990). It goes without saying that with the break-up of the USSR people's perceptions of where they would like to live will be rapidly and significantly changing. The large-scale exodus of Russians from the republics of Central Asia and the Transcaucasus is symptomatic.

In short, the increased stratification of Soviet society over the whole post-Stalin era was being reflected to an ever increasing extent in the social geography of towns, as moves by individuals and their families brought about, however slowly, a sorting of the population on the basis of status, occupation, education and income. The individual was creating what the plan certainly did not seek. If, until the latter decades of the Soviet Union, spatial social distinction in cities was more commonly by building rather than by district, this has been gradually changing and segregation by area was being reinforced rather than diminished. By the mid-1980s a Soviet geographer could comment that, "Populations fairly distinctive in composition are concentrated in different districts within towns" (Vasil'yev 1985: 61).

December 1988 saw a development that was set to bring about considerable further development of the trends outlined in this chapter, namely the decree permitting Soviet people from 1989 to purchase their flats from the State with the help of 50 per cent ten-year mortgages (*The Independent*, 23 December 1988). One can immediately see parallels with the sale of council houses to tenants in Britain. Inevitably, even if the Soviet system had persisted, this must have resulted in the development of a housing market on a basis of cash sales, rather than on terms of exchange with space compensation. Movement between residences would be accelerated by this development and, with the movement, the further crystallizing out of socially differentiated areas within towns. In practice, the end of the Soviet system came before this measure had much effect. The post-Soviet situation, with flat-holders registering their ownership and thus having the right to sell, is already beginning to reinforce the trends described here; the "fashionable" areas of Moscow, especially the west centre, are showing steep rises in property value.

Ethnic patterns and problems

The most common type of social distinction, which existed before the revolution and which continued to be reflected in spatial patterns throughout the Soviet period and up to the present, was ethnic differentiation. The USSR was of course a multiracial society embracing over a hundred nationalities. Unfortunately, statistics relating to ethnic groups in general have always been very scarce and until now the situation has remained even bleaker concerning availability of data relating to ethnic groups in urban areas. Only the censuses of 1959 and 1970 were published with any material on ethnic numbers in towns, and then only for oblasts as a whole; republican capitals were the only individual towns for which nationality breakdown was given. Since then there have been only scattered snippets of information in secondary sources. As a result, little serious work has been done either inside or outside the Soviet Union on one of the most vital aspects of urban social geography. For example, the eminent specialist Vakhtang Dzhaoshvili, in his otherwise seminal work on the urbanization of Georgia, never mentions ethnic issues even when dealing with demographic matters, other than in a brief two-page description of the numerical membership of ethnic groups in the four censuses up to 1970 (Dzhaoshvili 1978a: 148–50).

The colonizing process, which dominated the whole of Russian history, constantly brought Russians into the territories of other nationalities. In the initial stages of Russian advance and down to the nineteenth century, the Russian settlers were moving into very thinly populated and empty areas in the steppes of European Russia and the forests of Siberia. Such indigenous peoples as there were in these lands were mostly nomadic or semi-nomadic; they were rarely town builders or town dwellers and numbered but few. Towns were Russian foundations and non-Russians have ever since formed at most a small element within them.

In the nineteenth century, Russian military conquests in the Caucasus and Central Asia brought them into areas of established urban cultures, much older than the Russian culture. Russians moved in as colonial administrators, military personnel and merchants. In the countryside they never formed more than a tiny minority, but in the towns they were a substantial component. Before the revolution some two-thirds of the population of Georgian towns were alien in-migrants, including Russians, but also with an even larger Armenian component. Armenians enjoyed a developed urban culture so that they not only formed a clear majority in their own towns, but also dominated the towns of Georgia and Azerbaydzhan, even as late as the 1926 census (Dzhaoshvili 1978b: 106). In addition to forming an ever-growing share in the population of non-Russian towns, in towns of Russian foundation (for example, military posts such as Vernyy, later Alma Ata and now Almaty, the capital of Kazakhstan) the Russians were a large majority and have usually remained so. In the 1970 census Russians still made up 70.3 per cent of Almaty's population.

In the Soviet period, Russians were outstandingly the most mobile ethnic group and, as rapid industrialization got under way and spread to the previously lightly

151

industrialized non-Russian areas, it was the Russians who moved in to set up, manage and man the new factories. In consequence, the difference in degree of urbanization between the Russians and all the other nationalities of the Soviet Union (except the Jews) has increased over the Soviet period (Lewis et al. 1976: 334). At the same time the Russian share of urban population in other republics tended to increase markedly in the early Five Year Plans. In Georgia, between the censuses of 1926 and 1939 the Russian share of urban population rose from 11.8 to 18.4 per cent, although it then stabilized and after the Second World War began to fall as more and more Georgians moved into the towns (Dzhaoshvili 1978a: 149).

In new industrial centres such as Karaganda in Kazakhstan, the population has all along been predominantly Russian. In 1970, Russians constituted 57 per cent of the 1 259 377 urban inhabitants of Karaganda Oblast, whereas the Kazakhs made up only 11 per cent, scarcely more than the 10.5 per cent of Ukrainians (the second most mobile nationality). Indeed, in Kazakhstan, where the Russian share of total population is greater than in any other Union Republic, Russians in 1970 outnumbered the Kazakhs in the urban population of all but two oblasts, sometimes by ratios of five or six to one.

Russians also form an extremely significant constituent in the major towns of the Baltic Republics; in 1970 they outnumbered Latvians in Riga. In Vil'nyus the Lithuanians were outnumbered by the Slav nationalities as a whole – Russians, Poles, Ukrainians and Belorussians. Moreover, in the Baltic States, with the highest standard of living in the Soviet Union, the inflow of Russians after the 1970 census continued to be considerable.

The Russians in the towns of non-Russian areas have played a major role in assimilating the indigenes who live there, especially in terms of language. Only a minority of Russians make a serious effort to learn the language of their host republic. In Karaganda Oblast in the census of 1970, of the 141 763 urban-dwelling Kazakhs, 6437 put Russian as their mother tongue and no less than 103 096 (72%) claimed fluency in Russian; of the 713 210 Russians in the oblast's towns, only 11 put Kazakh as their mother tongue and only 2226 (0.3%) could claim fluency in Kazakh (*Itogi* . . . 1973: 239).

In other republics, notably Georgia, an intensive nationalist cultural struggle has constantly and successfully been fought to maintain the pre-eminence of the Georgian language. In Tbilisi in 1970 less than 1 per cent of Georgians gave Russian as their mother tongue and only 43 per cent claimed fluency in Russian. Russians once again made a poor showing in their command of the host language, which was spoken fluently by a mere 18 per cent. The Armenians, who then outnumbered the Russians in Tbilisi, showed far greater willingness to learn other languages; 39 per cent had fluent Russian and 25 per cent fluent Georgian (ibid.: 258). Kasperovich (1985: 144) states that ethnic groups outside their own republic tend to linguistic assimilation and points out that Belorussians outside Belorussia most often change to the Russian tongue as the *lingua franca* of the USSR. Clearly, this does not apply to the Russians, no doubt reflecting persistent colonial attitudes of mind, if only at a subconscious level.

Kasperovich (1985: 143) further suggests that the towns have had an effect in "internationalizing" material cultural phenomena such as housing and clothing. Although this is undoubtedly true, in Central Asia there appears to have been a trend in recent years to revert more frequently to wearing traditional clothing, more noticeably among women. There is also a widespread hostility to the replacement of traditional types of housing by modern "international" ones.

Studies in 1974–5 in Kazan', Al'met'yevsk and Menzelinsk in the Tatar Autonomous Republic suggested that Russians and Tatars showed some variation in employment structure. In all three towns a larger proportion of Tatars than of Russians worked in the manufacturing and building industries and also in trade and public catering. Science, education, health and cultural occupations employed significantly higher proportions of Russians, while in finance and administration the share of both groups was similar in Kazan' and Al'met'yevsk, but rather larger among Russians than Tatars in Menzelinsk (Shkaratan 1986: 118). The same survey covered pay by social "layer" and age, but the results showed no clear pattern. In certain categories, in certain age groups, in one or another town, Russians received more pay; in other cases the Tatars had more. For instance, in Kazan' in the highly qualified managerial category, Tatars received substantially more (40%) than Russians; in Al'met'yevsk Russians in that category earned substantially more (56%) and in Menzelinsk Tatars received 12 per cent more (ibid.: 120).

The result of the last century and a half has been that all major towns of the USSR display a strong characteristic of ethnic diversity. There is evidence to suggest that with time the diversity may have increased, rather than diminished. Kasperovich has shown in his work on Belorussia that ethnic diversity has become most complex in the largest cities and republican capitals, which have usually been the nodes of attraction for migrants from other republics. Minsk has no less than 50 nationalities represented in its population. This in itself brings about an element of paradox, for it is the capitals such as Minsk that are the foci for national consolidation (Kasperovich 1985: 49). At the same time, in such cities the overall share of the indigenous nationality falls, as out-migrants are replaced by in-migrants from different republics (ibid.: 42). In the case of the Baltic Republics, the steep rise in the proportion of Russians in the population of the largest towns has taken place since these countries were occupied by the USSR in 1939. Elsewhere, as in Armenia, the Soviet period has seen a rise in the share of indigenous people in the urban population, often assisted by higher birth rates (Dzhaoshvili 1978b: 108–9).

The complex ethnic structure of the urban population has always been reflected, to a greater or lesser degree, in spatial differentiation. The various nationalities often display markedly different perceptions of, and attitudes to, the town and its functions. In many parts of the country the large-scale in-migration of Russians and other outside nationalities before the Revolution and the resultant domination of the town was seen as an alien imposition. Clearly distinct ethnic areas characterized the Tsarist town in the colonial areas, most noticeably in Central Asia, where Russian quarters were often as spatially and architecturally distinct from the older "native" towns as any British cantonment in India. Thus, Baku had its Armenian quarter in the north, a Muslim Azerbaydzhani area on the west, a Russian administrative area in the south and a predominantly Russian industrial area in the east (Altstadt-Mirhadi 1986: 282, 294–5). Marked spatial segregation has frequently survived to the present and even in new Soviet foundations segregation has developed. The old Azerbaydzhani town of Baku survives to this day. Its almost complete circuit of walls encloses the former palace of the Shirvan Shahs, mosques and narrow alleys lined with houses in traditional architectural style. Outside the walls are the wide streets on a rectangular pattern, fronted by large solidly built office buildings of the pre-revolutionary and Stalinist periods, which represent the first Russian town and the administrative and business centre of the city.

Equally distinct are the surviving "old towns" of Central Asian cities such as Tashkent, Samarkand and Bukhara. Along their irregular narrow streets and alleys are traditional single-storey houses made of wattle and daub, with few, if any, outward-facing windows and arranged around an interior courtyard. Although the indigenous Uzbeks share with Russians and other nationalities the new microregions surrounding the historic cores, they form the overwhelming majority in the old centres. The traditional house, although it may possibly be less well provided with amenities, suits the lifestyle and usages of the extended family unit and is widely preferred to the little boxes of modern apartment blocks.

Statistical information about ethnic distributions within Soviet cities is limited in the extreme and very few Soviet researchers have undertaken work in this sensitive field. One of the rare exceptions is Vladimir Rukavishnikov, whose researches in the 1970s were primarily in the Tatar Autonomous Republic, especially its capital, Kazan', and in Tallin, the capital of Estonia. The near uniqueness of his studies have led him to be widely quoted in Western literature, with frequent reproductions of his maps (Bater 1984: 152–3, 156; French 1987: 312; Bater 1989: 120–22; Smith 1989: 24).

In the Tatar Autonomous Republic, Rukavishnikov found a high degree of separation of the two major ethnic groups, Russian and Tatar. In Kazan', some town areas were 60 to 80 per cent Tatar, while other areas had 60 to 100 per cent Russian population (Rukavishnikov 1978: 85). The pattern of areas with one or the other nationality predominating was complex, but inner parts of Kazan', the Russian town of pre-revolutionary times with the regular street pattern of the Catherine plan era had 80 to 100 per cent Russian inhabitants. This was the administrative focus of the city. Immediately south was a belt with concentrations of the Tatar population, in some areas forming 60 to 80 per cent of the total. These were the areas of pre-revolutionary Tatar segregation, the so-called Old and New Tatar Suburbs. Farther out from the centre, the proportion of Russians in the population increased and many of the outer microregions were entirely Russian.

In Al'met'yevsk, now the fourth largest town of Tatarstan, but then the second, it is perhaps significant that the areas of Russian preponderance included the city centre and nearby areas of better quality housing from the Stalin period. In contrast, an extensive area east of the city centre, mostly with dormitory-type build-ings (*baraki*) and lacking in amenities, was predominantly inhabited by Tatars (ibid.: 86). Further work by the same author in Tallin discovered similar patterns. In parts of the Estonian capital Russians formed up to 68.8 per cent of the popula-tion and in others Estonians made up 83.8 per cent (Rukavishnikov 1980: 181). Rukavishnikov found that the ethnic component was significant in three of his five factors in the factorial structure of Tallin, but he was criticized later by Raitviir (1988: 146) for not giving enough weight to ethnicity.

In the RSFSR the long-standing tendency for non-Russians to be found in the less desirable parts of cities was exemplified in Samara. There, the Gornaya district of the central part of the town beyond the Glebuchev ravine consisted in the late 1950s of poorly built one- and two-storey houses in chaotic distribution; it was the home of many Tatars and people from the Caucasus engaged in retailing, crafts and mar-ket gardening, all occupations of lesser status at that period (Sklyar 1958: 121).

The spatial differentiation of ethnic groups has, not unnaturally, considerably reduced the level of contact between them. Koroteyeva found in her surveys of Tashkent and Tbilisi that, in areas predominantly of one nationality, people had almost no links with other groups. In Tashkent, Uzbeks living in Uzbek areas had 91.7 per cent of their contacts with other Uzbeks, and Russians in their own areas had 82.4 per cent of their contacts with other Russians. The equivalent figure for Georgians in Georgian sectors of Tbilisi was 92.7 per cent. In marked contrast, Uzbeks in Russian areas had 57.2 per cent of contacts with Russians, and Geor-gians in Russian areas had 50.7 per cent Russian contacts in the respective cities (Koroteyeva 1988: 151–2).

This lack of communication between ethnic groups carries worrying implica-tions. In the unstable and changing situation of the post-Soviet Union in the 1990s, the ethnic geography of the urban areas is likely to become increasingly signifi-cant and to carry risks, perhaps serious risks, of ethnic conflict. Until the era of *glasnost*, the rigid police control, the suppression of all genuine nationalist expres-sion, the lack of free media communication all effectively suppressed interracial tensions. An early consequence of the freedom of expression and communication that emerged under *glasnost* was the use of that freedom to give voice to ancient but deep ethnic resentments. The change came swiftly. In a survey of the urban and rural populations within and outside the Tbilisi metropolitan region at the end of the 1980s, problems of ethnic relations ranked last, or last but one, in a list of 25 social problems; only 3–9 per cent of those interviewed considered them a problem (Gachechiladze 1990a: 479). It is highly unlikely that they would now rank so low. The Transcaucasus witnessed one of the first major ethnic distur-bances, when in 1988 the clash between the Christian Armenians and Islamic Azerbaydzhanis over the administration of the Nagorno–Karabakh Autonomous District was rapidly followed by outbreaks of violence between the two commu-nities in Baku and especially in its oil-refining satellite, Sumgait. The pogrom of Armenians, leading to the death of at least 32 people, was in turn followed by fur-ther violence in both republics and mass emigrations of Armenians out of the

Azerbaydzhani towns and of Azerbaydzhanis out of Armenia. By 1992, Georgia was riven internally by strife between the Georgians and smaller groups who lived in autonomous areas within the republic: the Ossetians and the Abkhaz.

The break-up of the Soviet Union has left many millions of people within newly independent States consisting predominantly of other nationalities. Inevitably there must be grave potentialities for clashes, especially where there are local concentrations of minorities. Within the Russian Republic, the Tatars are heavily concentrated in the middle Volga region and there are already more than murmurs in favour of an independent Tatarstan. A local, substantial and long-established local Russian minority lives in Moldova, in a zone along the River Dnestr including the second largest town of the Republic, Bendery. Here, the opposition of the Russians to an independent Moldova, which might one day seek reunification with Rumania, has already led to serious armed clashes.

The urgent need to modernize the economy, to get rid of inefficient over-manning, together with the likely reduction in the size of the armed forces, will increase still further the burgeoning unemployment in all the republics. Under these circumstances of a diminished labour market, people of outside nationality tend to become the focus of resentments. Nowhere is this more likely to be true than in the Donbas heavy industrial region. The huge Soviet metallurgical industry, buoyed up for so long by the demands of the military, protected from competition with the outside world and characterized by considerable overcapacity and generally obsolescent technical inefficiency, will be undergoing considerable cutbacks in coming years. At the same time, the coal mining of the region has for a considerable time been undergoing recession, as seams and pits become worked out. In the intervals between the 1959, 1970 and 1979 censuses, the majority of significant towns which declined absolutely in population were mining centres, mostly coalmining and including a number of Donbas towns. The possibility of ethnic clashes between Ukrainian workers, who have just achieved national independence, and Russians, who make up nearly half the population, cannot be lightly dismissed. Similar situations may be found in a number of regions of the Soviet Union, including those where the cultural and religious differences are more sharply marked than between Russians and Ukrainians.

Uncertainties on such scores since the collapse of the Soviet Union have brought about a reversal of trends towards diversity in many areas of the former USSR, as minority populations leave for their "home" republic; thus Armenians and Azeris have in large measure left each other's republic as a result of the conflict between them. The scale of Russian emigration from the Central Asian republics has become considerable. Where the Russians are choosing to migrate back to their home republic, the possibilities of ethnic clashes may be reduced, but industries such as the metallurgy and coalmining of Karaganda will be crippled by the shortages of skilled management and workforce. At the in-migration end, the influx of Russians to the Russian Republic is causing severe housing problems. By December 1992 the official estimate of refugees in Russia was 500000, of whom 120000 had still not found employment.

Of the characteristics of the new society envisaged in the aftermath of the 1917 revolution, a unity of ethnic groups within a classless society was taken as axiomatic by everyone. One might well feel that, of all the objectives of the planned city, such unity has made the least progress. The individual's perception of his or her ethnicity has remained clear and strong; in many instances it has become stronger, as groups which had never previously enjoyed national status or defined territory, sometimes never had their own written language, acquired these adjuncts to ethnic identity. The plurality of Soviet urban society threatens to be a weakness of the post-Soviet city.

CHAPTER 7

The onset of the tyranny of the car

The growth of traffic

It has been suggested in earlier chapters that, by the 1980s, the Soviet city was entering a fourth stage in its development, in which the role of individual choice was increasingly bringing about geographical patterns other than those sought by the plan. This fourth stage saw another major factor steadily emerging, which reinforced the element of individuality. It also was proving far more intractable to manipulation by the planner; it will in all probability leave any plan and its compilers, whatever the system of urban management in coming years, lagging as helplessly behind as did industrialization and housing construction in the early Soviet stages. That factor is of course the rise of road traffic and in particular the growth in private car ownership.

It is true that both road traffic and car ownership even now have a long way to go to be comparable with countries such as the USA or Great Britain. In 1970, car ownership per 100 families was only two, in 1980 it was ten and by 1988 it had reached 17, that is to say, still only 52.8 per cent of the Soviet officially determined "rational norm" (Sarkisyan 1983: 167). Where commercial freight movement is concerned the Soviet Union had the lowest proportion of its turnover moving on the roads of any developed country, lower even than most of its east European CMEA partners. In 1990, road transport hauled just 1.71 per cent (in tonne/kilometres) of the total freight turnover on forms of public transport. However, this figure is somewhat misleading; in terms of absolute tonnage carried, there was a substantial increase throughout the Soviet period. In 1990 6344 million tonnes (51.4 per cent of the national total, and more than on the railways) were dispatched by public road haulage. In fact the tonnage carried on the roads was far higher than this, since the majority of construction organizations and manufacturing enterprises and many other bodies had their own fleets of trucks. Total deliveries by road transport in the same year came to 27 263 700 000 tonnes (all these and subsequent figures for 1990 derive, unless otherwise specified, from *Narodnoye Khozyaystvo SSSR v 1990g.* 1991).

The implication of these figures is that freight on the roads moved, and still moves, very short distances compared with other forms of transport, and this is indeed the case. The average length of haul on the roads in 1990 was 21 km, as

159

against 963 km on the railways, to which the roads were for the most part merely feeders. The lack of an adequate national network of hard-surfaced all-weather roads seriously limited rapid development of long-distance freight carriage. In 1990, there were 2 175 500 km of roads, of which 1 375 800 had any kind of hard surface and, of those, only about half had all-weather surfaces (concrete, asphalt, tarmacadam). Even in towns, of the 340 500 km of streets, only 220 900 were hard-surfaced. In other words, road freight haulage was largely confined to the towns, their immediate vicinity and short trips between neighbouring towns. Within towns, pressures of commercial road traffic had already become considerable by the end of the 1980s.

Since the commencement of the Five Year Plans, visitors to the Soviet Union have commented on the dominance of city traffic by trucks; during the 1980s the proportion of cars on the streets gradually increased, but the absolute number of trucks rose markedly. Over the 1960s and 1970s, the annual production of trucks more than doubled and it continued growing to a peak figure of 866 000 in 1987. Thereafter, to 1990, there was a fall-off in production to 774 000. Sagars (1991b: 436), in reporting this drop, attributes it to shortages of inputs. It may also be that the growing emphasis during *perestroyka* on economic realism was causing enterprises and trusts to get more mileage out of their existing fleets and to reduce purchases of new vehicles.

Certainly, trucks have remained a very substantial proportion of the 700 000 motor vehicles that use Moscow's roads daily (Glushkova 1986: 87). Significantly, the quantity of freight being shifted by container – an indicator that one would expect to have grown considerably in the *perestroyka* drive for improved technological efficiency – increased on the roads from 66 million tonnes in 1970 to 122 400 000 tonnes in 1989. At that point it was more than double the container weight carried on the railways (*Narodnoye Khozyaystvo SSSR v 1989g.* 1990: 550), indicating that, where container movement was concerned, the roads were more than just feeders to the railway.

This rise in road haulage put steadily increasing pressure on the road networks of the towns, a pressure not eased by the failure to shift out environmentally noxious industries, which are often those generating largest volumes of freight, as in the case of Moscow's centrally located "Hammer and Sickle" steel works. The pressure was becoming all the greater with the rising use of heavy "juggernaut" trucks. At the end of the 1970s they were to all intents and purposes absent in the Soviet Union, except for international loads carried on East German and Bulgarian trucks. A decade later their number was steadily growing and surely made up for any fall in the number of new trucks coming on to the roads. The greater weight of trucks, which until recently were small by Western standards, caused more wear and tear on the roads, which in any case suffer considerable annual damage from frost.

Growth in passenger transport

Considerably faster than the expansion of freight carriage was the growth of passenger movement by public road transport. The number of bus passengers rose from 600 million in 1940 to over 50000 million in 1990 (Table 7.1). Of this latter figure about three-quarters (37000 million) consisted of intra-urban bus travellers, for whom the average journey was only 5.8 km. A further 11 300 million were carried on suburban bus routes. Although the fastest increase has been in the number of buses and the number and length of routes, at the same time the length of line, the number of vehicles and number of passengers carried on trolley bus systems were all increasing very rapidly (Table 7.2). Between 1960 and 1986, the number of trolley buses in service increased by five times. This rapid expansion of trolley bus services reflected their ecological advantage in the urban environment and thus their popularity. In the same way, trams, which like trolley buses are environmentally less harmful than motor buses, have reversed their earlier decline and are now once again increasing in length of route and usage. Because of the inflexibility and hindrance to other traffic of both these transport modes, there is increasing effort being made to put them into separated fast tracks, particularly trams. Although in only a small number of instances is this feasible in the foreseeable future, Volgograd, Tallin, Staryy Oskol and Cherepovets, among others, have all recognized the expediency of such express trams (Agas'yants & Gorbanev 1985: 16).

The largest cities of the Soviet Union were generally well provided with public

Table 7.1 Passenger transport by bus, 1940–90 (thousand millions).

Year	Passengers	Turnover (passenger/km)
1940	0.6	3.4
1960	11.3	61.1
1970	27.3	202.0
1980	42.2	390.0
1990	50.3	480.7

Source: Narodnoye Khozyaystvo . . . (1987, 1990, 1991).

Table 7.2 Passenger transport by tram and trolley bus, 1940–90.

	1940	1970	1990
Tram			
Kilometres of track	4475	8261	9975
Number of cars	11400	22100	22101
Passengers (million)	7283	7962	8517
Trolley bus			
Kilometres of track	329	8151	17874
Number of cars	800	15800	28505
Passengers (million)	377	2294	11448

Source: Narodnoye Khozyaystvo . . . (1987, 1990, 1991).

161

transport. They had a variety of modes, with fixed-route taxis as well as buses, trolley buses and trams. Very large cities had suburban electric trains and those with over a million inhabitants could qualify for the most efficient mode of all, the metro underground system. By the end of the Soviet period, 12 cities had operating metros – in order of commissioning, Moscow, St Petersburg (Leningrad), Kiev, Tbilisi, Baku, Khar'kov, Tashkent, Yerevan, Minsk, Nizhniy Novgorod (Gor'kiy), Novosibirsk and Yekaterinburg (Sverdlovsk). Where they were built, they obviously did much to reduce pressure on surface forms of public transport, but only Moscow (with 138 stations and 222.3km of line in 1989) had a well developed system. Leningrad, the next largest, had only 48 stations on three routes; the remainder had mostly one or two lines only; the last five commissioned have so far under ten stations each. However, not every city saw an underground transport system as the most desirable way of coping with increased volumes of passenger movement; in Riga, opposition to the building of a metro on conservation grounds brought about at least a postponement of construction. Now, with independence, it may very well never be built.

As the population size of a town decreased, so too did the adequacy of public transport provision. Normally only the very large cities had more than one mode of transport, that is to say, the bus; places with multi-modal public transport constituted only about two per cent of all urban settlements (Litovka 1976: 59). Smaller places had no internal public transport. In 1989, 2534 towns and settlements of town type, out of a total of over 6000, had public intra-urban bus services. Those with such services included all towns and settlements of town type with over 20000 population. It was considered essential that towns of such size should have an internal transport system, but it was not thought necessary for places with under 20000 people and with a compact layout less than 1.5–2km across (Markov & Ryazanov 1975: 144); it is not likely therefore that there will be much further provision of services to towns lacking them. The figure for towns with internal bus services would almost certainly include all places with alternative forms of public transport.

Much more significant for future increase in urban public transport is the heavy pressure of ridership on existing networks and fleets in towns of every size, including the largest. In Minsk in 1981, some 800 buses carried 369300000 passengers, that is 1265 per bus per day, assuming even passenger usage every day of the year and making no allowance for the certainly significant number of buses out of commission at any moment. The city's 120 suburban bus lines were served by only 202 buses (*Minsk . . . 1983*: 70–71). In consequence, dissatisfaction with public transport has grown. In a survey of Leningrad in 1978, complaints about public transport came in third place after housing and ecology; a repeated survey in 1984 found transport at the head of the list of twelve problem issues (Mogilevskiy 1987: 42). Even in Moscow, the best provided city in the country, the growth in the fleets of buses and trolley buses did not keep pace with the growth of new housing in outer districts. This meant that the frequency of service declined, as vehicles had to be taken off existing routes and transferred to new ones in recently developed districts. It was said that services "do not satisfy current demands" and that they needed reconstruction and renewal (Glushkova 1986: 87). The lack of spare capacity was never more obvious than in the annual school summer holidays, when convoys of city buses (headed by a police car and with an ambulance bringing up the rear) transported children out to Young Pioneer camps, and every bus stop had a notice warning passengers of consequential extended intervals between buses.

The rise in living standards sought by *perestroyka* included considerable improvements in forms of surface passenger transport. Many of the hindrances to improvement, noted by Crouch at the end of the 1970s, continued in force. For instance, the operation of metros, suburban electric services, taxis, buses, trams and trolley buses was by various different ministries, or departments of ministries, or by local large industrial enterprises (Crouch 1979: 233). Yet again, service and maintenance facilities are grossly inadequate; spare parts and trained personnel are equally in short supply (ibid.: 245). But whatever the problems, there can be no doubt that the number and intensity of services, and the regional distribution of public transport, will surely increase. Even by the end of the USSR, the growth in road haulage and public transport was putting greater pressure on urban streets and pressure on the planners to make provision for the higher levels of traffic control, road design and maintenance, as well as support requirements – loading and container yards, bus stations, garages and repair workshops.

The increase in private car numbers

In the long run, however, the most significant development will undoubtedly be the growth in the number of private cars. This process is one that, until the very last period of the Soviet era, received little attention from the planners, although as early as 1975 the Soviet Sociological Association set up a special section for "The social problems of automobilization" (Yefimov & Mikerin 1976: 128). There was in general an unwillingness to face the inevitability of an urban environment dominated by the private car. Khrushchev declared bluntly that this possibility would not be permitted to arise; instead, he envisioned every town having its park of hire cars, as a substitute for private ownership. Even after Khrushchev's departure, this concept lingered on. It was iterated as late as 1975 at a round table discussion, where it was stated that improved public transport would obviate the demand for the use of private cars in towns; if necessary, such use would be forbidden, and cars would be used only for holidays and recreation (ibid.: 129–30).

By the 1980s such views were becoming a thing of the past and the process referred to in Soviet writings as "automobilization", that is the growth of private car ownership, was not only increasingly widely accepted as a reality, but was being described as "a progressive phenomenon" (Lyubitseva 1985: 59). It was not to be rejected, but included in complex development planning for all forms of transport (Listengurt 1976: 69).

Until very recently there was little for the planners to accept. As late as the early 1970s, only 5–10 per cent of all urban passengers were carried by motorcycle and car, including taxis, and a book then published could say that "in practice, for the time being in our cities such transport has no actual significance" (Sigayev 1972: 45). In Tallin, well in advance of most Soviet cities, 3.9 per cent of passenger traffic was by private car, 2.7 per cent by private motorcycle and 2.7 per cent by "company" car on a year round basis; in summer, the shares rose somewhat to 6.8 per cent for cars, 5.3 per cent for motorcycles and 3.9 per cent for official cars. In Novosibirsk the equivalent figures were 2.1 per cent for motorcycles and a mere 0.8 per cent for private cars (ibid.: 46–7). In the USSR as a whole only 2 per cent of families owned cars in 1970; even in Estonia, the best provided republic, only 5 per cent had their own car.

Nationally, the picture of increase in private car ownership reflects that outlined for the Ukraine by Lyubitseva (1985: 60) – a slow rise, beginning in the late 1950s, and giving way to more rapid growth after 1970. In the USSR as a whole, the number of cars increased by over six times between 1970 and 1980, since when it has roughly doubled. By the end of the 1980s, movement by car in the USSR was increasing by 5–8 per cent annually (Tulayev 1989: 6). This growth in numbers was largely the result of the opening of the huge car plant on the Volga at Tol'yatti, built by Fiat for the Soviet government. Largely due to this factory, making some 650000 cars a year during the 1980s and rising to 730000 by 1988, the USSR as a whole was manufacturing over 1300000 cars annually, together with over 1100000 motorcycles and mopeds. The agreement signed with Fiat in late 1989 to build a plant at Yelabuga to make some 300000 Fiat cars a year (rising eventually to 600000), if and when carried out, will further increase the number of cars coming on to the nation's roads as well as providing further exports.

Export of cars has been about 300000 a year (in 1986, 306000), leaving an annual increment of approximately one million cars on the roads of the Soviet Union. One must of course subtract from this figure the unknown number of cars taken off the road, but one can feel certain that this was very small; the normally quite brief useful life of cars in the West and the expectation of their replacement in two to five years are not yet the norms in the Soviet Union. A feature of the present-day post-Soviet city is the increasing number of old cars in poor condition; not infrequently one comes across cars 18–20 years old. As a result, the absolute number of cars on the road rose from just under 1400000 in 1970 to over 15 million in 1988 (Sagars 1991a: 62) and to 17294327 by 1 January 1991 (*Za Rulem* 1991 no. 12: 7). Of this last figure, 11682777 cars were urban based; Moscow alone had 629028 cars.

The republican totals reflect considerable regional variation in levels of private car ownership, coinciding with the broader picture of the highest levels of the quality of life in the Baltic and Slav Republics and lowest levels in the Islamic Republics of Central Asia and Azerbaydzhan. The Baltic States could boast over 90 cars per 1000 population with up to 126 per 1000 in Estonia. Of other republics only Georgia (81) and Armenia (67) surpassed 60 per 1000, but the third Transcaucasian republic, Azerbaydzhan, lay at the very bottom of the table with only 34, well below even the Central Asian republics with 40-odd cars per 1000 (Table 7.3).

Table 7.3 Private cars per thousand population.

Republic	1970	1980	1988
USSR	6	30	53
Russia	6	29	52
Ukraine	6	31	57
Belarus	4	25	49
Estonia	20	76	126
Latvia	13	60	91
Lithuania	11	47	110
Moldova	3	21	42
Georgia	11	47	81
Armenia	9	37	67
Azerbaydzhan	5	22	34
Kazakhstan	5	27	44
Uzbekistan	3	22	40
Kyrgyzstan	5	23	41
Turkmenistan	3	28	49
Tadzhikistan	4	19	41

Source: Transport i Syvaz' (1990: 89).

Figures for ownership have not been consistently available for units less than Union Republic, other than the RSFSR, where figures were published by major economic region up to 1989 (Table 7.4; Sagars 1991a: 64). These made it clear that there was considerable variation within republics. The increment in car numbers was primarily an urban phenomenon, as one would expect in a country where some two-thirds of the population were urban. In the Ukraine in 1985, 70 per cent of private cars and 66.1 per cent of the population were in towns. Regional levels

Table 7.4 Cars per thousand population in the RSFSR.

Region	1970	1980	1987
RSFSR	5.5	29.9	55.1
North	2.7	22.5	43.1
Northwest	7.7	27.6	55.1
Centre	7.3	28.7	50.6
Volga–Vyatka	3.0	21.0	37.6
Central Chernozem	3.7	26.3	55.3
Volga	4.9	29.2	55.4
North Caucasus	7.1	39.1	69.2
Urals	5.5	30.8	54.6
West Siberia	4.8	32.6	60.7
East Siberia	4.5	35.4	66.0
Far East	4.2	27.0	53.6

Source: Sagars (1991: 64)

of ownership varied with the degree of urbanization. Within the RSFSR, ownership was highest in West and East Siberia, where the proportion of urban inhabitants was high (Table 7.4), although, as Sagars (1991a: 64) points out, this regional variation related also to level of income and to special factors such as the use of car availability as a lure for migrants to Siberia. Urban occupations, Sagars reminds us, tended to be more highly paid than rural ones; in 1985 Zaporozh'ye Oblast, with 74.9 per cent of its inhabitants in urban areas, had 47 cars per 1000 people, while Rovno Oblast, only 44 per cent urbanized, had 17 per 1000. Table 7.4 indicates that the highest rate of car ownership in the Russian Republic is in the North Caucasus region; one cannot but wonder if there is a correlation to be found here with the association of car crime (thefts and a black market in cars and spares) in Moscow with the so-called "Chechen mafia".

There is also a marked difference in l3evel of car ownership between towns. Data for individual towns are rarely available; Table 7.5 has been compiled from various sources and for various dates, but it gives some indication of the disparities. For example, medium-size and smaller places have considerably lower ownership levels, as low as 16 per 1000 in the Ukraine (Lyubitseva 1985: 60–61). Onega in 1980 had "over 300" cars; at that time there were 12 520 employed persons, although its population at that date is not known, as the town was under the 50 000 threshold and therefore its population was not published. By January 1991 its population was 26 400 and it is not unreasonable therefore to assume a population in the vicinity of 25 000 or 12 cars per 1000 (Kalinin 1980: 102).

Table 7.5   Cars per thousand population for selected towns.

Town	Date	No. of cars
Moscow	1960	9
	1980	38
	mid-1980s	44
	1986	53
	1989	60
Kiev	mid-1980s	28–32
Leningrad	mid-1980s	28–32
Donetsk	1983	28
Minsk	1981	43.5
Alma Ata	1982	59.9*
Dubna	1981–2	50
Transcaucasian towns	mid-1980s	50
Baltic republic towns	mid-1980s	60–70

* Including motor-cycles.
Sources: various.

According to Glushkova the number of private cars in Moscow has risen from 9 per 1000 population in 1960 to 14 in 1970, 38 in 1980 and 44 per 1000 in the mid-1980s (Glushkova 1986: 87). On 1 January 1986 there were in Moscow 465 000 private cars (and 48 000 motorcycles) registered by GAI (the traffic police), that is 53 per 1000, or one to every 18.7 people (*Gorodskoye . . .* 1986 no.

11: 23). As one would expect, the Moscow figure is higher than the national average. St Petersburg and Kiev had only 28–32 per 1000 in the mid-1980s; Donetsk, with 29500 cars in 1983 (together with 24700 motorcycles and mopeds), had 28 per 1000 (Belenko 1983: 18).

Nevertheless, Moscow had by no means the highest ratio of cars to population in the country; Minsk, with 43.5 cars per 1000 in 1981 (*Minsk . . .* 1983: 73), had then a slight lead over Moscow, while Transcaucasian and Baltic Republic towns, with 50 and 60–70 per 1000 respectively in the mid-1980s, have always led the way in this respect (Glushkova 1986, loc. cit.). A small town with a high proportion of professional people, such as the science town of Dubna, may well have a higher level of ownership. It was estimated that, in Moscow alone, the number of cars was increasing in the 1980s by 30000–40000 a year and there were expected to be some 650000–700000 cars in the city by 1990 (*Gorodskoye . . .* 1986 no. 11: 23). At a national level it is estimated that, by the year 2000, car ownership will be running at 240–50 per 1000 population (Artem'yev 1979b: 21), a marked rise from the 1970 level of only 6 per 1000. The change in circumstances since that estimate was made makes it highly problematical today; the actual figure at the end of the century could be much higher or, if difficulties continue, even lower.

Cars in the Soviet Union were, as they still are, expensive items representing for most workers several years' gross income, but the lack of goods meant that it was easy for many to accumulate savings; the slow growth in car numbers had less to do with cost than with supply. Purchasers had to endure long waits of up to two years for a new car. As more cars became available, there was no shortage of willing buyers. Indeed, at the opening of the 1990s a person lucky enough to head the waiting list at his place of work and to buy a Zhiguli (Lada) car for 9000 roubles could instantly resell it for three times that amount and have no difficulty in finding purchasers. At the same time, growing car numbers will inevitably strengthen the second-hand market, with consequent widening of the car-owning sector of the population to those at present unable to afford a new one.

The needs of the private car

Undoubtedly, the first pressure to be put on the planners by the increase in numbers of cars, together with increasing lorry traffic and stepped-up public transport, will be to improve the present low standards of road provision. This includes the network density between towns, the network within towns, the capacity of existing roads and the quality of surfacing, and resistance to weight of traffic and climatic conditions. Already the effect of increased traffic is being felt. In 1954 some 21359 cars a day were using Tver' (then Gor'kiy) Street, one of the busiest in Moscow; even by 1968 that figure had risen to 45880 a day. Tver' Street is broad, widened in the years of the early Five Year Plans before the Second World War. On Bogdan Khmel'nitskiy Street, still the narrow two-lane road it was before the

Revolution, daily car traffic rose from 7690 in both directions in 1954 to 11842 in one direction in 1968 (Sigayev 1972: 35). Glushkova considered that 30 per cent of Moscow's main roads were at maximum capacity by the mid-1980s and that 80 per cent of main intersections were suffering from severe traffic pressure (Glushkova 1986: 87). In Yerevan, where street construction has fallen behind the growth in numbers of vehicles, many roads and junctions have reached maximum traffic load (Valesyan 1990: 575). Of the expressways devised for Moscow in the 1971 Genplan, not one was built. The greater realism nowadays towards cost allows one to rule out with confidence the 1974 proposal of the then chief architect of Moscow for a network of underground expressways or "automotive traffic tunnels" (Posokhin 1974: 122). Such a concept does, however, illustrate the lack of realistic understanding of the problems of the car in the modern city on the part of many Soviet planners.

In the largest cities such as Moscow and St Petersburg it is possible even now to find roads without a proper hard surface, although this is rare. As one moves down the size hierarchy of towns, such unmade roads become more and more common. Less than 20 years ago, even such giant cities as Nizhniy Novgorod (Gor'kiy), Samara (Kuybyshev) and Novosibirsk had no more than 40 per cent of their roads hard-surfaced (Bater 1977: 197). Moreover, even hard-surface roads have often not been constructed to cope with the increasing weight both of traffic and of individual vehicles.

Bad road conditions caused the accident rate to rise with the growth in traffic. In 1986 39000 people were killed in the USSR and almost 260000 injured in some 241000 accidents. One accident in seven was attributed to poor road conditions. This may well help to explain the fact that the accident rate is worse in rural areas than in towns (CDSP 1987 39 no. 25: 23). One might hazard a guess that this also reflects less experienced drivers and lower driving standards in the countryside. In fact, 1986 was a relatively good year for traffic accidents; after a decline during the first half of the 1980s, the USSR death rate from road accidents rose steeply from 39012 to 58651 in 1989 and 63362 in 1990 (Table 7.6). In the case of 31770 (50%) of these fatalities in 1990, the blame was attributed the drivers of private

Table 7.6 Fatalities in road accidents.

| Year | Total | Caused by | |
		Private driver	Other driver
1980	48935	17460	21386
1985	41492	16930	16430
1986	39012	18349	14057
1987	39822	19582	13108
1988	47197	24563	14366
1989	58651	30563	17169
1990	63362	31770	17880

Source: Norodnoye Khozyaystvo SSSR v 1989g. (1989: 586), *Norodnoye Khozyaystvo SSSR v 1990g.* (1991: 616).

vehicles; in 28 per cent of cases, blame was laid on drivers of public and "company" vehicles, with the remainder (22%) presumably attributable to pedestrians (*Narodnoye Khozyaystvo SSSR v 1990g.* 1991: 616).

In Belorussia the number of motor accidents rose from 7600 in 1980 to 8500 in 1984; the highest rates (0.91 to 1.2 incidents per km of road) were recorded on the Republic's most modern highway, the Minsk Ring Road (Belov 1989: 103), which undoubtedly reflected the heavy traffic concentration on this road.

Hardly less urgent was and is the growing need for more parking and garaging space. This was made all the more pressing by the combination of two factors. First, Soviet private cars were stationary for a high proportion of the time. In 1986 the average daily run of a Moscow taxi was 285 km and of a service car 98 km; for a private car it was only 18 km. That is to say that private cars were on the move for only 1–1½ hours a day, or 300–400 hours a year. For the rest of the time, they were parked (*Gorodskoye* . . . 1989 no. 11: 17). At the same time the appalling shortage of spare parts means that any car left unattended is liable to be stripped of parts. For many years it has been standard practice for Soviet drivers to remove the windscreen wipers on leaving the car in a public place; nowadays, thieves are just as likely to remove the entire windscreen! The unfortunate owner then must face either an endless wait for a spare part at an ill afforded 100 roubles (in 1989 prices) or a near-impossible bill of 1000 roubles for a black market spare.

Soviet town planners were confident that all the problems of garaging and parking cars could be met by building underground carparks, smaller parks on a single level for 25, 50, 75 or 100 cars and larger two- or three-level parks for 200–300 cars (Borisov et al. 1981: 128). In Moscow this would allow city growth to be contained within the ring motorway (Segedinov & Tomsen 1964: 43–4), an intention already overtaken by events. Realization of the colossal cost of providing adequate underground garages in both city centres and residential districts, and the strain on an already heavily engaged construction industry, engendered a greater sense of reality during the 1980s, but it is still widely felt that simple answers to much of the parking problem will be found below ground.

Moscow now has its first two-storey park for 800 cars on Miklukho–Maklay Street (in, of course, the favoured southwest sector), but this is not underground and it occupies a not inconsiderable surface area. Construction of an eight-storey carpark for 2080 vehicles was started near to VDNKh, the huge permanent Exhibition of Achievements of the National Economy, but it was reported in late 1989 to be taking longer and costing more than was expected. At the same time a 400-car park planned for Teplyy Stan in the southwest was described as "problematic" (*Gorodskoye.* . . 1989 no. 11: 17).

Even now, there appears to be less than full comprehension of the likely future scale of the problem. For the time being, a partial solution has been found in open-air fenced compounds, often with guard huts, located beside the microregions (Fig. 7.1). It is an extensive rather than intensive use of space and does nothing to protect vehicles from the severities of the Soviet climate. Wealthier members of society join together to erect covered and guarded co-operative garages. Tbilisi in

Figure 7.1   A fenced compound for private cars, near Belyayevo, Moscow.

1980 had 22 pay parks (French 1987: 316). Minsk in 1981, then a city approaching 1.5 million population, had about 58000 private cars, to accommodate which there were only 21 carparks with 5948 places, together with garage spaces for 620; the first carpark was not opened there until 1967 (*Minsk . . . 1983*: 73). Thus, even a major city and republican capital had storage spaces for less than one car in nine. The situation was closely similar in Alma Ata (Almaty), where in 1982 there were 6800 permanent parking sites for over 60000 cars and motor-cycles (Kozybayev et al. 1983). In St Petersburg (Leningrad) in 1975 almost a quarter of the private cars were parked on roadways (Litovka 1976: 63). The Baltic capitals of Riga and Tallin, the frequent front-runners, in the early 1970s had garage parking for 83.2 and 72.5 per cent of all cars, figures presumably including both private and official vehicles (Sigayev 1972: 48); with the growth in car numbers since then it would not be surprising if these high percentages have fallen.

The compounds of lock-up garages, which began to appear in the late 1980s, were located on the outskirts of towns, where space could be found and allocated. This was, of course, highly inconvenient to the owners, who had to use public transport for access to their cars. It reinforced the widespread habit of using cars, not daily for an assortment of purposes, but only at weekends and on holidays for recreation.

As one might expect, Moscow was rather better provided with garaging than most places, although still far from adequately. In 1985 there were storage places for 221000 private cars, 47.5 per cent of the total number; of these, 64000 were in co-operative garages; 48000 in collective and individual garages and 109000 consisted of open standings – 62000 in 265 large parks and 47000 in over 800 small parks (*Gorodskoye* ... 1986 no. 11: 23). All the remainder, over half the total, had to be parked in the courtyards of apartment complexes, or on roadways, with consequent disruption of traffic flows and of mechanized street cleaning and the hampering of emergency services (Glushkova 1986: 88). Even this less than satisfactory provision marks a great advance over the situation only eight years earlier in 1977 when Moscow had 59 carparks for the use of which charges were made; 50 of these were long-stay parks.

The inadequacy of provision inevitably resulted in resort to the second, or black, economy. Of Moscow's 48000 collective and individual garage spaces in 1985, more than half, 26000, were put up illegally; many self-organized garage or parking groups were failing to pay rent; some were illegally connected up to the public electricity supply. Moreover, there seems little prospect of any improvement in the situation in the foreseeable future – indeed it has been getting worse. The decision was taken in 1985 to provide additional garages and parking spaces during the Twelfth Five Year Plan, 1986–90, for 49500 cars, comprising 11400 in co-operatives, 23080 in garages and 15020 in open standings; that is to say, the plan set out to cater for only about a quarter of the expected *increment* of cars in the plan period; to make matters more difficult, every year some 3000–5000 storage places are lost through various redevelopments (*Gorodskoye* ... 1986 no. 11: 23).

Some authorities are pessimistic about the problem. As early as 1979 it was being suggested that, in all towns with over 10000 inhabitants, there was no possibility under existing planning to set aside sufficient parking spaces to meet forecast levels of car ownership (Artem'yev 1979b: 25). Agas'yants & Gorbanev (1985: 17) were suggesting in 1985 that every living region should have short-term parking for 25 per cent of the total number of cars. Solutions are now being seen in the making of carparks along the railway lines into Moscow, underneath electricity pylon lines and all along the Moscow Orbital Motorway, a length of some 100km. The service road for these last parks would act as a duplication of the Orbital Motorway. Other possible sites for both open-air standings and garages include gullies, other uneven ground, and alongside factories. Greater use of collapsible prefabricated garages is being urged. It has been further suggested that GAI should not register a car until parking space has been allocated (*Gorodskoye* ... 1986, no. 10: 8; ibid. no. 11: 24).

In addition to a huge increase in available storage space, cars will require an equally massive improvement in the provision of petrol stations and service and repair workshops. Every foreigner who has taken his car to the USSR has been only too sharply aware of the extremely sparse network of petrol stations, although the 1980s saw a rapid increase in number from an extremely low base. Moreover, perhaps no more than half the stations may be for public use, the rest being for official cars only. Minsk in 1982 had twelve petrol stations (*Minsk* ... 1983: 71); by 1985, when the city had reached over 1.5 million people, the figure was only 13, of which 7 were public. Moscow's 8.5 million inhabitants in the same year were proportionately better served, with a total of over 200 stations, both public and service (French 1987: 315); although this represented a quadrupling in number over the previous two decades, it was still far from adequate, especially in view of the regularity with which any given station ran out of petrol of one or all grades. According to a map published in 1985, Tallin, a capital in the more advanced consumer economies of the Baltic republics, had ten petrol stations to serve its 470 000 inhabitants, a level of provision comparable to that of Moscow.

Provision of repair centres was even less adequate, and the Soviet private car owner needed to be, and usually was, competent at do-it-yourself maintenance, servicing and repair. In 1983, Tver (sometime Kalinin), a town approaching half a million population, had eight repair stations for all vehicles, including one at the fibreglass factory and four in settlements and villages on the outskirts (Zakharov 1983: 198). Tallin, with a very comparable population in 1985, had five repair stations. Attempts have been made to work out a methodology for forecasting future demand for car repairs (Mel'nikov et al. 1979). Meanwhile, the shortage of spare parts has inevitably meant a thriving black market. In Moscow it was based on the Orbital Motorway and it continued to operate despite frequent police raids (CDSP 1987 39 no. 31: 26). Car servicing and repair did not prove to be one of the areas taken up with much enthusiasm in the development of private co-operative enterprises by individuals and families, which was permitted under *perestroyka*. The principal problem to date has been the near impossibility for such co-operatives to obtain supplies, other than on the black economy. Certainly, by 1990 there were only five co-operatives working on car servicing in Moscow and they were extremely narrowly specialized in the operations they undertook (*Vsya Moskva 1990–1991*: 357).

The use of the car for commuting, shopping and leisure

The rise in the number of cars is inevitably going to affect, however gradually, the patterns of daily activity by the urban population and, in the first place, the journey to work. In the 1990s, only a very small proportion of car owners use their vehicles for daily travel to work. It is usual to see cars sitting in the open carparks or courtyards, sheeted in plastic covers throughout the working week, or even more commonly throughout the winter season of the year, awaiting pleasure use at weekends or in summer. But already in the 1980s there were the beginnings of change in this occasional or seasonal use of cars. One reason was that the Zhiguli (Lada) make of car, unlike most of its fore-runners, was capable of being reasonably easily started after a winter night parked out in the open.

Another reason for the limited car commuting has been that the majority of car owners, even in the later Soviet stages, were the wealthier, more influential members of society, who tended to concentrate in central areas of the city and therefore to live nearer to their employment. Many had a chauffeur-driven car provided by their place of work. Moreover, the more influential citizens were concentrated in the largest cities, where on the one hand inner-city parking problems were often greatest, but on the other hand, and more importantly, the provision of public transport was at its best.

In these large cities it may be expected that, in the foreseeable future, the efficiency of public transport will continue to discourage the use of the private car. Set against this, it is the largest cities which have grown the fastest and the mush-rooming of so many new microregions has often outstripped the extension of ade-quate services, or caused the siphoning-off of public service vehicles from existing routes. Thus, lengthening times of journeys to work have been a consistent feature of the Soviet city since the late 1950s and this inevitably makes the private alter-native more attractive. A survey taken in 1979 showed private cars as having a clear time advantage over public transport in a number of major cities (Table 7.7).

Table 7.7 Average door-to-door journey to work (minutes).

City	Public transport	Private car
Moscow	44.0	30.3
Leningrad (St Petersburg)	34.5	29.5
Kiev	33.0	16.5
Kuybyshev (Samara)	26.3	16.6
Riga	30.5	17.4
Tallinn	28.3	15.4
Gor'kiy (Nizhniy Novgorod)	35.4	24.1

Source: Chuverin (1979: 33).

In fact these figures may underestimate the time taken on public transport. A more recent source for Moscow gives the average journey to work in 1970 as 52 minutes; by 1986 it had risen to 60 minutes, a duration 50 per cent more than the norm prescribed in the General Plan. This longer time reflects in part an increase in the average distance travelled to work, from 8.3 km in 1970 to 11.52 km in 1986, but in part also the decline in efficiency and frequency (*Gorodskoye* . . . 1986 no. 7: 19). Counterbalancing this, of course, is the increase in journey time by private car as congestion on the roads becomes more common. Either way, this trend, which the planners have so far vainly combated, must inevitably increase the pres-sure on car owners to use them on a daily basis. Chuverin's 1979 enquiry among Muscovite car owners found that 49 per cent gave time as the reason for preferring to use their car to get to work, as against 37 per cent citing convenience and only 6 per cent indicating poor access to public transport. As car ownership spreads in smaller towns, with their lower levels of transport services, again there is likely to be greater car commuting.

At the same time, as was indicated in Chapter 4, employment continues to rise in inner urban areas, in spite of the best efforts of the planners to prevent this. Under the 1971 Genplan for Moscow, the share of employment in the inner area (i.e. within the ring railway) was to be greatly reduced, so cutting the volume of commuting to the centre. In practice, since the plan began, the excess of work-places over working population in the centre has increased by more than twice (Fedorov 1986: 8) and still industry is coming in.

Even greater use of the car to get to work may well be stimulated by the increase in long-distance commuting. This has been encouraged particularly in the largest cities by the restrictions on in-migration and the resultant labour shortages. There has been rapid population growth in the *prigorody*, the suburban zone, beyond the official limits of such closed cities. It has been estimated that as many as one-third of all suburban trips are by non-public transport; such is already the case in Belorussia (Filina 1987: 730). In cases such as Moscow, where the city is surrounded by a designated forest-park amenity zone of controlled development, many commuters have to live still farther out beyond the green belt.

Until now, the weight of commuting from these outer areas has been carried by the *elektrichka,* the electric suburban train, but at such distances out, the density of public services is obviously much lower and, unless a person lives very close to an *elektrichka* stop, the time advantage of public transport is significantly lessened. People who failed to get permission to reside in restricted cities and therefore had to commute from small suburban settlements to central workplaces, were dominated by the low-qualified groups, who could not usually obtain cars. In Moscow 73 per cent of those in such situations were low-qualified, 16.5 per cent were office workers, 7 per cent engineering and technical workers and 3 per cent students (Pravotorova 1986: 22). As car ownership spreads downwards through society, commuting by these groups will inevitably increase.

As yet the use of the car for shopping journeys has been minimal, whether by urban dwellers moving about town or by rural dwellers coming into town. In any case the chronic shortages at the opening of the 1990s caused general discrimination against out-of-town shoppers. Nevertheless, among the growing group of professional and middle-class car owners, the practice is slowly beginning of using the car to accelerate the hunt for scarce commodities. The considerable physical effort and time loss involved in shopping certainly encourage the use of cars where possible. Moreover, even the largest towns have often only one emporium for a particular speciality and it may well be located in an outer suburb of microregions. Again, the new supermarkets and department stores, as they are built, are most usually in between the newer microregions. There is thus some use of the car to travel outwards to these retail outlets, rather than inwards to the traditional city centre.

This use of the car did not increase very rapidly in the USSR, but in the post-USSR the trend to this aspect of "automobilization" is as inevitable as it has been in the developed Western countries. So far, shopping precincts with planned incorporation of parking facilities simply do not exist, but already one can find quite sizeable shops well outside city limits, intended to serve surrounding rural districts. For example, such a store lies in a small village half way between Samarkand and Pendzhikent on the Uzbek/Tadzhik border, a village too small to sustain a department store and accessible only by the rather infrequent bus service between the two towns. Vehicles from the farms in the area and even coming out from the towns are the principal forms of transport for the store's customers.

The last two decades of the Soviet period saw a gradual increase in the amount of leisure time enjoyed by the average citizen and, for those who possessed cars, leisure represented the principal form of use. Although, as the Kaluga survey discovered, cultural visits tended to be exclusively to city centres, where theatres, most important museums, principal cinemas and best restaurants were located (Bakshteyn et al. 1986: 91), it remained the case, as with commuting, that public transport was generally used for this type of leisure excursion in the largest cities, where such attractions were most numerous. Rather, the car served to facilitate weekend and holiday recreation. In various northern Soviet cities, where long and severe winter conditions make outdoor parking and operation of cars difficult, it has been quite common for car owners to keep their vehicles in central or southern regions of the country and to use them only for vacations.

Each year the proportion of the population taking holidays away from home has steadily risen. A survey of over 2000 people in the small Lithuanian town of Shaulyay revealed that only 22 per cent stayed at home over their annual holidays; 23 per cent went to the countryside, including those visiting relatives, 16.4 per cent travelled as tourists, 14.2 per cent travelled "wild" (i.e. not in an officially organized group) in resort areas, 12.1 per cent went to a sanatorium or house of rest, and 8.8 per cent stayed on their dacha (Vosilyute 1984: 143–4). It can safely be assumed that, among car owners, there is a higher share of those travelling away from home, especially "wild". Shaulyay might be said to be typical only of the Baltic Republics, but it is perhaps an indication of the direction in which the other republics are, or will be, moving. The USSR had established its first motels; two stand on Moscow's Orbital Motorway, the Mozhayskiy Motel at the junction with the Mozhayskoye Chaussee on the west and the Solnechnyy Motel on the south, at the junction with the Varshavskoye Chaussee.

Leisure use of the car is still, however, largely a development for the future. As recently as 1982, an examination of people's time budgets at work and away from work did not consider it necessary to make any reference to time spent making use of the car, whether for pleasure, shopping or journey to work (Artemov et al. 1982). But already at that time there were straws in the wind. It was reported that cars were swamping the inadequate parking facilities at Arkhangel'skoye, the eighteenth-century mansion (now a museum) and its park to the northwest of Moscow (*Gorodskoye* . . . 1983 no. 10: 28).

The fourth stage in the development of the Soviet city, the idea of which was advanced in an earlier chapter, has been truncated before developing very far by the end of the Soviet system as such. If the trends which it began to display are now continued, as one might expect once present difficulties are overcome, then they will fairly certainly be characterized by rising living standards, even if the rise is slow in coming and whatever the political future of the area may be. If the increased capital investment (including foreign involvement) and effort in meeting consumer demands required by the post-*perestroyka*, post-Soviet era really do come about, then the rise might eventually be quite rapid. Either way, the imperatives of the car, which are mostly technical imperatives and occur regardless of political system, will be as dominant as those of industrialization and housing in earlier stages. In the same way, they will leave plans and their compilers lagging helplessly behind.

With the inevitability of a flood-tide, the car is coming to form an ever greater element in the life of the ex-Soviet republics. Already, investigators are studying the psychological impacts of the car on its owner, as Abramyan & Pikichyan (1989) have done in the context of Yerevan; there, in a manner many Westerners will recognize, owners give their vehicles a personality and even a name (often a Western female name such as "Linda"!) and seek to obtain "prestige" registration numbers. Equally, the republics are having to face the social problems associated with the car. By 1986, traffic violations had topped 40 million; although many of these were trivial infringements of movement controls, which one would scarcely expect to be noticed in most Western cities, the figures included 1 500 000 convictions for drunken driving (Dienes 1988: 798).

There are, as we have seen, a number of shortcomings inherited from Soviet city life – the need for more and substantially improved housing, the need for more, better and more fairly distributed consumer goods, the need for better services of every kind. It is not impossible to foresee these deficiencies being made good, given the will to accord them high priority and given the prerequisite upturn in the economy. But, as Western countries have discovered over more than half a century, the problems presented by the car are not easily met, either by city planning or by free-market competition, and efforts to meet them more often than not create a host of undesirable side-effects. Nothing in Soviet town planning experience suggests that they discovered better, or more easily achieved, solutions.

CHAPTER 8

Incorporating the past in the present

As the previous chapters have stressed, by the end of its existence the Soviet Union was not only an urbanized country, it was by and large a country of young towns. In 1987 there were 2176 towns and 3992 settlements of town type; the latter, with very few exceptions, and 1290 of the former were founded or raised to urban status in the Soviet period, a significant number since the Second World War. In the 900 or so remaining towns, which date from the pre-revolutionary period, the vast majority of buildings have been put up since the Revolution, indeed since 1957. Yet these older towns include nearly all the largest and most important cities, and almost none of these are totally without trace of the past. Even places, which have been defined as urban since 1917, have often grown from pre-existing villages, or have enveloped villages as they spread and thus may contain surviving churches, monasteries, mansions or other old buildings.

Early ideas and efforts in conservation

With the development of the Soviet command economy and the coming of town plans intended to shape the urban geography of the country to a degree never previously experienced, it became necessary to consider what should be done about this inheritance from previous times. Much of the legacy clearly had no place in the new City of Socialist Man, or indeed in any modern city; its replacement has been merely a question of the availability of resources to do so. That old and inadequate housing should be replaced as soon as opportunity allowed was and is an obvious and general view; no-one argued over the need to modernize the weakly developed urban infrastructures. Even more urgent, especially in Stalin's eyes, was the need to replace small-scale antiquated industrial enterprises and workshops with large modern factories.

Changes of other inherited features were less obviously pressing but also were less easy to deal with, particularly street patterns of the past, which tend to be one of the most enduring traits of any town in any socio-economic system. Despite the opening up or widening of central squares such as Red Square and Manezh Square (sometime Square of the Fiftieth Anniversary of the October Revolution) and the

177

straightening and widening of streets such as Tver' (sometime Gor'kiy) Street, the street pattern of central Moscow still reflects clearly and closely the ring and radial pattern of pre-revolutionary, indeed largely medieval, times; in the oldest inner city areas of Kitay Gorod, parts of the Belyy Gorod and Zamoskvorech'ye, many of the alleys display their medieval provenance in their names as much as in their form. St Petersburg's street pattern no less clearly reflects the regularities of eighteenth-century town planning. The central squares and radiating main streets, laid out in the town plans which Catherine the Great required of all her towns, are frequently the principal features in the inner areas of many regional centres of European Russia.

A major legacy of the pre-Soviet period comprised the buildings of architectural merit and historical interest. It was a bequest of great richness and variety; towns were rare indeed that could offer no treasure in stone, brick or wood, no building associated with the events and figures of history. More than any other aspect of the relationship between the past and the plan, the question of what to do with this inheritance has evoked controversy and more than one change in attitude over the whole period since 1917.

In the debates of the early Soviet period on the nature of the forthcoming socialist city, few of the participants paid serious heed to the pre-existing fabric of the town. Most of that fabric had survived the Revolution and the Civil War. The latter was focused along the railway lines and had only rarely caused more than superficial damage, save in a few railway junction towns; very little damage was caused in the oldest and largest cities. But the theoreticians planning the city of the future usually assumed that the past had no relevance, since society in all its aspects was to be changed. For them, such symbols of outmoded concepts and social relations as churches and palaces should indeed be rejected. The City of Socialist Man would start afresh, based on new principles and constructed *ab initio*.

Kirillov (1976: 215), writing half a century later, has attempted to show that from the start there was the desire to harmonize the transmogrification of the old cities into Cities of Socialist Man, with conservation of all that was of aesthetic value. In reality, of all the dreamers of a new city for a new society, only a few exceptions paid attention to saving the historic heritage. Thus, Shchusev and Zholtovskiy, the traditionalists, incorporated many elements of existing Moscow and carefully saved buildings of historic and architectural merit in their plan for the Moscow's development; indeed, around these elements would be a controlled zone of height restriction (ibid.: 217). But such exceptions were rare.

If the dreamers of new societies in new settings of work and residence ignored the past, the men of action did not. Lenin, the realist, was more sharply aware of the role of heritage in societal consciousness. A decree of 12 April 1918 was published "On monuments of the Republic". A further decree the same year concerned "registration, taking account of and protection of memorials of art and antiquity in private, societal and institutional hands" (Potapova 1988: 142). On 5 October 1918, yet another decree of the Council of Peoples' Commissars (*Sovnarkom*) was issued, with the aim of encouraging the protection, study and popularizing of the treasure houses of art and antiquity in Russia (Ratiya & Dogina 1952: 177). It proclaimed, "Citizens, do not touch even one stone, protect the monuments, the old buildings . . . all this is your history, your pride.".

At a practical level, also in 1918, the Collegium for Museum Affairs was transformed into the Department of Museums and the Preservation of Ancient Monuments (Berton 1977: 199), and work was planned to commence on the restoration of St Basil's cathedral, the Simonov monastery and the former English Club (Potapova 1988: 142). Another decree in 1921, signed by Lenin, sought to protect nature, gardens and parks, linked with architectural objects (Ratiya & Dogina 1952, loc. cit.).

The man put in charge of the new Department of Museums was the painter and art historian, Igor Emmanuelovich Grabar'. Before the revolution he had been a key figure in the architectural revivalist movement, whose interest in traditional Russian architecture and art had led him to edit and contribute significantly to the six-volume *History of Russian art*. In 1910 he had been involved in the foundation of the Society for the Defence and Preservation in Russia of Monuments and Ancient Times (Berton 1977: 198). The roots of this group can be seen in the Society for the Protection of Ancient Buildings, founded in Britain in 1877 by the poet, novelist and painter, William Morris. Morris, as a socialist, had considerable influence on Russian liberal and revolutionary thought, more particularly through the person of Prince Petr Kropotkin, who was equally an admirer and supporter of Ebenezer Howard and his concept of the Garden City (Starr 1976: 231).

Grabar' now began with energy to undertake the work of conservation, including the tasks of listing buildings of architectural merit and carrying out repair work on them. In his activities, he himself acknowledged the influence of Morris and, indeed, in 1923 he visited London to talk to the Society for the Preservation of Ancient Buildings. But Grabar' parted company from Morris's views in a fundamental way, which has influenced Soviet ideas of architectural preservation ever since. Morris followed the views of the British art critic, John Ruskin, in holding rigidly that the contemporary generation had no right whatsoever to touch the creations of the past, the "monuments of a bygone art, created by bygone manners that modern art cannot meddle with without destroying" (from Morris' *Manifesto for the Society for the Preservation of Ancient Buildings*). Such monuments belong to past and future generations; they should be preserved from destruction, but under no circumstances should they be restored. In this, Morris was echoing the magisterial pronouncement of Ruskin that restoration:

> . . . means the most total destruction which a building can suffer, a destruction accompanied with false description of the thing destroyed. Do not let us deceive ourselves in this important matter: it is *impossible*, as impossible as to raise the dead, to restore anything that has ever been great or beautiful in architecture.. . . that spirit which is given only by the hand and eye of the workman, can never be recalled. (Ruskin 1889: 194)

Grabar' tried to avoid the maledict word "restoration", saying that "our main care must be directed not to restoration, but to repair and the very word 'restoration' in our days is largely anachronistic" (Grabar' 1969: 380). Under the guise of "repair" he undertook what Ruskin and Morris would undoubtedly have regarded as restoration, notably on the Sukharev Tower in Moscow, built by Peter the Great for his School of Mathematics and Navigation. He justified this activity in an essay written during the 1920s, entitled *Restoration in Soviet Russia*: "One must not forget that there is restoration and restoration, and if Morris struggled against 'restoration' in inverted commas, against unfounded and undocumented reconstructions, then scientifically based restoration does not meet opposition" (ibid.: 379). One must have grave reservations as to whether Morris would have agreed with this modification of his views, but it is certain that the attitude expressed here by Grabar', accepting the supremacy and virtue of science in validating restoration, has been the bedrock of subsequent Soviet thought on the matter.

In another way also, Grabar' departed from the Morris principle that the past cannot be touched; for him not all the past heritage was sacrosanct. "Without tearing down, the town cannot grow, it is necessary to remove the old and give place to the new, but all this must follow a strictly worked out plan, accompanied by maximum guarantees with the aim of saving everything historically and artistically valuable" (ibid.: 359). In pursuit of this double objective of making room for development, while saving the worthwhile, Grabar' approved the destruction of the bell tower of the Kazan' Cathedral on Red Square in order to widen the square, justifying it on the grounds that the tower was a vulgar nineteenth-century accretion and thus its removal would leave the seventeenth-century church in its pristine state. This was exactly the attitude of those British architects, members of the Cambridge-based Camden Society, who had provoked Ruskin and Morris to their condemnations of interference with historic buildings. But once again, a principle was being enunciated that remained widespread in Soviet approaches.

In the short run, however, the ideas and the work of Grabar' went for very little. By the late 1920s, preservation was giving way to wholesale destruction of architectural treasures. Not only the bell tower, but the whole of the Kazan' Cathedral was pulled down, as were the Sukharev Tower and the Golitsyn Palace, both devotedly restored by Grabar'. Hardly surprisingly, Grabar' resigned in 1930 and the Central Restoration Workshops, of which he had been director, were closed. Significantly, his paper on restoration existed in three manuscript versions from the 1920s, but was never published until 1969.

All through the 1930s, the vandalism continued on a massive scale, with the demolition of thousands of major buildings across the country and countless lesser ones. Losses in Moscow included the Iverskiye Gates to the Red Square and the huge nineteenth-century Spasskiy (Saviour) Metropolitan Cathedral, the latter to make a site for the Palace of the Soviets, which in fact was never built. Even the unique Cathedral of St Basil the Blessed on Red Square came very close to being pulled down in 1936. Altogether, approximately half the 520 churches in Moscow were lost (Daniloff 1983: 66).

The damage was not only in the removal of buildings; those which were left standing were converted to other uses, generally as a temporary measure while awaiting clearance. They therefore received no maintenance or repair; crude and careless adaptations were made to fit them for their new functions as workshops, warehouses, offices or residences. Serious deterioration of their fabric was allowed to occur.

War and the rediscovery of the past

This wholesale extirpation of the architectural heritage continued until the Second World War. The war itself contributed to further destruction and damage in the towns within the zone of fighting, with the loss of over 3000 buildings and monuments (ibid.). But at the same time, it brought about a change of attitude on the part of the government. In the desperate struggle to survive, Stalin needed to call on patriotism, rather than *partiynost'* (party loyalty), and on the symbols of the Russian past. Religious practices were once more permitted, which helped to save a small number of churches by making the upkeep of those which were reopened the responsibility of their congregations. Victorious tsars, like Peter the Great, were now admitted to the Soviet pantheon. Peter's statue by Falconet on the bank of the Neva, the "Bronze Horseman" of Pushkin's poem, was carefully protected throughout the ravages of the siege of Leningrad. So too the cultural achievements of the Russian past were emphasized. In 1943, at the height of the war, an Architectural Committee was established, with a Chief Directorate for the Protection of Architectural Monuments (Ratiya & Dogina 1952: 185); a year later the Central Restoration Workshops were reopened, with Grabar', by then 73 years old, as scientific director.

The reawakened pride in the national heritage was given powerful emphasis by the ruthless vandalism of the German invaders, who blew up or burned buildings in a deliberate effort to destroy that heritage. The Russians refused to accept this robbery of their past, in exactly the same way as the Poles refused to accept the levelling of the old town of Warsaw after the 1944 uprising. When the war was over, the Soviet government began the process of restoration of the ruined buildings. In most instances, this involved far more than repair or heavy restoration; it involved large-scale building of facsimiles of what had formerly existed. Scrupulous care and the meticulous use of documentary and all other historical evidence has been applied to the task, with results which in their striking visual splendour do much to promote the tourist trade in such towns.

Among the buildings, where work first began on the huge task of restoration from nothing more than burnt-out shells, were the summer palaces ringing Leningrad – Peter the Great's palace at Petrodvorets, with its famous cascade of fountains and pools running down to the Gulf of Finland: the palace at Pushkin, designed by Rastrelli for Elizabeth and much developed by Cameron for Cather-

Figure 8.1 Catherine the Great's summer palace at Pushkin (formerly Tsarskoye Selo), as rebuilt after the Second World War.

ine the Great (Fig. 8.1), and Brenna's palatial hunting lodge at Pavlovsk. In each of these cases, although the walls could be massively repaired and restored, there had to be wholesale re-creation of totally destroyed roofs and interiors, including painted ceilings, frescoes, mouldings and the like. In Leningrad itself, many of the eighteenth-century palaces of the nobility, such as the Yelagin and Yusupov palaces, churches such as that at Smol'niy, and other public buildings, which had suffered severely from shellfire and bombing, underwent similar heavy restoration or reproduction.

The immediate post-war period saw the revived patriotism and conscious efforts to increase the sense of national pride continue, linked strongly with the "cult of the personality". A work published in 1952, entitled *Save Monuments of Architecture*, declared, "In order to help the state protect for long centuries the cultural treasures, the patriotic pride and glory of the Soviet people, it is essential that each Soviet citizen is imbued with love for the history of his country, for its ancient monuments" (Ratiya & Dogina 1952: 3). In 1948 Stalin issued an order concerning measures to improve the protection of cultural legacies and considerable funds were made available. An All-Union Scientific Research Institute of Restoration was set up. By 1952, almost every republic had its restoration workshops (ibid.: 179).

This connection between national self-esteem and the conservation of the architectural heritage has continued through most of the post-Stalin era. Considerable efforts have been made to arouse popular interest in the task and to encourage the man in the street to take part in preserving the country's legacy of art and

182

architecture. Indeed, the new Soviet constitution of 1977 laid down in Article 68 that, "Concern for the preservation of historical monuments and other cultural values is a duty and obligation of citizens of the USSR." In 1965, the All-Russian Society for the Protection of Historical and Cultural Monuments was established. It eventually boasted over 13 million members across the country (Daniloff 1983: 67). The Moscow branch alone claimed 800000 members, or one in ten of the entire population (Baldin 1986: 35). Members played an active role in the work itself. In 1984 the Moscow branch organized 180 days of voluntary work on Saturdays and Sundays, a total of 11500 man-days, on 52 projects (ibid.: 36). Not least among the contributions made by members was the identification of buildings, interiors and works of art which stood in need of preservation.

The emphasis on national prestige meant that considerable attention was paid in the first instance to the restoration of the Kremlin in Moscow, as seat of government. Although the Kremlin had suffered no significant loss of the fabric of its buildings due to war damage, there had been much neglect in making good the ravages of time. Over the period since the Second World War gradually all its churches, palaces, towers and walls have been repaired, repainted, regilded and the stonework touched up.

Work on the Kremlin continued even in Khrushchev's time, but in all other respects his administration was a second period of vandalism and destruction. He had scant respect for the historical relics of bygone times and in consequence between 1959 and 1964 there was a further large-scale removal of old buildings. Fortunately, his fall from power in 1964 brought about an immediate change of policy. One of the first beneficiaries of a more enlightened attitude was the row of churches and secular buildings on Razin Street in Moscow's medieval trading quarter, the Kitay Gorod, which were due to be pulled down to make way for the giant Rossiya Hotel. They included the churches of St George on Pskov Hill, built in 1657, St Barbara in late eighteenth-century classical style and the cathedral church of the Znamenskiy monastery, dating from 1679–84. These were now reprieved, heavily restored and incorporated into the general development ensemble; so too was the fifteenth-century church of "The Conception of St Anna, which is in the corner" on the other side of the hotel, its quaint name deriving from its location in the angle of the former walls in the extreme southeast corner of the Kitay Gorod.

Through the 1960s and 1970s, tourism increased, particularly foreign tourism with its invaluable supplies of hard currency. It was gradually realized that historical buildings were high on the list of things that tourists wished to see and as a result the two decades saw the tempo of restoration stepped up and spread across the country. In particular, the years leading up to the 1980 Olympic Games were a period of exceptionally busy activity. Among the more notable buildings of central Moscow, heavily restored in the 1970s, were the seventeenth-century "Moscow baroque" style churches of the Trinity in Khokhovskiy Alley (1676–82), Trinity in Nikitiny (1635–53) and St Nicholas in Khamovniki (1676–82). In the east central Bauman District of the capital, one of the smallest districts by area, there are no less than 72 buildings in government conservation (*Gorodskoye* . . . 1986 no. 3: 27). Altogether, at the time of the 1971 Moscow General Plan, the city had 405 ensembles and individual features under conservation orders, to which the plan envisaged adding a further 455 (Promyslov 1972: 396).

Exceptional examples of restoration on a grand scale are found in the so-called "Golden Ring" of historic towns around Moscow at distances conveniently managed by day-excursion coaches – Zvenigorod, Yaroslavl', Suzdal, Vladimir, Rostov Velikiy (where a hurricane in 1953 caused massive damage on a wartime scale) and Sergiyevsk (sometime Zagorsk). All were places of first-rank importance in medieval times, and both Suzdal and Vladimir were for a time capital of Russia before Moscow. Sergiyevsk has the largest and most important monastery, that of the Trinity and St Sergius, which continued functioning as such in the USSR. All these towns have complexes of kremlins, cathedrals, churches, convents and monasteries, now resplendent with colour and gilding. With the exception of Vladimir with its range of industries and the large textile town of Yaroslavl', these are today all very small centres and tourism is now outstandingly their most important economic activity. In 1970, as well as Zvenigorod and Sergiyevsk (Zagorsk), the Moscow Oblast towns of Dmitrov, Kolomna, Mozhaysk, Zaraysk, Serpukhov and Istra were all added to the list of towns with historic ensembles of national importance (Potapova 1988: 145).

Farther away from Moscow, the commencement of restoration swiftly followed the opening up of towns to foreign visitors, particularly in the ancient cities of Central Asia and the Transcaucasus. At Samarkand the three madrassas (religious schools) surrounding the Registan central square, together with the Gur Emir, Tamerlane's tomb, and the necropolis of Shakh-i-Zinda were all repaired; one of the minarets of the madrassa of Ulug Beg was brought back to the upright from a perilous slant, and all the buildings were refaced with mosaics of coloured tiles, made from the same raw materials and by the same techniques as in the time of Tamerlane. The most recent achievement has been the nearly total rebuilding of the great mosque of Bibi Khanum, which had been reduced by time and earthquake to a few precarious ruins.

Policies and principles in Soviet conservation

The case of the Bibi Khanum mosque illustrates a trend in the Soviet approach to restoration that steadily became more pronounced. As the task of putting surviving buildings back into good repair achieved more and more of its goals, there were ever more frequent examples of the creation of what were largely, or even wholly, facsimiles. An example is provided by the *Angliyskoye podvor'ye* (the "English court") in Moscow on Razin Street (Fig. 8.2). The original building had reputedly been used to house the English merchant-ambassadors in the sixteenth century; it was wholly rebuilt in the late seventeenth century and largely destroyed

Figure 8.2   The "English Court", Razin Street, Moscow: a replica of a sixteenth-century building.

by the fire of 1812. On little more than some stonework foundations, long incorporated into a sequence of later buildings, a replica of the sixteenth-century building has been erected. Since no plans or architectural drawings exist from the period of its first construction, one can only wonder how far informed imagination played a role in the project. In 1994 a replica of the lost Kazan' Cathedral on Red Square was reconsecrated.

The USSR never built its Williamsburg, the famous US re-creation of the early colonial town, but the trend increasingly developed to establish reproductions in a very similar manner. Bauman Street in the eastern pre-revolutionary working class district of Moscow consists of old buildings and houses, mostly of one or two storeys. It was planned to pull them down to widen the street, but this proposal was replaced by another to turn the street into a pedestrian precinct, on the lines of the Arbat, west of the Kremlin, which has already been pedestrianized. Any buildings of architectural merit were to be saved, and the rest were to be cleared and replaced by shops and service establishments, built in a style replicating the medieval "foreigners' quarter", Nemetskaya Sloboda, which once stood there (*Gorodskoye . . .* 1986 no. 3: 27). In fact this project never came to pass before the Soviet demise. It is worth noting *en passant*, that the most distant fort built by the Russians in their eastward expansion, Fort Ross in California, where only one original wooden hut survived, has been recreated in replica by the Americans.

In certain instances there has been conservation of old buildings by moving them to new sites. For example, the sole surviving tower of the *ostrog* (wooden fort) at Bratsk was shifted to a new location when its original site was drowned by the building of the dam on the Angara River. At Suzdal a museum of wooden architecture includes not only a number of wooden houses and mills, but also two wooden churches, all brought from elsewhere. Several republican capitals, notably Riga and Tbilisi, have open-air ethnographic museums containing re-sited examples of vernacular architecture from various parts of the republics.

A feature of the 1970s and 1980s was the designation of certain towns as "historic", ranging in size from Moscow and St Petersburg (Leningrad) to small towns with little other than their ancient buildings, such as Suzdal, Mtskheta (the old capital of the Georgian kings), and Kargopol'; in the RSFSR alone there were 115 such designated towns by 1973 (Gulyanitskiy 1973: 200). In Uzbekistan, Khiva has been designated a UNESCO World Heritage City and similar recognition is being sought for Bukhara.

Frequently, modern inner-city redevelopment has taken place with little or no regard to the scale of existing historic buildings and streets. This has led to considerable protest, notably in Moscow over the Palace of Congresses within the Kremlin (dubbed at the time by furious Muscovites *stilyag mezhdu boyarami* – "lout amidst the nobility"), the Rossiya Hotel covering almost half the ancient Kitay Gorod quarter, the towering new Intourist Hotel behind the pre-revolutionary National Hotel and, above all, the line of giant high-rise office and apartment blocks along the new Kalinin Prospect, which was driven through one of the older parts of inner Moscow.

To control further disproportionate developments of this kind within historic towns, whole streets and even quarters were set aside as conservation areas, where modern buildings were prohibited or very strictly controlled, especially as to height. The entire centre of St Petersburg has been so protected, successfully maintaining its splendid eighteenth-century skyline. There, no less than 2167 buildings have been designated under conservation orders as architectural or cultural monuments, not to mention 222 buildings preserved as having an association with Lenin (Ruble 1990: 85).

In Moscow a regulation as early as 1926 had banned buildings over six storeys within the Garden Ring, but it had from the start remained a dead letter (Khan-Magomedov 1983: 404). In 1974 nine conservation areas were designated (Fig. 8.3), including Zamoskvorech'ye, the area of old houses and churches directly across the Moskva River from the Kremlin and associated with a number of artists and literary figures including Chekhov, Ostrovskiy, Yesenin and Akhmatova. Another conservation area is Kropotkin Street, with very few buildings dating from after the Revolution and with an array of classical buildings that include the Tol'stoy home, now a museum, and the Khrushchev–Seleznev house, now the Pushkin museum; both were designed by Grigor'yev in 1814 and 1822 respectively. Yet another designated area is the pedestrianized Arbat. Altogether, the nine Moscow conservation zones cover about 30 per cent of the area within the Garden Ring and include 237 architectural, historical and cultural monuments (Potapova 1988: 147).

Four former mansions and estates of the crown or nobility, now within Moscow, are designated as conservation parks: the former Sheremet'yev estate at Kuskovo, Kuz'minki (once the Golitsyn estate), Kolomenskoye and Tsaritsyno, the last with its unfinished palaces, designed first by Bazhenov and then by Kazakov for Catherine the Great, who refused to be content with either version.

Minsk has two such areas: the "Upper Town" in the centre, where most of the very few surviving historic buildings in that much-destroyed city are to be found, and the Calvary cemetery, with its nineteenth-century gate, to the west in Frunze District. The seven conservation zones of Irkutsk include an area of several city blocks in the centre consisting of one- and two-storey wooden buildings in the typical pre-revolutionary Siberian style; among them is the house of Prince Tru-

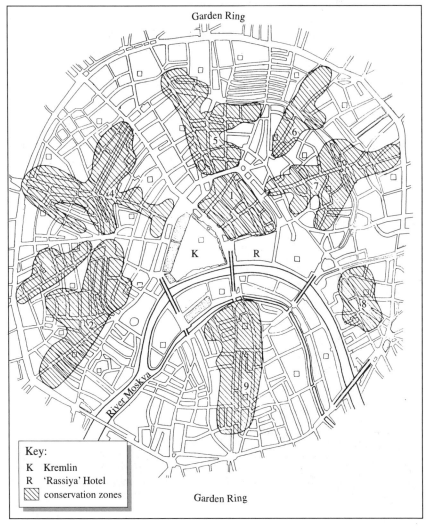

Figure 8.3   Conservation zones in Moscow.

betskoy, the Decembrist exile, now a museum. The centre of Yaroslavl' was designated in 1990 as a conservation zone (Ruble 1992: 214), although Kostroma, down stream on the Volga, was in the same year still fighting for a similar designation. Another conservation area covers much of the old town in Tbilisi, where there has been considerable restoration of old houses in traditional Georgian styles. Indeed, in Georgia, with many of the oldest cities in the former USSR, thought is given to protecting the panoramic views of downtown conservation areas (Baburov 1977: 5).

This development is entirely admirable and it should help to prevent the overwhelming of historic buildings by grossly disproportionate modern ones. In Moscow, where the huge Rossiya Hotel overshadows the churches on Razin Street (Fig. 8.4), and the tower blocks of Kalinin Prospect hang threateningly over the small seventeenth-century gem of St Simon Stylites church, it is perhaps already too late. As Kirillov (1976: 214) comments wryly, "One can hardly acknowledge as harmonious with the past, the attempt to build up Kalinin Prospect, or the building of the Rossiya Hotel in Zarad'ye, or the Intourist Hotel on Gor'kiy Street".

Yet the policy of area conservation presents its own problems, nowhere better exemplified than in central Bukhara in Uzbekistan. The old town is almost totally free of modern twentieth century buildings; as well as the many, often outstandingly beautiful, mosques and madrassas, traditional houses with their blank mud and wattle walls line the maze of alleys, many of which are too narrow to permit motor vehicles. Cupola bazaars span three of the major road intersections. The whole town centre is a living museum, but it is scarcely possible to provide the

Figure 8.4   The Church of St George on Pskov Hill, Razin Street, Moscow, and the 1960s Rossiya Hotel.

inhabitants with a standard of living appropriate to the late twentieth century in these conditions. Gradually, the people who once lived there, especially the younger generation, are moving out to the new blocks of flats on the town's outskirts. For the most part, they move unwillingly, for many of the town's Uzbek population consider the traditional house, with its capability to accommodate an extended family, far preferable to the standardized all-Union style flat with one to three rooms in a high-rise apartment block. Nevertheless, the living museum is slowly, but apparently inevitably, becoming a dead one. At Khiva, also in the Uzbek Republic, this has already happened and the old town now forms an empty museum at a distance of several kilometres from the modern town of Urgench.

Another conservation problem, which has emerged as the number of buildings involved has grown, is the question of finding contemporary, non-harmful uses for buildings designed for other purposes. In at least one case, an historical complex of buildings has been restored to something close to its original purpose; in 1988 the Danilov monastery, one of the ring of medieval monasteries that guarded the southern approaches to Moscow and is nowadays deep within the city, was handed over after heavy restoration to the Moscow patriarch as his religious headquarters. The new freedoms for religion and the upsurge in religious adherence that followed the introduction of *glasnost* has led to a rapid and considerable increase in the number of churches restored to their original purpose. The Soviet press reported that, by the beginning of 1991, 550 churches and ensembles of religious buildings had been returned to the Orthodox church; in the process 54 museums were displaced (CDSP 1991, 43 No. 7: 30).

A certain number of buildings have been converted into museums with appropriateness. Some commemorate individuals who once lived there, such as the Pushkin and Tol'stoy museums on Kropotkin Street in Moscow or the wooden house of the exiled Decembrist, Prince Trubetskoy, in Irkutsk. The palace of Ostankino in northern Moscow, built entirely of wood in *trompe l'oeil* fashion by the serfs of Prince Sheremet'yev, is a museum of serf art, although this skirts around the fact that the palace was designed by the Italian architects Quarenghi and Camporesi.

Other buildings have become specialist museums; the Novodevichiy and Donskoy monasteries in Moscow are museums of architecture for which their own buildings provide the most striking exhibits. Similarly, the Church of the Trinity in Nikitini, built in 1628–53, is a museum of seventeenth-century architecture and painting. Rather less appositely, the seventeenth-century Church of St Simon Stylites on Moscow's Kalinin Prospect was a museum of mineralogy; happily, it is one of the churches restored to its original religious purpose. Greatest of all the Soviet museums is the former Winter Palace in St Petersburg, the whole of which has become the Hermitage Art Gallery; previously the gallery was only a small part of the palace.

Some other uses are not wholly inappropriate. The lovely Pashkov House, dating from 1785–6 and perhaps the finest creation of the architect Bazhenov, was later the Rumyantsev Museum and is today part of the Lenin Library. The Moscow clas-

sical style house on Vorovskiy Street, which Tol'stoy used as the model for the Rostov home in *War and peace*, became the headquarters of the Writers' Union, and
a statue of Tol'stoy presides over its courtyard. Other latter-day functions are less
related to previous uses. The thirteenth-century Church of The Virgin in Metekha,
Tbilisi, was for a time a theatre, although it has now reverted to its original purpose;
the house, built in a highly fanciful revivalist style in 1894 for the wealthy Morozov
family, was translated into the House of Friendship for the reception of foreign del-
egations; the classical house behind the Lubyanka Prison on Moscow's Lubyanka
(Dzerzhinskaya) Square served as the Reception Hall of the KGB.

Even when lessees are found for the restored buildings, problems have arisen
over infringements by the occupiers of the strict conditions laid down in the terms
of the lease and there is an urgent need to tighten controls, especially against sub-
letting (Baldin 1986: 36). When the Rosmonumentisskustvo Association took
over the rental of the Simonov monastery in southeast Moscow from the "Saturn"
factory, it found the buildings in an appalling state of ruin; the site was overgrown
with weeds, and 150 tonnes of rubbish had to be cleared (*Gorodskoye* . . . 1986,
No. 4: 39).

One-fifth of historic buildings in Moscow still continue to be used as warehouses, small workshops, eating places or service establishments, in defiance of
the law on historic conservation, although the proportion used for dwellings is
down from 30 to 5 per cent. Clearly, it is the general intention that restored historic
buildings should no longer be used for residence; in Moscow's Zhdanov District
the people living in its 35 historic buildings have all been moved out and, after restoration, it is intended that the properties should be used for cultural purposes
(*Gorodskoye* . . . 1985, No. 12: 19). Over the whole city, up to 80 per cent of such
buildings are in the occupation of cultural, educational or administrative organizations. Local authorities do not usually include in their estimates sums for the
upkeep of historical buildings and are therefore not ideal tenants (Baldin 1986:
36). A further problem arises where there are streets predominantly of restored
and conserved buildings that have been taken over as public buildings; there is no
longer a significant number of inhabitants and the streets become "deserts" at
night (Potapova 1988: 149), a localized version of the problem in museum towns
such as Khiva.

The increased tempo of restoration has meant that corners have sometimes
been cut. Thus, in replacing carved limestone lions at the gates of several Moscow
buildings, concrete has been used (*Gorodskoye* . . . 1985, no. 6: 23). In general,
however, in the task of salvaging ancient buildings the Soviet restorers followed
closely the principles laid down by Grabar' – the reliance on a scientific approach
using all historical evidence as to the former appearance, use of proper materials
and techniques and every modern scientific method of carrying out the work. In
Tashkent, a research institute studies, with devoted exactitude, traditional methods
of producing the ceramic tiling that so beautified the great Islamic monuments of
the past.

But in this search for scientific precision in restoration, the conservation specialists are following, even if unconsciously, those precepts of the Cambridge Camden Society in nineteenth-century Britain, which Ruskin and Morris attacked with such vehemence. *The Ecclesiologist*, the journal of the Camden Society, stated that, "To restore is to revive the original appearance . . . lost by decay, accident or ill judged alteration" (quoted in White 1962: 159). This is precisely the line taken by the Soviet specialists – the removal of accretions of later periods as false, "ill judged alterations", in order to recreate a perceived or imagined original state.

In a work on restoration in St Petersburg, the authors write, "Accumulated experience in individual cases has permitted, not only the reconstruction of the destroyed, but also the revelation of the original form of the monument and thus resurrect long-lost features of the Leningrad townscape" (Kedrinskiy et al. 1983: 310). A classic example of this is displayed by the former Kunstkamera in Leningrad on the north bank of the Great Neva, today the Anthropological Museum. Originally designed by Matarnovi and built in 1718–34, only 13 years later in 1747, it was damaged by fire and the upper part of its tower was destroyed. When restoration was carried out two centuries later in 1947 the original tower was replaced, together with rustication and many details of the original facade, all on the basis of old documents and drawings.

The "false", which must be removed, could include more than the additions of later periods; additions, which were perceived as inappropriate in a sociopolitical sense, could also be considered undesirable. This applied especially to monuments of wooden architecture, which tended to be seen as popular, or folk, art. A work devoted specifically to the restoration of wooden buildings laid down the principles definitively, if less than succinctly:

Before deciding questions of renovation of actual losses, one must decide questions of stratified depositions; that is, one must thoroughly investigate which in the existing conglomeration of multifarious elements are genuine, authentic and most valuable, which are accidental or neutral, and which are false, borrowed or foreign, which came hither from another world of aesthetic ideals, from another non-popular, artistic culture, which enveloped the authentic architecture of the monument with alien decorative orders and which do not possess intrinsic merit.

In short, before starting renewal of losses, one must precisely define what indeed must be renewed, what must be religiously preserved and carefully restored, what may be retained temporarily, or with certain reservations, and what not only must not be saved and even less restored, but on the contrary must be removed as alien and destructive of the authentic form of the monument.   (Opolovnikov 1974: 7)

The Ecclesiologist would have applauded such an approach. Morris would have termed it "scrape", as opposed to his own "anti-scrape" views.

This search for a perceived original perfection of national, or vulgar, architecture has engaged the strongest support during the 1980s and since from the unof-

191

ficial Russian nationalist society, *Pamyat'* ("Memory"). The society's sinister qualities include a chauvinism, indeed at times an hysterical xenophobia, which enthusiastically embraces the principle of ridding buildings of "alien" additions, advanced in the quotation above, in order to recreate an imagined "golden age" of national expression unsullied by other cultures. Fortunately, the work of restoration is not to any significant extent in the hands of such extreme proponents.

One area of conservation, which as yet has attracted little attention or work, is that of industrial archaeology. In part the view of Soviet industry as the cutting edge of economic development led to the removal of old plant and buildings; at the same time, intense pressures to meet ever higher plan targets often led to the continued operation of antiquated factories. As a result of this second circumstance, there are still buildings to be saved. So far, almost the only examples of industrial preservation are the wooden wind and water mills, saved in museums of wooden architecture or ethnography. In Yekaterinburg (Sverdlovsk), the re-mains of the original ironworks in the centre of the city have been preserved as a museum of the Urals iron industry.

In the more traditional aspects of architectural preservation also, despite the good work achieved, much still remains to be done. In Yaroslavl' Oblast, over half the 750 historic monuments are in need of repair (CDSP 1986, 38 no. 46: 13). The unique collection of wooden ecclesiastical architecture at Kizhi Pogost' on the shores of Lake Ladoga, including the remarkable Preobrazhenskiy Church, is but the best known of a series of wooden structures throughout the north that are suffering from grave neglect and failure to carry out restoration work. Despite a resolution of the RSFSR Council of Ministers in 1980 on the preservation of historic monuments, by 1985, only 18 of 202 wooden historic buildings in the Karelian Autonomous Republic had been repaired (CDSP 1986, 38, no. 24: 26). Part of the problem was the shortage of staff. Only four art institutes in the former USSR offered courses on restoration, each admitting 8–15 students a year (Daniloff 1983: 72). Another difficulty has been the lack of a State body with full powers (Potapova 1983: 145). Most restrictive of all has usually been lack of funds, a problem which has become very much worse with the demise of the USSR.

Despite the 1971 Moscow Genplan incorporating measures to conserve historic buildings, losses of historic areas through the invasion of modern buildings and the construction of modern economic operations have "become perceptible" (Potapova 1988: 144). The construction of a new Metro station near the Lenin Library is threatening the foundations and the very survival of the Pashkov House. In Nizhniy Novgorod (Gor'kiy), the creation of the Cheboksary dam and reservoir on the Volga, down stream of the city, with its consequent raising of the water table, caused subsidence in the city kremlin (Gutsalenko 1989: 117).

The republics of Central Asia are currently witnessing the development of a grave threat to some of the world's loveliest buildings and finest examples of Islamic architecture, due to heedless economic activity. Faulty irrigation practices, especially the failure to line canals or to restrict flow of scarce water, have caused a rise in the water table. The water, heavily impregnated with salt, has reached the foundations of buildings in Samarkand, Bukhara and Khiva. Rising damp brings the salt up through the buildings and, as the water evaporates from the surfaces of buildings, the salt crystallizes out, breaking up the brick, stone and mortar and extruding the coloured ceramic tiling that forms the main decoration of walls. In time, if not dealt with, the whole fabric becomes at risk of collapse. Much of the tile and other repair work carried out since the 1960s is already itself suffering, often as a result of using salt-impregnated water to make the cement (Akiner et al. 1992).

Certainly, there was certainly a growing concern during the 1980s about the need for greater conservation efforts. Equally, the necessity incumbent on town planners to make due accommodation for the historic heritage and to blend it with new developments was generally recognized. "In the architecture of their buildings, in the laying out of their streets and squares, [towns] embody the links of time, they delight by the union of old and new. It is mindless to drown the voice of history in them, to wipe out the imprint of past eras.... Town planners must manifest genuine art, in order that on the road to the future of the town, they do not waste the impressive heritage of the past" (Lappo 1987: 223). A Georgian writer put it in even stronger terms: "It is fundamentally abnormal, if architectural and urban heritage is seen as an obstacle to planners, instead of being seen as a 'genotype' of compositional development and continuity" (Baburov 1977: 8). A questionnaire survey carried out in Kaluga found that architectural monuments played an important role in people's perceptions of the social significance of urban core areas (Bakshteyn et al. 1986: 92–3).

Nevertheless, there is not infrequently a difference in perception of what is of historic and architectural significance between the "experts" in art history and the urban population at large. Surveys in Tver' (Kalinin), Kaluga and Staraya Russa showed that some surviving churches and historic buildings were ignored by the townsfolk, while others long disappeared were still referred to (Savkin 1989: 109). In Kaluga it was found that, while architectural buildings of significance were a major element in the environmental and social worth of a given part of town, historical monuments located by service establishments were those most commonly mentioned by interviewees (Bakshteyn et al. 1988: 93). Savkin has suggested a need for an intermediate plan between the framework plan of past monuments and developmental projects for conservation zones, which would incorporate both people's perceptions of the role of the past and the need to find a role for the elements of the past in the future city.

In 1986, in response to the call for a national body with weight, a Soviet Cultural Fund was established, with Academician D. S. Likhachev as chairman of its board, to promote national culture and national consciousness of cultural heritage; its responsibilities included the restoration of historic buildings (CDSP 1986, 38 No. 46: 12–14). Branches of the Culture Fund in individual towns have fought to raise funds and get protection orders for individual buildings and conservation zones. In Kostroma, the Culture Fund has been striving to secure a conservation order for the whole city centre, representing as it does one of the most complete fulfilments of a town plan drawn up under Catherine the Great's decree.

In the post-Soviet city, as it has been formed over the Soviet era, restored or facsimile buildings of past eras form a vividly colourful and varied element in a townscape only too often monotonous, an element usually appreciated by native and visitor alike as giving visual pleasure, cultural depth and aesthetic richness. There can be no question that, whatever the town plans of the future will be, they and republican and local authorities will have to take into consideration and incorporate that which the past has bequeathed. As Sazonov & Strashnova commented (1988: 96), "in considering social concepts in the paths for Moscow's development, it is an historically individual city" and "even if not a question of conserving all these traditions in an untouched form, they all require taking into account and their relationship carefully considered". Even more strongly, Lavrov (1977: 175) stated that, "former achievements will take part in the establishment of the present planned environment and its perfecting in the future." Perhaps there is no better symbol of this re-evaluation of the past than the reversion of the name of Leningrad to St Petersburg. What is certain is that the question of preservation of the past in the former Soviet Union exemplifies clearly the complex relationships between plans, government policies and wishes for State grandeur, and the wishes and emotions of ordinary people, together with the no less complex results of success and failure in urban development.

CHAPTER 9

The consequences of
Soviet urban planning
– an evaluation

The preceding chapters have indicated that the evolution of the Soviet city fell into several clearly distinct stages, each of which saw its own set of relationships between the realities of urban development and the ideals and objectives of the planners. Certain threads can be traced throughout the three-quarters of a century after the storming of the Winter Palace. Most importantly, in all stages up to the end of the USSR, government, party, planners and populace at large all saw themselves as creating a socialist State on Marxist principles, as the necessary preliminary stage to achieving a final communist society. Even as late as August 1991 and after the attempted coup, Gorbachev, as head of a State on the verge of extinction as a communist country, proclaimed his belief that the socialist way forward was desirable. No other country has had as long a period in which to experiment with ways of attaining this goal, no other country has been so well endowed with every needful resource for doing so. To this one must add the flying start given by the preceding Tsarist regime, which, for all its manifold inadequacies, had brought Russia to the position of the fifth most industrially developed and powerful country in the world. Equally important in the context of the city, it had established an exceptional, widespread tradition that towns should have formally constituted plans, even if the plans were rarely fulfilled entirely and had faded into the background by the time of the Revolution. It is fair then to judge the Soviet Union as the prime exemplar of Marxist socialist planning in all its aspects and in particular of socialist town planning.

The Soviet era saw huge changes in the urban environment of the USSR and, now that era is over, it is possible to make an assessment of its achievements and its failures and to examine what that period means for the successor States today. Several questions at once present themselves. First, how far did the plans succeed in creating a "City of Socialist Man" as envisaged in theory before and just after the 1917 Revolution, a city that expressed the aims and ideals of communist thinking? Then, secondly, how did the city that did evolve differ from cities in other countries that continued to develop under various forms of capitalist and mixed

195

economies? The final question is, what legacy has been inherited by the post-Soviet society that is now gradually, and perhaps painfully, coming into existence?

A City of Socialist Man?

The first necessity was to establish the role of a socialist town, of what nature it should be in order best to fulfil that role, and how to give it that nature. Over these questions ranged the cut and thrust of argument through the decade of the 1920s. Communist theory gave little practical help. The founding fathers of Marxism believed, correctly, that it would be the urbanized and industrialized proletariat who would make the revolution. For all the faults and appalling conditions of the capitalist town in Russia, it was better than the "idiocy" of rural life; the urban workers were at least marginally better educated and informed than their rural counterparts. When the revolution occurred, therefore, it was generally accepted that the new society would be housed in towns, where the ultimate in quality of life could eventually be provided. Even the Disurbanists were not concerned with destroying the urban level of life, but rather with destroying the existing artefact and replacing it with urban life in the setting of countryside, a flourish of romanticism that was perhaps more Russian than Marxist and certainly more directly influenced by Ebenezer Howard than by the authors of the *Communist manifesto*.

The failure of the theoreticians of the 1920s to come to any consensus and the hard economic realities of the day meant that town planning at that period had no existence in fact. The very little that was constructed rarely consisted of more than single buildings in isolation. But for all the impractical dreams of the 1920s debates, various principles were worked out, were generally accepted and have throughout the Soviet period been considered fundamental by Soviet town planners. Some of these principles, although not many, have been specifically Marxist; some have been aesthetic or concerned with the quality of urban life; yet others have expressed national or indeed "imperial" pride. Fundamental principles were that the town should be planned in its development and form, and that it should be planned to achieve the highest quality of life for the society it contained, by constraining unlimited growth in town size, by generous use of greenery and amenity space, by restricted length of journey to work, and by establishing and applying adequate and equitable norms of provision for all types of services. It is not unreasonable to consider the development of these tenets as the most important contribution of the entire Soviet period to town planning in general. They were spread throughout the world by international participants in the process such as le Corbusier and Gropius. Indeed, for decades, the rest of world was more frequently influenced by the new ideas than was the Soviet Union.

The onset of the Stalin era brought to an end abstract theorizing about towns and their plans, and simultaneously introduced the national economic plan as the controlling system of the country's development. At the level of the national econ-

196

omy, the plans of the Stalin period broadly achieved the tasks they were given, to allocate the priorities between economic sectors and to bring about rapid growth in the priority sectors. This meant heavy industry, defence and, in rather poor third place, agricultural collectivization and mechanization, with the consequent opportunities to release labour for the new urban factories.

Urban development was the inevitable concomitant of these priorities, but providing for it was not a priority. Just as the existing railway network was in the main expected to cope with vastly increased burdens, and what capital investment there was in transport was mostly directed to building railways where none had existed before, in exactly the same way existing towns were expected to absorb the huge numbers of new in-migrants, yet with most capital investment going to build towns where none had existed before. In consequence the number of towns increased greatly and existing towns grew rapidly in population, but the quality of urban life seriously deteriorated. Above all, the housing situation reached crisis point by the time that Stalin died. The drawing up of plans was on a most limited scale; only a handful of towns – the very largest and the completely new – actually got them. Of those that were drawn up, little or nothing was realized, even in places on greenfield sites. The overriding dominance of industry and its controlling ministries in decision-taking again and again frustrated the aims of the planners. In the greater freedom of the era of *glasnost*, a Soviet geographer could write, "In the process of urbanization of our country, the economic policy of Stalin and the maintenance of socio-economic tendencies established at that time have proved negative." (Gornostayeva 1989b: 41).

Stalin created a society which by his death was significantly urbanized, with almost half the population living in towns. Yet it is not too exaggerated to compare the urban situation in the USSR in 1953 with, for example, Pittsburg or Sheffield in the mid-nineteenth century. Heavy industry dominated and polluted, living conditions were appalling, the workers had inadequate rationed access to food and all daily requirements. If some efforts to green the towns could be put on the credit side, the slave conditions of so many of the workers in the Gulag system, who did a substantial share of the construction in the Stalinist town, were more evil than anything the early Industrial Revolution had produced, even in Russia. Perhaps one might find something of a comparable Western capitalist evil in the employment of child labour down coalmines and in factories. The Soviet city at the height of the command economy was Mumford's "Coketown" with the addition of electricity and, in the case of Moscow alone, of a grandiose Metro. Lenin's famous dictum was displayed for so long by every power station in the country, "Communism is all power to the Soviets plus electrification of the whole country". Lenin could hardly have foreseen that the reality of Stalin's Soviet Union was no more than precisely that.

This legacy of abased urban life put pressure on the entire period following Stalin, giving national and local governments little option but to give total priority to the programme of housing construction, with no less disregard for town plans than industry had shown in the earlier stage. The fringes of all the larger and medium-size urban places were built over in countless microregions of apartment blocks, where planned norms of service provision were rarely achieved or were only achieved years after the housing was occupied. Smaller places usually acquired a cluster of four- or five-storey prefabricated blocks of flats, standing in the midst of old single-storey wooden housing. Old housing in central areas of bigger places could but infrequently be renewed in the prevailing shortage of accommodation; when it was, there was only "point" renewal by individual buildings, rather than by planned areas.

Thus, all along, town plans were forced to yield their priorities to the short-term needs of the government of the day, or to particular pressure groups, especially industries, which continued to play an overriding role throughout the Soviet period. As a result, plans were left on the shelf or, at best, given only marginal attention. Moscow's 1935 General Plan was not merely not carried out, but was only fully replaced by a new plan in 1971 and even that date was only achieved on paper, by back-dating the start of the plan to four years before its real date of promulgation in 1975. Some other towns paid so little attention to their plans that their planning offices were kept happily busy drawing up one new plan after another, with none being applied. Often enough, the need to revise the plan at such frequent intervals was the result of totally inadequate assessment of the town's future development, especially in the matter of population growth. The plan was not helped by its rigidity, which meant that changed circumstances required a wholly new plan; flexible rolling plans never were promulgated, although planners themselves increasingly saw the need for them.

The 1980s witnessed the start of a shift to a further stage in Soviet urban development, when it seemed likely that people, by their choices of where they wished to live and expectations of enhanced living standards, and cars, by their technical demands, were beginning to impose their imperatives on plans just as forcibly as ever industry and housing construction had done in the past. Features associated with the capitalist city became ever more readily apparent – socially distinct areas within towns, traffic problems, growing consumerism. Asking the townsfolk for their views, unheard of in Stalin's time, became increasingly a feature of the latter-day Soviet Union. The questionnaire survey, if slow in first being used, by the 1980s was a regular tool of the Soviet sociologist, geographer and planner.

In the latter days of the Soviet system, the impact of these previously unfelt forces of individuality and non-Communist Party controlled local groups was undoubtedly becoming greater as the political and economic changes of the Gorbachev regime increased the role of devolved, democratic decision-taking. This brought about new freedoms of action for individual republics, ethnic groups and economic entities, and shifted the weight of emphasis still further from the collective to the individual.

For some time, well before the beginning of *perestroyka*, planners perforce had to adapt their concepts of what was desirable. The ideas of the nature and function of the city had long been far removed from early idealisms and broad supranational theories. Ever since the Second World War there had been general recognition of the national heritage and pride, certainly of nationalist consciousness (although at first only at an all-USSR level, which tended to draw a rather feeble distinction between "Soviet" and "Russian") and perhaps also of instinctive popular conservatism. No longer was it generally believed that the socialist city had an active or determining social role to play in moulding society to a new form of living. Rather, the task of the planners was to satisfy the growing material demands for improvements to the quality of life. The majority of Soviet people, as much as the majority in Western capitalist countries, measured quality of life in material goods and convenience of day-to-day activity, not in social goals.

By the opening of Gorbachev's *perestroyka* programme, these changes in attitude in Soviet society had brought about a transition to the fourth stage of urban development, a transition gradual and prolonged, unlike the quite swift transitions from first to second stage in 1928–31 and from second to third in 1957. In consequence, the late 1980s saw frequent calls in Soviet literature for new approaches to the drawing up of town plans. One such approach was to begin to consider the town in its regional context, to plan for land-use zoning for agglomerations as a whole (Grebennikov et al. 1987: 248), even for urban corridors and regions (Lappo 1987, Polyan 1988). Others were asking for rolling plans, yet others for social rather than purely physical planning for the cities.

Thus, even before the end of communism, Soviet town planning had evolved to resemble far more closely planning for the Western city. Planners had very generally come to accept that hard realities had swept aside earlier ideals, in particular that there should be a maximum size for cities. Far from seeing the ultra-large cities as a thoroughly undesirable end-product of capitalism, to be avoided at all costs in the socialist world, the fact that the USSR had 28 of them over the million mark, and would in future have more, was increasingly put forward as a matter of satisfaction; the largest cities changed from being undesirable and anti-socialist, to being desirable and most economic.

The acceptance of very large cities and the parallel start in planning for the wider areas of metropolitan regions and urban agglomerations led some writers to face up to the prospect of that bourgeois development, suburbanization, which they began to present as a desirable trend for Soviet cities. Others saw the Marxist objective to abolish the distinction between the town and the countryside coming about as the result of a rural–urban continuum, in which towns are merely trend-setting foci for people who maintain an urban standard of life in rural areas; "If earlier urbanization processes manifested themselves primarily in the growth of towns and of urban population, now they encompass all types of settlement from the largest towns to villages. Towns thus play the role of nodal points of urbanization, since in them are worked out the bases of perfecting material and spiritual activity and culture, which then permeate the life of all socialist settlements" (Trushkov 1983: 4).

While this view (*mutatis mutandis*) might seem at present rather more applicable to spatially small, highly urbanized Western countries like Great Britain than to the Soviet Union, by the end of the 1980s it was possible to detect in the USSR the first faint beginnings of counterurbanization. Gorbachev urged young city dwellers to buy houses in the country, either as second homes or as commuting bases, as part of the effort to revivify villages with many houses abandoned in the migration to urban areas or in the key village concentration programme. Yet if indeed there was such a start to suburbanization and counterurbanization, there was no time before the end of communist power for the plan to reflect or take account of these processes.

The concept of grades of housing was propounded; in the past there was indeed a clear difference in housing for different social groups, but the fact was played down, or more usually denied, in Soviet literature. It was even suggested by Gorbachev, in his report to the Central Committee of the party in 1987, that there should be differential rents according to size. This was not an entirely new concept; even before *perestroyka* the idea had been mooted that accommodation should be free up to the established norm of living space, but that there should be differential rents for all space over the norm. This idea was far from universally acceptable. Sarkisyan (1983: 187) attacked it on the grounds that families should be given space in accordance with need, not at a minimum level, and that it was wrong to give anyone space over the norm while there were still people unprovided with their own accommodation. The concept of differentiated rents may not have been socialist, but it represented a sense of reality in building what people wanted and were willing and able to pay for, rather than building for purposes of social engineering, or government economics, or even national vainglory.

Increasingly, as more and more people were rehoused and it began to be taken for granted that eventually every household could hope to get an individual apartment, it appeared that what large numbers wanted was an individual dwelling, or a least that blocks should be small enough for there to be some sense of community. Families, having at first joyfully accepted their own flats in high-rise blocks, after years in communal apartments, now began more frequently to feel loneliness and alienation. As one old lady, rehoused from a communal flat to a self-contained one-roomed flat in a new block, commented to the author, "I know no-one in the block." The Baltic Republics, as in so many aspects of Soviet life, led the way in restoring a human scale to the built environment and started to design complexes of two-storey buildings arranged to form a small community. "Today 'the small world' is fully rehabilitated" (Yanitskiy 1986: 70). The substantial survival of the private sector in housing after 70-odd years of socialism reinforced this renewed role for the small and individual as opposed to the giant and collective. Changes in Soviet law on private ownership in the early 1990s, if ever brought into force, would certainly have increased very greatly the role of the private sector, with an inevitable concomitant development of a housing market. By 1994 it was already becoming clear that those citizens of the Russian Republic who could afford to do so were building substantial houses for themselves in the forest-park belt and adjacent areas around Moscow.

This move towards capitalist relationships in the last years of the Soviet Union, and the increasing obviousness of social distinctions in the quality of urban life, are perhaps the clearest indicators that the Soviet attempts to create a new society and a new city for it to live in failed in their own terms. Fisher, writing in 1962 and on the basis of cities in the CMEA countries of eastern Europe, although extending his evaluation to the Soviet Union, considered that the answer to the question whether the planners had failed was a "qualified 'no'", but he conceded that "the contemporary cities fall far short of the ideal socialist goal." The reasons he gave for the shortfalls were: the war devastation and costs of reconstruction, the political rigidity of Stalinism, the lack of technical knowledge and skill, and the priority for investment in heavy industry (Fisher 1962: 265). Since then, 30 years have passed; other countries as gravely damaged by the war, such as Germany, have created prosperous societies and cities. The USSR developed technical skills that led the way into space and the priorities for heavy industry weakened from the day that Stalin died. Yet the last 30 years did not see the Soviet city progressing towards the ideal goals. Far from bringing about a better life for town dwellers in terms of democracy, social relations, fairness between individuals and groups, welfare and material benefits, the urban plan under the command economy produced minimal results. In consequence, life in the Soviet town was in few, if any, respects better than in its capitalist equivalent; in many respects it was just as bad and, far too often, it was distinctly worse.

Poverty, inequality, ethnic tensions and discrimination were not eliminated. "One form or another of privatism and privilege has come to shape urban cultural values in subtle ways, and to shape some parts of the Soviet city itself" (Bater 1984: 157). In many parts of the non-Russian republics, especially in Central Asia and above all in its smallest towns, urban conditions were not significantly better than in many Third World countries. Even in the RSFSR, a majority of small towns were only marginally better places in which to live in 1991 than in 1914. In the country at large, the level of housing provision, for all the desperate efforts to make good its deficiencies, still had far to go by 1991. If actual homelessness was not as frequent as in, say, the British city of the early 1990s, this advantage was counterbalanced by the far more common condition of desperate slum-level overcrowding and inadequate accommodation. Service provision of every type, the supply of foodstuffs and consumer goods, were far below what was needed and imposed wearisome, time-consuming burdens on the urban population. Although the end of the Soviet period saw the bulk of the urban population in clearly better conditions than in 1917, over the same time period the capitalist city made even greater strides, and the gap between the two systems was wider rather than narrower.

If the Soviet Union failed to provide a better quality of life than in Western countries, equally it failed to achieve the Marxist aim of abolishing the distinction between town and countryside. The advance achieved in the towns, however lagging behind Western developments, was still far faster than in the villages. In many respects, life in thousands of the wholly agricultural villages differs from pre-revolutionary times in little more than the presence of electricity and more farm machinery. Those still living in the yurts (portable huts of skins) of the arid lands of Central Asia in 1991 would in all likelihood not have even these modern blessings. The 34 per cent of the population at the national level, who lived in rural areas in 1989, rose in the least developed republics to 59 per cent in Uzbekistan, 62 per cent in Kyrgyzstan and 68 per cent in Tadzhikistan. Of the country's employed population, 19 per cent were engaged in agriculture and forestry. For a sizeable minority of the population and for a majority in Central Asia, any urban standards of life were nowhere in sight.

Moreover, in some respects other than material standards of living, the gap between town and country had widened. Before the Revolution, the large annual pendulum migration between town and country had formed a social link. This was reinforced by the fact that a very high proportion of urban dwellers were first-generation migrants, who still had families living in the villages and working the land and whom they would visit, especially at harvest time. These urban–rural links are today very weak, at least in the Slavic and Baltic republics. The countervailing processes that have linked town and country in western Europe and North America – suburbanization, commuting, second homes and the achievement of urban living standards in rural areas – have only developed to a very limited extent so far in the former USSR and have had little or no effect except in the vicinity of the largest cities.

Reasons why a truly socialist city was never achieved are debatable and surely manifold. Some would consider the very concept to be an idealistic dream and therefore never achievable in reality. Others maintain that the Soviet Union was never a true example of Marxist fulfilment, although the failure of the many different efforts in different countries to set up an efficiently working Marxist system weakens such a case. Realities of power politics and of human nature are cruel to ideals and idealists. No less ruthless are the technological imperatives of such things as the motor vehicle or building methods. Beyond question, outside factors such as the Second World War and the military requirements of the Cold War period made huge diversionary demands on resources, although of course these factors applied just as much to most Western countries. Undoubtedly, a major reason for the failure to implement plans is that they lacked the force of law; "the status of the General Plan for the Development of Moscow is that of recommendation, not requirement" (Khorev & Glushkova 1991: 181). According to the authors of that statement, such a lack of planning law was characteristic only of Cyprus, Mongolia and the USSR!

But above all, the powerful individual can distort the plan, whether it be President Jackson siting the US Treasury in defiance of L'Enfant's plan for Washington, in order to shut out his view of the Capitol from the White House, or Stalin's industrial ministers inverting Milyutin's plan for Stalingrad in order to give their factories the best sites. Perhaps finally, that long-suffering, but ultimate power, the people, will exert their pressure to distort the plan, if it fails to provide the way of life that they want.

If, then, the answer to the first question is that the Soviet Union did not create that qualitatively different city with a qualitatively different way of life, which was its professed aim, one must turn to the second question and consider the degree to which the Soviet city in its development was on a convergent path with the capitalist city. Some have denied convergence on the grounds that the Western city has not become more like the Soviet city, but of course convergence need not depend on both elements moving towards each other, but may come about by the approach of only one towards the other. Moreover, any convergence has not been of the theory; rather, as the socialist system tried to advance, it found itself (perhaps inevitably?) adopting more and more capitalist measures or measures resembling capitalist ones and therefore they converged in practice. In the context of town planning, it is the end-product on the ground that counts, rather than the theories that brought it about.

In contrast, Enyedi (1992) has suggested that there is just one global process of urbanization and that socialist cities participate in it. Since cities have functions that they must carry out regardless of system, the Soviet city has been advancing along the same inevitable developmental path, but with a substantial time-lag behind the Western city. This interpretation is undeniably true of certain issues; one such is considered in this book, the increase in the ownership and use of private cars. Both ownership and use in statistical terms are far behind those of the Western city, but both are rising in the same way as they did many decades earlier in the West. As they do so, all the same problems are met and similarly inadequate solutions are sought and sometimes tried. The pipe-dream of Soviet city planners that they could cope by building large numbers of underground carparks can be compared with the equally unrealistic proposals for dealing with traffic in British towns put forward in the Buchanan Report of 1963.

The gradual process of the emergence of socially distinct areas of towns is another way in which the Soviet town was slowly becoming closer in its geography to the Western town. In some respects, such as ethnically distinct areas within towns, the Soviet city, having inherited them had always resembled cities in other pluralist societies. However, this was not a process that one can describe as trailing along the same path as the Western city, which always had clear spatial separation of social groups. There was a long period at the height of the command economy in the USSR, when such spatial distinction was extremely weak and the building rather than the area denoted status. Convergence yes, but hardly a successive progression.

Finally, there is the question of what has been the legacy of the Soviet Union for the 15 republics which now succeed it. Undoubtedly, for all republics the most important achievement has not been directly a matter of town planning – the development of an educated population, thereby enhancing their human resources. For the Slavic and Baltic Republics, perhaps next in importance has been the urbanization of the population. In the southern republics there has been a movement towards greater urbanization, but in most the process has a long way still to go. Indeed, one of the most significant legacies of the Soviet period in general has been the creation of a north/south divide, or at least the failure to remove such a divide. The Slavic and Baltic republics – the north – in their culture and standard of living relate to the countries of western Europe, however much they may lag behind. The south – Central Asia and Azerbaydzhan – shares in many respects the problems of the less developed countries; ethnic turmoil is already sharply reducing the quality of life in several of these republics and is similarly having a negative effect on the intermediate republics of Armenia, Georgia and Moldavia. Kazakhstan, the last of the intermediate republics, with its near balance of Russian and Kazakh populations, stands poised between north and south, with the potential of going either way.

Although the level of urbanization varies considerably between republics, the planned urban artefact that the Soviets built was remarkably consistent everywhere. The features which give cultural individuality to towns in different areas are almost always old, pre-revolutionary in origin, occasionally with superficial modern borrowings from the past. The apartment block, normally of five storeys in smaller towns, higher in the larger centres, arranged in designated microregions, is the hallmark of the Soviet city. Such areas can be found elsewhere in the developed countries, for example Sarcelles in Paris, and they were exported on an extensive scale to the countries of the CMEA, but nowhere has such housing been so widespread. The standardization, resulting from planning norms, which was seen as a goal of the socialist city, has left an enduring stamp on housing and townscape. As the preceding chapters have stressed, the Soviet city suffered from and has left behind it a vast array of problems: inadequate housing supply, lack of service provision and effective infrastructure, environmental disruption, social disruption, growing traffic complications and many more. All of these are shared in varying degrees by the city produced by the market economy. Convergence of the two systems, in the sense of both having acquired the same problems and the same limited success in dealing with them, cannot be gainsaid. The difference in many such areas of difficulty is rather a matter of intensity. With the exception of traffic problems, most of the negative features of the ex-Soviet city are worse than in its Western counterparts, although in countries like Britain the housing situation may well be as bad and in the USA crime may well be even worse.

The post-Soviet city is having to face these inherited woes and to try to find solutions for them. In doing so, perhaps the first task will be to set up effective local government, with the concerns of the city at heart and the power to act to improve affairs. For 70 years or so, local government has been entirely under the control of the Communist Party and therefore of the central government. The finances raised by the Soviet city or town largely went to the central government, which then allocated resources back to the town. Central control of local government finance does not inevitably loosen in a market economy, as Britain has seen in the recent period of rate-capping by the central government of local authorities' revenue raising, but independent local authorities can at least fight to try to obtain the resources they need and should have some powers to distribute them. In distributing resources to solve the problems, the post-Soviet city will have to build on, and improve, the legacy of planning experience from the previous regime.

For all the changes in the economic situation, in the political structure and in concepts about the city, a plan is still necessary. Almost all societies recognize the need for some level of control over the development of towns, whether by Town and Country Planning Acts, or zoning laws, or whatever. The Soviet Union in its ultimate phase still saw town plans as part of the process of bringing about *perestroyka,* and new plans were being drawn up. That plans in the past have not been 100 per cent successful is a universal experience and certainly does not mean that there should be no plan. What the plans will need is to be flexible, as they were not in past; they cover a long time period, during which circumstances may change considerably. They must also have force of law.

The most probable development of all in the rapidly changing and unstable situation of the post-Soviet republics is that the basic role of the plan will change, from being the innovator of urban form and function, to being the controller of what individual persons and organizations choose to do, from being compulsory to being restrictive. In other words, the plan of the future, like the British Town and Country Planning Acts or the US zoning laws, will not tell people what they must do, but rather will seek to prevent them from doing things that harm the quality of the urban environment for others. In the future, plans will still be made; without question, in spite of them, decisions will often continue to be taken on pragmatic grounds. Equally surely, the people will be the final arbiter in making the city the place in which they want to live and work.

BIBLIOGRAPHY

Abbreviations

AN   Akademiya Nauk
GO   Geograficheskoye Obshchestva
IG   Institut Geografii
LO   Leningradskoye Otdeleniye
MGU   Moskovskiy Gosudarstvenniy Universitet
SO   Sibirskoye Otdeleniye
TGU   Tartuskiy Gosudarstvenniy Universitet
TSNIIP   Tsentral'nyy Nauchno-Issledovatel'skiy Institut Proyektov
VGO   Vsesoyuznoye Geograficheskoye Obshchestvo
VNII   Vsesoyuznyy Nauchno-Issledobatel'skiy Institut

Abbakumova, G. A. 1976. Sozdaniye torgovykh tsentrov – osnovnoye napravleniye sovershenstvovaniya seti torgovo-bytovogo obsluzhivaniya. In *Sovershenstvovaniye Seti Uchrezhdeniy Kul'turno-bytovogo Obsluzhivaniya*, 22–3. Moscow: TSNIIP Gradostroitel'stva.
Abramyan, L. A. & R. V. Pikichyan 1989. Zametki po etnografii sovremennogo goroda. II Avtomobil'naya kultura Yerevana. In *Etnokontaktnyye Zony v Yevropeyskoy Chasti SSSR (Geografiya, Dinamika, Metody Izucheniya)*, I. I. Krupnik (ed.), 148–59. Moscow: Moskovskiy Filial GO SSSR.
Agafonov, N. T. & O. P. Litovka (eds) 1979. *Geografiya v Sisteme Kompleksnogo Ekonomicheskogo i Sotsial'nogo Planirovaniya*. Leningrad: GO SSSR.
Agafonov, N. T. & M. N. Mezhevich 1985. Marksizm o sotsial'no-ekonomicheskoy obuslovlennosti rasseleniya (stat'ya vtoraya). *Izvestiya VGO* **117**(2), 110–19 (for first article, see S. B. Lavrov & M. N. Mezhevich).
Agafonov, N. T. & V. P. Pavchinskiy 1972. Moskva-Leningrad: proizvodstvenno-territorial'naya sistema? *Vestnik MGU Seriya 5 Geografiya*, No.4, 55–60.
Agafonov, N. T., Ye. D. Klimenko, V. I. Meleshchenko 1978. Regional'nyye narodnokhozyaystvennyye kompleksy kak ob'yekty planirovaniya i upravleniya (na primere Leningrada i Leningradskoy Oblasti). *Voprosy Geografii* **109**, 130–43.
Agafonov, N. T., S. B. Lavrov, B. S. Khorev 1983. On some faulty concepts in Soviet urban studies. *Soviet Geography* **34**(3), 179–87.
Agafonov, N. T., M. N. Mezhevich, B. N. Starinskiy 1985. Promyshlennyy kompleks krupnogo goroda i protsessy aglomerirovaniya. *Izvestiya VGO* **117**(1), 10–15.
Agas'yants, A. A. & R. V. Gorbanev 1985. Odna iz klyuchevykh problem. *Gorodskoye Khozyaystvo Moskvy*, No.2, 15–18.
Aitov, N. A., B. I. Gobako, F. A. Igebayeva 1982. *Gorod. Naseleniye. Trudovyye Resursy*. Ufa: Bashkirskoye Knizhnoye Izdatel'stvo.
Aitov, N. A., V. G. Mordkovich, M. Kh. Titma 1988. *Sovetskiy Gorod: Sotsial'naya Struktura*. Moscow: Mysl'.
Akhiyezer, A. S. 1981. Otsenka prostranstvenno-predmetnoy sredy kak problema kul'tury. In *Chelovek i Sreda; Psikhologicheskiye Problemy*, 19–22. Tallin.
Akhiyezer, A. S. & P. M. Il'in 1975. Zadachi razrabotki sotsial'nykh otsenok territorii v usloviyakh nauchno-tekhnicheskoy revolyutsii. *Izvestiya AN SSSR; Seriya Geograficheskaya*, No.1, 86–92.
— 1977. Iyerarkhiya otsenok urbanizirovannoy territorii. In *Gorodskaya Sreda i Puti yeye Optimizat-*

sii, Yu. V. Medvedkov (ed.), 157–63. Moscow: Institut Geografii AN SSSR.

Akhiyezer, A. S., M. N. Nochevnik, O. N. Yanitsky, L. B. Moskvin (eds) 1980. *Nekotoryye Problemy Urbanizatsii i Gradostroitel'stva (sotsial'no-ekonomicheskiye aspekty)*. Moscow: AN USSR.

Akiner, S., R. U. Cooke, R. A. French 1992. Salt damage to Islamic monuments in Uzbekistan. *Geographical Journal* **158**, 257–72.

Alekseyev, A. N. & O. I. Shkaratan (eds) 1973–5. *Planirovaniye Sotsial'nogo Razvitiya Gorodov*, Vyp.1 1973; Vyp.2 1975. Moscow: Institut Sotsiologicheskikh Issledovaniy et al.

Alekseyev, V. V. 1987. *Urbanizatsiya Sovetskoy Sibiri*. Novosibirsk: Nauka SO

Alekseyeva, T. I. 1987. *Regional'nyye Osobennosti Gradostroitel'stva v Sibiri i na Severe*. Leningrad: Stroyizdat LO.

Altstadt-Mirhadi, A. 1986. Baku: transformation of a Muslim town. In *The city in late Imperial Russia*, M. F. Hamm (ed.), 283–318. Bloomington: Indiana University Press.

Alymov, A. N. 1974. Sotsial'no-ekonomicheskoye planirovaniye razvitiye gorodov. *Kommunist Ukrainy*, No.6, 67–76.

Andrusz, G. 1984. *Housing and urban development in the USSR*. London: Macmillan.

— 1987. The built environment in Soviet theory and practice. *International Journal of Urban and Regional Research* **11**, 478–98.

— 1990. Housing policy in the Soviet Union. In *Housing Policies in eastern Europe and the Soviet Union*, J. A. A. Sillince (ed.), 228–330. London: Routledge.

Animitsa, Ye. G. 1969. *Malyye i Sredniye Goroda Sverdlovskoy Oblasti, Geograficheskiye Problemy ikh Razvitiya*. Avtoreferat. Moscow: Institut Geografii AN SSSR.

Annenkov, V. V. & O. P. Litovka 1980. Geograficheskoye issledovaniye territorial'noy organizatsii goroda. *Izvestiya VGO* **112**(5), 446–51.

Anokhin, A. A. 1984. *Sotsial'naya geografiya SSSR (Problemy Metodologii i Teorii)*. Leningrad: AN SSSR; GO.

Artemov, V. A. 1986. Izmeneniya usloviyy zhiznedeyatel'nosti gorodskogo naseleniya. In *Sotsiologicheskiye Issledovaniye Problem Goroda i Zhilishcha 1970–1980 gg.*, B. P. Kutyrev (ed.), 69–77. Novosibirsk: Nauka SO.

Artemov, V. A., N. A. Balykova, Z. I. Kalugina 1982. *Vremya Naseleniya Goroda: Planirovaniye i Ispol'zovaniye*. Novosibirsk: Nauka SO.

Artem'yev, S. S. (ed.) 1979a. *Avtomobilizatsiya i Rasseleniye (Voprosy Sistemnogo Analiza)*, Vyp.1, Moscow: VNII Sistemnykh Issledovaniy.

Artem'yev, S. S. 1979b. O granichnykh usloviyakh avtomobilizatsii. In *Avtomobilizatsiya i Rasseleniye (Voprosy Sistemnogo Analiza)*, Vyp.1, S. S. Artem'yev (ed.), 21–6. Moscow: VNII Sistemnykh Issledovaniy.

Ausmane, A. Ya. 1980. K voprosu opredeleniya granits rizhskoy aglomeratsii. *Voprosy Gradostroitel'stva* 7, 11–20.

Baburov, A. 1977. *Historic Cities of Georgia: some aspects for Preservation*. Tbilisi: Academy of Sciences of the Georgian SSR.

Baklanova, T. A. 1977. Territorial'naya podvizhnost' naseleniya kak proyavleniye otsenok sredy v usloviyakh krupnogo goroda. In *Gorodskaya Sreda i Puti yeye Optimizatsii*, Yu. V. Medvedkov (ed.), 55–60. Moscow: IG AN SSSR.

Bakshteyn, I. M., N. B. Barbash, A. A. Vysokovskiy, K. M. Savkin 1986. Sotsial'no-territorial'nyye obshchnosti v gorode i gradomorfologicheskoye rayonirovaniya (na primere g. Kalugi). In *Problemy Razvitiya Sotsial'no-Demograficheskikh Grupp i Sotsial'no-territorial'nykh Obshchnostey; Sbornik Trudov*, Vyp.4, O. S. Pchelintsev & N. N. Nozdrina (eds), 86–94. Moscow: VNII Sistemnykh Issledovaniy.

Baldin, V. I. 1986. Zavisit ot nas, *Gorodskoye Khozyaystvo Moskvy*, No.3, 35–6.

Baranov, A. V. 1981. *Sotsial'no-demograficheskoye Razvitiye Krupnogo Goroda*. Moscow: Finansy i Statistika.

Barbash, N. B. 1975. Vyyavleniye otnoshenii naseleniya k elementam gorodskoy sredy. *Izvestiya AN SSSR Seriya Geograficheskaya*, No.6, 97–109.

— 1977. Opyt' issledovaniye faktornoy ekologii Moskvy. In *Gorodskaya Sreda i Puti yeye Optimizatsii*, Yu. V. Medvedkov (ed.), 37–53. Moscow: IG AN.

— 1978. Sopostavleniye aspektov gorodskoy sredy Moskvy i ikh territorial'noy organizatsii. In *Urbanizatsiya i Formirovaniye Sistem Rasselenia*, G. M. Lappo & Yu. L. Pivovarov (eds), 116–23. Moscow: Moskovskiy Filial GO.

— 1979. Faktornoekologicheskaya struktura rasseleniya v Moskve. In *Geograficheskiye Issledovaniya Gorodskoy Sredy*, Yu. V. Medvedkov & I. V. Kantsebovskaya (eds), 39–59. Moscow: AN.

— 1980. Territorial'noye sootnosheniye mest s dopolnyayushchimi funktsiyami v g. Moskve. *Izvestiya AN SSSR Seriya Geograficheskaya*, No.3, 53–66. Translated as: Spatial relations among places with complementary functions within the city of Moscow. *Soviet Geography* 1982, **23**, 77–94.

— 1982. Analiz pokazateley fizicheskogo razvitiya novorozhdennykh kak kharakteristika sostoyaniya gorodskoy sredy. In *Vzaimodeystviye Khozyaystva i Prirody v Gorodskikh i Geotekhsistemakh*, 83–92. Moscow: IG AN. Translated as, Physical development of infants as an indicator of the condition of the urban environment,. *Soviet Geography*, 1983, **24**, 204–13.

— 1983. Nekotoryye sotsial'no-demograficheskiye osobennosti rasseleniya v Moskve. *Izvestiya AN SSSR Seriya Geograficheskaya*, No.1, 72–81.

— 1984a. Otsenka naseleniyem uchastkov gorodskoy sredy (na osnove dannykh o zayavkakh na obmen zhil'ya). *Izvestiya AN SSSR; Seriya Geograficheskaya*, No.5, 81–91.

— 1984b. Sotsial'no-geograficheskiye osobennosti rasseleniya v krupnom gorode (na primere g. Moskvy). In *Prikladnyye Sotsial'no-geograficheskiye Issledovaniya*, T. Raitviir (ed.), 58–61. Tartu: Kafedra Ekonomicheskoy Geografii TGU et al.

— 1985. Osvoyeniye naseleniyem gorodskogo prostranstva. *Izvestiya VGO*, **117**(6), 552–9.

— 1986. *Metodika Izucheniya Territorial'noy Differentsiatsii Gorodskoy Sredy*. Moscow: IG AN SSSR.

Barbash, N. B. & A. E. Gutnov 1980. Urban planning aspects of the spatial organization of Moscow. *Soviet Geography* **21**, 557–73.

Bater, J. H. 1973. The development of public transportation in St Petersburg, 1860–1914. *The Journal of Transport History*, NS **11**(2), 85–102.

— 1974. The journey to work in St Petersburg 1860–1914. *The Journal of Transport History*, NS **12**(4), 214–33.

— 1976. *St Petersburg: industrialization and change*. London: Edward Arnold.

— 1977. Soviet town planning: theory and practice in the 1970s. *Progress in Human Geography* **1**(2), 177–207.

— 1978. Planning problems in Siberian new towns. *Bloomsbury Geographer* **9**, 55–62.

— 1980. *The Soviet city: ideal and reality*. London: Edward Arnold.

— 1984. The Soviet city: continuity and change in privilege and place. In *The city in cultural context*, J. Agnew, J. Mercer, D. Sopher (eds), 134–62. London: Allen & Unwin.

— 1986a. Some recent perspectives on the Soviet city. *Urban Geography* **7**(1), 93–102.

— 1986b. Between old and new: St Petersburg in the late imperial era. In *The city in late Imperial Russia*, M. F. Hamm (ed.), 43–78. Bloomington: Indiana University Press.

— 1989. *The Soviet scene: a geographical perspective*. London: Edward Arnold.

Belenko, A. I. 1983. *Vse o Donetske: Spravochnik*. Donetsk: Donbas.

Belkin, Ye. V. & F. E. Sheregi 1985. *Formirovaniye Naseleniye v Zone BAM*. Moscow: Mysl'.

Belousov, V. N. (ed.) 1980. *Kompleksnaya Rayonnaya Planirovka*. Moscow: Stroyizdat.

Belov, S. I. 1989. A geography of motor vehicle accident trauma in Belorussia. *Soviet Geography* **30**(2), 103–8.

Berton, K. 1977. *Moscow: an architectural history*. London: Studio Vista.

Bil'chak, V. S. 1984. Rol' geografii v kompleksnom planirovanii ekonomicheskogo i sotsial'nogo razvitiya oblastnogo tsentra (na materialakh Kaliningrada). *Izvestiya VGO* **116**(5), 454–7.

Bliznakov, M. 1976. Urban planning in the USSR: integrative theories. In *The City in Russian History*, M. F. Hamm (ed.), 243–56. Lexington: University Press of Kentucky.

Bobylev, S. N. & O. V. Korotkova 1984. Utilizatsiya otkhodov i ispol'zovaniye gorodskikh territorii. In *Ekonomiko-geograficheskiye Problemy Ekologii*, T. S. Khachaturov (ed.), 15–27. Moscow: Izdatel'stvo MGU.

Bocharov, Yu. P. & N. R. Frezinskaya 1970. *Sotsial'nyye Problemy Gorodov-tsentrov Nauchnoy Dey-atel'nosti*. Moscow: Sovetskaya Sotsiologicheskaya Assotsiatsiya.

Bocharov, Yu. P. & O. K. Kudryavtsev 1972. *Planirovochnaya Struktura Sovremennogo Goroda*. Moscow: Stroyizdat.

Bocharov, Yu. & V. Lyubovnyy 1976. Kompleksnoye razvitiye krupnykh gorodov. *Planovoye Khozyaystvo*, No.12, 78–91.

— 1979. Gorod – tselostnyy sotsial'no-ekonomicheskiy kompleks. *Kommunist*, No.2, 48–58.

Bogayenko, V. A., S. I. Ishchuk, A. V. Stepanenko 1980. *Kompleksnoye Planirovaniye Sotsial'no-eko-nomicheskogo Razvitiya Goroda*. Kiev: Kievskiy Gosudarstvennyy Universitet.

Bond, A. R. 1984a. Transport development at Noril'sk. *Soviet Geography* **25**(2), 103–21.

— 1984b. Urban planning and design in the Soviet north: the Noril'sk experience. *Soviet Geography* **25**(3), 145–65.

— 1984c. Economic development at Noril'sk. *Soviet Geography* **25**(5), 354–68.

— 1984d. Air pollution in Noril'sk: a Soviet worst case? *Soviet Geography* **25**(9), 665–80.

— 1985. Northern settlement family-style: labour planning and population policy in Noril'sk. *Soviet Geography* **26**(1), 26–48.

— 1988. Moscow under restructuring. *Soviet Geography* **29**(1), 1–15.

Borisenko, G. G. 1982. The role of former rayon seats in the provision of services. *Soviet Geography* **23**(2),

Borisov, A. P., E. Ya. Bubes, N. G. Revunova 1981. *Ekonomika Gradostroitel'stva*. Leningrad: Stroyizdat LO.

Borshchevskiy, M. V. (ed.) 1988. *Sotsial'nyye Problemy Arkhitekturno-gradostroitel'nogo Razvitiya Moskvy*. Moscow: TSNIIP Gradostroitel'stva.

Borshchevskiy, M. V., Ye. V. Uspenskiy, O. I. Shkaratan 1975. *Gorod. Metodologicheskiye Problemy Kompleksnogo Sotsial'nogo i Ekonomicheskogo Planirovaniya*. Moscow: Nauka.

Boyko, V. I. (ed.) 1981. *Gorodskoye Naseleniye Tuvinskoy ASSR*. Novosibirsk: Nauka SO.

— 1982. *Sotsiologicheskiye Kharakteristiki Gorodskogo Naseleniya Tuvinskoy ASSR*. Novosibirsk: Nauka SO.

Bozhkov, O. & V. Golofast 1985. Otsenka naseleniyem uslovii zhizni v krupnykh gorodakh. *Sotsiologicheskiye Issledovaniya*, No.3,

Bradley, J. 1984. *Muzhik and Muscovite: urbanization in late Imperial Russia*. Berkeley: University of California Press.

— 1986. Moscow: from big village to metropolis. In *The city in late Imperial Russia*, M. F. Hamm (ed.), 9–41. Bloomington: Indiana University Press.

Broner, D. L. 1980. *Zhilishchnoye Stroitel'stvo i Demograficheskiye Protessy*. Moscow: Statistika.

Brower, D. R. 1990. *The Russian City between Tradition and Modernity 1850–1900*. Berkeley: University of California Press.

Brumfield, W. C. (ed.) 1990. *Reshaping Russian architecture: Western technology, Utopian Dreams*. Cambridge: Cambridge University Press.

Brumfield, W. C. & B. A. Ruble (eds) 1993. *Russian housing in the modern age*. Cambridge: Woodrow Wilson Center Press and Cambridge University Press.

Budina, O. R. & M. N. Smeleva 1989. *Gorod i Narodnyye Traditsii Russkikh*. Moscow: Nauka.

Bugromenko, V. N. 1974. Territorial'naya struktura goroda i vozmozhnosti yeye modelirovania. *Vestnik MGU Seriya 5 Geografiya*, No.4, 63–8.

— 1978. Kompleksnoye planirovaniye goroda i issledovaniye yego territorial'noy struktury. *Izvestiya AN SSSR Seriya Geograficheskaya*, No.1, 68–76.

— 1984. *Territorial'nyye Aspekty Razvitiya Transportnoy Infrastruktury: Sbornik Nauchnykh Trudov*. Vladivostok: AN SSSR.

Bunkse E. V. 1979. The role of a humane environment in Soviet urban planning. *The Geographical Review* **69**(4), 379–94.

Cattell, D. T. 1976. Soviet cities and consumer welfare planning. In *The city in Russian history*, M. F. Hamm (ed.), 257–75. Lexington: University Press of Kentucky.

Bibliography

Chislennost' Naseleniya RSFSR po Gorodam, Rabochim Poselkam i Rayonam na 1 Yanvarya 1991g. 1991. Moscow: Goskomstat RSFSR.

Chuverin, I. I. 1979. Vzaimodeystviye obshchestvennogo i individual'nogo transporta. In *Avtomobilizatsiya i Rasseleniye (Voprosy Sistemnogo Analiza)*, Vyp.1, S. S. Artem'yev (ed.), 28–34. Moscow: VNII Sistemnykh Issledovaniy.

Clark, Sir Kenneth 1964. *Ruskin today*. London: Murray.

Cooke, C. 1983. "Form is a function x": the development of the Constructivist architect's design method. In *Russian avant-garde art and architecture*, C. Cooke (ed.), 34–49. London: Academy Editions.

Crouch, M. 1979. Problems of Soviet urban transport. *Soviet Studies* **31**(2), 231–56.

Dadashev, A. & S. Sokolov 1983. Sotsial'no-ekonomicheskiye problemy upravleniya trudovymi resursami v krupnom gorode. *Planovoye Khozyaystvo*, No.11, 95–100.

Daniloff, R. 1983. Restoring a Russian heritage turns out to be a Byzantine task. *The Smithsonian* **13**, 64–72.

Davidovich, V. G. 1949. Formy rasseleniya v ugol'nykh basseynakh SSSR. *Voprosy Geografii* **14**, 3–28.

— 1956. O tipologii rasseleniya v gruppakh gorodov i poselkov SSSR. *Voprosy Geografii* **38**, 27–77.

— 1959. O razvitii seti gorodov SSSR za 40 let. *Voprosy Geografii* **45**, 37–71.

— 1965. O zakonomernostyakh i tendentsiyakh gorodskogo rasseleniya v SSSR. *Voprosy Geografii* **66**, 6–33.

Davidovich, V. G. & B. S. Khorev 1961. *Goroda-Sputniki; Sbornik Statey*. Moscow: Geografgiz.

Davidovich, V. G. & O. K. Kudryavtsev (eds) 1968. *Rasseleniye v Gorodakh (Kolichestvennyye Zakonomernosti)*. Moscow: Mysl'.

Demidenko, E. S. 1980. *Demograficheskiye Problemy i Perspektivy Bol'shikh Gorodov*. Moscow: Statistika.

Demyanovskiy, V. S. 1986. Dinamika naseleniya novogo goroda. *Izvestiya AN SSSR; Seriya Geograficheskaya*, No.3, 63–73.

Derbinova, M. P., I. G. Mikhnenko, L. S. Ostapenko, N. P. Terekhova 1985. Moscow's Lenin borough: ecological aspects of development. *Soviet Geography* **26**(7), 566–70.

Dienes, L. 1988. Crime and punishment in the USSR: new information on distribution. *Soviet Geography* **29**(9), 793–808.

Dimaio, A. J. 1974. *Soviet urban housing: problems and policies*. New York: Praeger.

Dmitriyev, A. V., A. M. Lola, M. N. Mezhevich 1988. *Gde Zhivet Sovetskiy Chelovek*. Moscow: Mysl'.

Dmitriyev, A. V. & M. N. Mezhevich (eds) 1982. *Gorod: Problemy Sotsial'nogo Razvitiya*. Leningrad: Nauka.

Dmitriyev, S., V. Loktionov, Ye. Saburov 1987. Zhilishchnoye stroitel'stvo na novom etape. *Planovoye Khozyaystvo*, No.2, 69–75.

Dmitriyeva, O. G. 1991. Regional policy and regional structure in the USSR. In *Economic diagnostics and forecasting of regional development*, R. Shniper & A. Novoselov (eds), 141–67. Novosibirsk: Institute of Economics and Industrial Engineering.

Dmitriyevskaya, N. F. 1981. O sotsial'no-geograficheskom aspekte prostranstvennoy podvizhnosti naseleniya. *Izvestiya VGO*, No.5, 411–18.

Dolgov, L. N. & S. I. Lapekin 1983. *Passazhirskiy Transport Moskvy: Spravochnik*. Moscow: Moskovskiy Rabochiy.

— 1986. *Passazhirskiy Transport Moskvy 1986: Spravochnik*. Moscow: Moskovskiy Rabochiy.

Dumnov, D. 1986. Byudzhet vremeni rabochikh, sluzhashchikh i kolkhoznikov. *Planovoye khozyaystvo*, No.6, 116–17.

Dzhaoshvili, V. Sh. 1978a. *Urbanizatsiya Gruzii: Genezis, Protsessy, Problemy*. Tbilisi: Metsniereba.

— 1978b. Etnicheskiye aspekty urbanizatsii Zakavkaz'ya. In *Geograficheskiye Problemy Regional'nogo Razvitiya i Gosudarstvennoye Planirovaniye*, V. V. Pokshishevskiy et al. (eds), 105–9. Tbilisi: IGAN USSR, IGAN Az SSR.

Ekkel, B. M. 1980. Polarization of the structure of urbanised areas with a view to improving living conditions and environmental protection. *Soviet Geography* **21**(2),

Ekonomicheskoye i Sotsial'noye Razvitiye g. Frunze: Statisticheskiy Sbornik. Frunze: Izdatel'stvo "Kyrgyzstan".

Elliot, D. & V. Dudakov 1989. *100 years of Russian art*. London: Lund Humphries.

Enyedi, G. 1992. Turning points of urbanization in East Central Europe. In *New perspectives in Hungarian geography*, A. Kertész & Z. Kovács (eds), 105–13. Budapest: Akadémiai Kiadó.

Fedorov, G. M. 1984. Teoreticheskiye i metodicheskiye osnovy geodemograficheskoy tipologii mikrorayonov. In *Sotsial'naya Geografiya SSSR (Problemy Metodologii i Teorii)*, A. A. Anokhin (ed.), 97–105. Leningrad: AN SSSR; GO.

Fedorov, Ye. P. 1980. Printsipy formirovaniya i pereraspredeleniya zhilishchnogo fonda v SSSR. In *Nekotoryye Problemy Urbanizatsii i Gradostroitel'stva (sotsial'no-ekonomicheskiye aspekty)*, A. S. Akhiyezer, M. N. Nochevnik, O. N. Yanitsky, L. B. Moskvin (eds), 21–7. Moscow: AN USSR.

Fedorov, Yu. D. 1986. Gradostroitel'nyye problemy razvitiya narodno-khozyaystvennogo kompleksa Moskvy i Moskovskoy oblasti v 1980–1990 gody. In *Geograficheskiye Problemy Razvitiya Narodnogo Khozyaystva Moskovskogo Rayona*, V. G. Glushkov & N. P. Matveyev (eds), 3–14. Moscow: Moskovskiy Filial VGO.

Fenin, L. N. 1971. Sotsial'nyye peremeshcheniya i sotsial'naya geografiya krupnogo goroda. *Trudy Ufimskogo Aviatsionnogo Instituta im. Ordzhonikidze* **37**, 38–45.

Filina, V. N. 1985. Vzaimosvyaz' osnovnykh sostavlyayushchikh razvitiya Moskvy: kontseptsii i tendentsii. *Izvestiya VGO* **117**(6), 511–17.

—— 1986. Mayatnikovaya migratsiya naseleniya i formirovaniye sistem rasseleniya. *Izvestiya AN SSSR; Seriya Geograficheskaya*, No.4, 37–46. Translated as, The influence of local commuting patterns on urban settlement systems. *Soviet Geography* **28**(10), 1987, 728–41.

Fisher, J. C. 1962. Planning the City of Socialist Man. *Journal of the Institute of American Town Planners* **28**(4), 251–62.

Fomin, G. N. 1989. *Gradostroitel'stvo i Arkhitektura: Problemy i Puti Sovershenstvovaniya*. Moscow: Stroyizdat.

Fomin, I. A. 1974. *Razvitiye Gorodov v Promyshlennykh Rayonakh*. Moscow: Stroyizdat.

French, R. A. 1979. The individuality of the Soviet city. In French & Hamilton (1979), 73–104.

—— 1983. The early and medieval Russian town. In *Studies in Russian historical geography*, 2, J. H. Bater & R. A. French (eds), 249–77. London: Academic Press.

—— 1984. Moscow, the socialist metropolis. In *Metropolis 1890–1940*, A. Sutcliffe (ed.), 355–79. London: Mansell.

—— 1987. Changing spatial patterns in Soviet cities – planning or pragmatism? *Urban Geography* **8**(4), 309–20.

French, R. A. & F. E. I. Hamilton (eds) 1979. *The socialist city: spatial structure and urban policy*. Chichester, England: Wiley.

Frolic, B. M. 1964. The Soviet city. *Town Planning Review* **34**(4), 285–306.

—— 1976. The new Moscow city plan. In *The city in Russian history*, M. F. Hamm (ed.), 276–88. Lexington: University of Kentucky Press.

Gabiani, A. A. & R. G. Gachechiladze 1982. *Nekotoryye Voprosy Geografii Prestupnosti*. Tbilisi: Izdatel'stvo Tbilisskogo Universiteta.

Gachechiladze, R. 1990. Social-geographical problems of a metropolitan region within a Soviet republic (a case study of the Tbilisi metropolitan region, Georgia, USSR). *Geoforum* **21**(4), 475–82.

Gachechiladze, R. G. & V. V. Gudzhabidze 1979. Issledovaniya kachestva gorodskoy sredy (na primere Tbilisskoy aglomeratsii). In *Geografiya Naseleniya v Sisteme Kompleksnogo Ekonomicheskogo i Sotsial'nogo Planirovaniya*, N. T. Agafonov & O. P. Litovka (eds), 90–96. Leningrad: Izdatel'stvo VGO.

Gladysheva, Ye. N. & O. P. Nazarevskiy 1950. Gorodskiye poseleniya Kazakhstana – novostroyki Stalinskikh pyatiletok. *Voprosy Geografii* **19**, 111–66.

Glazychev, V. L. 1984. *Sotsial'no-ekologicheskaya Interpretatsiya Gorodskoy Sredy*. Moscow: Nauka.

Bibliography

Glazyrin, M. V. 1983. *Upravleniye Sotsial'no-ekonomicheskim Razvitiyem Goroda.* Novosibirsk: Nauka.

Glik, F. G. & A. Ye. Rogovin 1977. *Razvitiye Sistemy Passazhirskogo Transporta v Krupnykh Gorodakh (na primere Minska).* Moscow: Stroyizdat.

Glushkova, V. G. 1981. Osnovnyye cherty razvitiya gorodskogo khozyaystva i demograficheskoy situatsii Moskvy v 1960–1970ye gody. In *Russkiy Gorod: Moskva i Podmoskov'ye,* 4, V. L. Yanin (ed.), 26–42. Moscow: Izdatel'stvo Moskovskogo Universiteta.

—1986. Sotsial'no-ekonomicheskoye sovershenstvovaniye Moskvy v sovremennykh usloviyakh nauchno-tekhnicheskogo progressa i perevoda ekonomiki na intensivnyy put' razvitiya. In *Geograficheskiye Problemy Razvitiya Khozyaystva Moskovskogo Regiona,* V. G. Glushkova & N. P. Matveyev (eds), 80–93. Moscow: Moskovskiy Filial, VGO.

—1989. Sotsial'naya sfera Moskvy: sovremennoye sostoyaniye, problemy i ikh razresheniye. In *Sotsial'nyy Faktor v Ekonomicheskoy Geografii,* O. A. Kibal'chich (ed.), 83–102. Moscow: Moskovskiy Filial Geograficheskogo Obshchestva.

Glushkova, V. G. & Yu. D. Fedorov 1986. Opyt perspektivnogo planirovaniya i proyektirovaniya razvitiya Moskvy. *Voprosy Geografii* 129, 138–46.

Glushkova, V. G. & B. S. Khorev 1986. Problema obespecheniya narodnogo khozyaystva Moskvy trudovymi resursami i ogranichaniye rosta goroda. In *Russkiy Gorod (Issledovaniya i Materialy)* 8, 237–254. Moscow: Izdatel'stvo Moskovskogo Universiteta.

Glushkova, V. G. & B. S. Khorev 1990. Problemy sotsial'no-ekologicheskogo razvitiya Moskvy v sovremennykh usloviyakh. In *Russkiy Gorod* 9, V. L. Yanin (ed.), 3–39. Moscow: Izdatel'stvo Moskovskogo Universiteta.

Glushkova, V. G. & N. P. Matveyev (eds) 1986. *Geograficheskiye Problemy Razvitiya Khozyaystva Moskovskogo Regiona.* Moscow; Moskovskiy Filial, VGO.

Glushkova, V. G. & A. S. Zholkov 1986. *Realizatsiya Planov Sotsial'no-ekonomicheskogo Razvitiya i Gradostroitel'nogo Sovershenstvovaniya Krupnykh Gorodov.* Moscow: MGTSNTI, Seriya "Problemy Bol'shikh Gorodov" No.6.

Gohstand, R. 1983. The geography of trade in nineteenth-century Russia. In *Studies in Russian historical geography,* Vol. 2, J. H Bater & R. A. French (eds), 329–75. London: Academic Press.

Gordon, L. A., E. V. Klopov, L. A. Onikov 1977. *Cherty Sotsialisticheskogo Obraza Zhizni: Byt Gorodskikh Rabochikh Vchera, Segodnya, Zavtra.* Moscow: Znaniye.

Gornostayeva, G. A. 1982. Izmeneniye funktsional'nykh osobennostey goroda v svyazi s yego rostom. *Vestnik MGU Seriya 5 Geografiya,* No.2, 68–73.

—1983. Urovni razvitiya sotsial'noy infrastruktury krupneyshikh gorodov. *Vestnik MGU Seriya 5 Geografiya,* No.6, 24–31.

—1988. Problemy razvitiya zhilishchnoy infrastruktury gorodov Moskovskoy oblasti. *Vestnik MGU Seriya 5 Geografiya,* No.6, 9–19.

—1989a. *Recent changes in the sizes of Siberian cities.* Soviet Geography 30(7), 525–38.

—1989b. *Osobennosti sovremennoy urbanizatsii v SSSR.* In Mirovaya Urbanizatsiya: Geograficheskiye Problemy, Yu. L. Pivovarov & O. V. Gritsay (eds), 39–51. Moscow: Moskovskiy Filial GO SSSR.

Gorodskoye Poseleniye RSFSR po dannym vsesoyuznoy perepisi naseleniya 1989 goda 1991. Moscow: Goskomstat.

Grabar', I. E. 1969. *O Russkoy Arkhitekture.* Moscow: Nauka.

Grant, S. A. (ed.) 1980. *Soviet housing and urban design.* Washington: US Dept. of Housing and Urban Development.

Grebennikov, V. G., O. S. Pchelintsev, S. S. Shatalin 1987. *Intensifikatsiya Obshchestvennogo Proizvodstva: Sotsial'no-ekonomicheskiye Problemy.* Moscow: Politizdat.

Grigor'yevaya, L. A., V. A. Sukhin, Yu. I. Tsymlyakov (eds) 1986. *Sotsial'naya Infrastruktura i Uroven' Zhizni Naseleniya Krupnogo Goroda.* Leningrad: Izdatel'stvo Leningradskogo Universiteta.

Gudzhabidze, V. 1978. Journey-to-work in the small and medium towns of Georgia. *Acta Universitatis Lodziensis: Nauki Matematyczno-Przyrodnicze,* Seria II, zeszut 15, 67–80.

Gulyanitskiy, N. 1973. Osobennosti sovremennogo podkhoda k razvitiyu istoricheskikh gorodov v

SSSR. In *Gorod i Vremya*, E. Gol'dzamt et al. (eds), 200–217. Moscow: Stroyizdat.

— 1985. Russkiy regulyarnyy gorod na traditsionnoy osnove. *Arkhitekturnoye Nasledstvo* **33**, 3–13.

Gutkind, E. A. 1972. *International history of city development*, 8: *urban development in eastern Europe, Bulgaria, Romania and the USSR*. New York: Free Press.

Gutnov, A. E. et al. 1970. *The ideal communist city*. New York: Braziller.

Hall, P. 1966. *The world cities*. London: Weidenfeld & Nicholson.

— 1984. Metropolis 1890–1940: challenges and responses. In *Metropolis 1890–1940*, A. Sutcliffe (ed.), 19–66. London: Mansell.

Hamm, M. F. (ed.) 1976. *The city in Russian history*. Lexington: University of Kentucky Press.

— (ed.) 1986a. *The city in late Imperial Russia*. Bloomington: Indiana University Press.

— 1986b. The breakdown of urban modernization: a prelude to revolution. In *The city in late Imperial Russia*, M. F. Hamm (ed.), 182–200. Bloomington: Indiana University Press.

Hanchett, W. 1976. Tsarist statutory regulation of municipal government in the nineteenth century. In *The city in Russian history*, M. F. Hamm (ed.), 91–114. Lexington: University of Kentucky Press.

Harris, C. D. 1970. *Cities of the Soviet Union*. Chicago: University of Chicago Press.

Hartley, J. 1984. Town government in Saint Petersburg Guberniya after the Charter to the Towns of 1785. *Slavonic and East European Review* **62**(1), 61–84.

Hausladen, G. 1984. The satellite city in Soviet urban development. *Soviet Geography* **25**(4), 229–47.

— 1987a. Planning the development of the socialist city: the case of Dubna New Town. *Geoforum* **18**(1), 103–15.

— 1987b. Recent trends in Siberian urban growth. *Soviet Geography* **28**(2), 71–89.

Herlihy, P. 1986. *Odessa: a history 1794–1914*. Cambridge, Mass.: Harvard University Press.

Hittle, J. M. 1979. *The service city: State and townsmen in Russia, 1600–1800*. Cambridge, Mass.: Harvard University Press.

Howard, E. 1965. *Garden cities of tomorrow*. London: Faber and Faber.

Igonina, L. N. 1979. Trudovyye mayatnikovyye poyezdki v zheleznorudnykh promyshlennykh uzlakh KMA. *Vestnik MGU Seriya 5 Geografiya*, No.2, 41–7.

Ikonnikov, A. 1988. *Russian architecture of the Soviet period*. Moscow: Raduga Publishers.

Il'in, I. A. 1982a. *Ekonomika Gorodov: Regional'yy Aspekt Razvitiya*. Moscow: Nauka.

— 1982b. Zelenograd. In *Russkiy Gorod (Issledovaniya i Materialy)* **5**, V. L. Yanin (ed.), 37–50. Moscow: Izdatel'stvo Moskovskogo Universiteta.

Il'in, M. A. 1963. *Moskva*. Moscow: Izdatel'stvo Isskustvo.

Il'in, P. M. 1972. O geografii zhilishchnogo khozyaystva. *Voprosy Geografii* **91**, 164–75.

Il'in, P. M. & M. I. Kagan 1979. Nekotoryye novyye tendentsii v formirovanii vnutrigorodskikh svyazey naseleniya. In *Geograficheskiye Issledovaniya Gorodskoy Sredy*, Yu. V. Medvedkov & I. V. Kantsebovskaya (eds), 39–59. Moscow: IGAN.

Istoriya Moskvy **6**(2), *Period Postroyeniya Sotsializma (1917g. – iyun' 1941g.)* 1959. Moscow: AN SSSR.

Itogi Vsesoyuznoy Perepisi Naseleniya 1970 goda, **4**, *Natsional'nyy Sostav* 1973. Moscow: Statistika.

Ivanova, A. K. 1972. *Ekonomicheskaya Effektivnost' Ispol'zovaniya Gorodskikh Territorii*. Moscow: GOSINTI.

Ivanova, F. A. 1970. Nekotoryye voprosy optimizatsii prigorodnykh zon krupnykh gorodov. *Izvestiya VGO.*, No.3, 278–82.

Ivanova, I. V. 1962. *Balkhash – Planirovka i Zastroyka*. Moscow: Gosudarstvennoye Izdatel'stvo Literatury po Stroitel'stvu i Stroitel'nym Materialam.

Jones, R. E. 1973. Urban planning and the development of provincial towns in Russia, 1762–1796. In *The eighteenth century in Russia*, J. G. Garrard (ed.), 321–44. Oxford: Oxford University Press.

Kabakova, S. I. 1973. *Gradostroitel'naya Otsenka Territoriy Gorodov*. Moscow: Stroyizdat.

— 1976. *O Povyshenii Effektivnosti Ispol'zovaniya Territorii, Otvodimykh dlya Stroitel'stv*. Moscow.

Bibliography

—1981. *Ekonomicheskiye Problemy Ispol'zovaniya Zemel' v Stroitel'stva*. Moscow: Stroyizdat.

—1986. Tsennost' Moskovskikh zemel', *Gorodskoye Khozyaystvo Moskvy*, No.12, 12–13.

Kagan, M. I. 1977. Prostranstvennaya differentsiatsiya podvizhnosti naseleniya v gorode In *Gorodskaya Sreda i Puti yeye Optimizatsii*, Yu. V. Medvedkov (ed.), 121–35. Moscow: Institut Geografii AN SSSR.

—1980. Razvitiye vnutrigorodskikh svyazey naseleniya v protsesse urbanizatsii. In *Nekotoryye Problemy Urbanizatsii i Gradostroitel'stva (sotsial'no-ekonomicheskiye aspekty)*, A. S. Akhiyezer, M. N. Nochevnik, O. N. Yanitsky, L. B. Moskvin (eds), 51–6. Moscow: AN USSR.

Kaganovich, L. M. Undated, 1931? *Socialist reconstruction of Moscow and other cities in the USSR*. New York: International Publishers.

Kalinin, G. D. 1980. *Onega*. Arkhangel'sk: Severo-zapadnoye Knizhnoye Izdatel'stvo.

Karabanova, L. (ed.) 1986. *Passazhirskiy Transport Moskvy: Spravochnik*. Moscow: Moskovskiy Rabochiy.

Kasperovich, G. I. 1985. *Migratsiya Naseleniya v Gorode i Etnicheskiye Protsessy*. Minsk: Nauka i Tekhnika.

Kazanskiy, N. N. 1978. Problemy planovogo regulirovaniya razvitiya krupneyshego goroda (na primere Leningrada). *Voprosy Geografii* **109**, 144–58.

Kedrinskiy, A. A., M. G. Kolotov, B. N. Ometov, A. G. Raskin 1983. *Vosstanovleniye Pamyatnikov Arkhitektury Leningrada*. Leningrad: Stroyizdat.

Khanin, S. Ye. 1971. Sovremennoye rasseleniye v Barnaule. *Vestnik MGU Seriya 5 Geografiya*, No.2, 102–6.

—1991. Opyt izucheniya samoorganizatsii gorodov SSSR. *Izvestiya AN SSSR Seriya Geograficheskaya*, No.3, 129–40.

Khan-Magomedov, S. O. 1983. *Pioneers of Soviet architecture: the search for new solutions in the 1920s and 1930s*. London: Thames and Hudson.

—1986. *Alexandr Vesnin and Russian constructivism*. London: Lund Humphries.

Khodzhayev, D. G. 1983. Gosudarstvennoye ekonomicheskoye i sotsial'noye planirovaniye i problemy upravleniya razvitiya gorodov. In *Sotsialisticheskiy Gorod kak Ob'yekt Issledovaniya i Upravleniya*, I. I. Sigov et al. (eds), Leningrad: Nauka L. O.

Khodzhayev, D. G., V. S. Vishnyakova, N. K. Glabina, 1983. *Effektivnost' Rasseleniya: Problemy i Sudzheniya*. Moscow: Mysl'.

Khokhlov, R. F. & Ye. V. Yakuto 1979. Pamyatniki arkhitektury Dmitrova. *Russkiy Gorod* **2**, 71–94.

Khorev, B. S. 1971. *Problemy Gorodov*. Moscow: Mysl'.

—(ed.) 1972. *Malyy Gorod: Sotsial'no-demograficheskoye Issledovaniye Nebol'shogo Goroda*. Moscow: Izdatel'stvo Moskovskogo Universiteta.

—1975. *Problemy Gorodov*, 2nd ed. Moscow: Mysl'.

—(ed.) 1979. *Krupneyshiye Goroda – ikh Nastoyashcheye i Budushcheye*. Moscow: Statistika.

Khorev, B. S. & V. G. Glushkova 1991. Aktual'nyye voprosy sotsial'no-ekologicheskogo razvitiya Moskvy. *Izvestiya VGO* **123**(2), 178–85.

Khorev, B. S., V. L. Baburin, V. G. Glushkova (eds) 1989. *Problemy Uluchsheniya Ekologicheskoy Situatsii i Ratsional'nogo Prirodopol'zovaniya v Moskovskom Regione*. Moscow: AN SSSR/Moskovskiy Filial GO SSSR.

Kibal'chich, O. & V. Lyubovnyy 1976. Opyt i problemy regulirovaniya razvitiya krupnykh gorodskikh aglomeratsiy v Sovetskom Soyuze. In *Problemy Urbanizatsii i Rasseleniya*, V. V. Pokshishevskiy & G. M. Lappo (eds), 239–50. Moscow: Mysl'.

Kilesso, S. K. 1982. *Donetsk: Arkhitekturno-istoricheskiy ocherk*. Kiev: Budivelnyk.

Kirillov, V. V. 1976. Idei rekonstruktsii Moskvy v proyektakh 20-x – nachala 30-x godov XXv. In *Russkiy Gorod: (Istoriko-metodologicheskiy sbornik)*, 214–45. Moscow: Izdatel'stvo MGU.

—1979. Iz istorii gradostroitel'stva Podmoskov'ya v pervyye gody sovetskoy vlasti (proyekty i praktika stroitel'stva). In *Russkiy Gorod (Issledovaniya i Materialy)* **2**, 3–48. Moscow: Izdatel'stvo MGU.

—1983. Russkiy gorod epokhi barokko. *Russkiy Gorod* **6**, 127–62.

—1986. Russkoye gradostroitel'stvo na perekhode ot srednevekov'ya k novomu vremeni. *Russkiy Gorod* **8**, 3–30.

Kirkh, A. (ed.) 1985. *Sotsial'naya Mobilnost' Gorodskogo Naseleniya*. Tallin: AN Estonskoy SSR.

Kochetkov, A. V. 1975. Kompleksnoye prognozirovaniye i planirovaniye razvitiye seti naselennykh mest SSSR. In *Planirovaniye Sotsial'nogo Razvitiya Gorodov*, Vyp.2, A. N. Alekseyev & O. I. Shkaratan (eds), 9–33. Moscow: Institut Sotsiologicheskikh Issledovaniy et al.

Kogan, L. B. 1973. K opredeleniyu zadach i napravleniy gradostroitel'no-sotsiologicheskikh issledovaniy. In *Planirovaniye Sotsial'nogo Razvitiya Gorodov*, A. N. Alekseyev & O. I. Shkaratan (eds), 200–203. Moscow: AN SSSR.

— (ed.) 1976, *Razvitiye Gorodskoy Kul'tury i Formirovaniye Prostranstvennoy Sredy*. Moscow: TSNIIP Gradostroitel'stvo.

— 1986. Urbanizatsiya i gorodskiye protsessy: sushchnost' i zadachi issledovaniya. In *Sotsiologicheskiye Issledovaniye Problem Goroda i Zhilishcha 1970–1980 gg.*, B. P. Kutyrev (ed.), 5–18. Novosibirsk: Nauka SO.

— 1989. *Razvitiye Sotsial'no-kul'turnykh Funktsii i Prostranstvennoy Sredy Gorodov*. Moscow: Avtoreferat.

— (ed.) 1990. *Byt' Gorozhanami*. Moscow: Mysl'.

Kogan, L. B. & A. A. Pravotorova 1976. Sotsial'no-kul'turnyye svyazi v aglomeratsii krupneyshego goroda i yego razvitiye. *Arkhitektura SSSR*, No.1, 20–23.

Kogan, L. B. & I. P. Shumnaya 1980. Sotsial'no-funktsional'nyye osobennosti razvitiya novogo goroda-nauchnogo tsentra. In *Nekotoryye Problemy Urbanizatsii i Gradostroitel'stva*, A. S. Akhiyezer, M. N. Nochevnik, O. N. Yanitsky, L. B. Moskvin (eds), 35–50. Moscow: AN SSSR.

Kolosov, V. A. & Ye. V. Sidorova 1989. Geografiya vyborov v SSSR: osnovnyye cherty i spetsifika krupnykh gorodov (na primere Moskvy), In *Politicheskaya Geografiya: Sovremennoye Sostoyaniye i Puti Razvitiya*, V. A. Kolosov & A. V. Novikov (eds), 3–13. Moscow: Moskovskiy Filial GO SSSR.

Kolosov, V. A., N. V. Petrov, L. B. Smirnyagin (eds) 1990. *Vesna 1989: Geografiya i Anatomiya Parlamentskikh Vyborov*. Moscow: Progress.

Konstantinov, O. A. 1947. Izmeneniya v geografii gorodov SSSR za sovetskiy period. *Voprosy Geografii* 6, 11–46.

Kopp, A. 1967. *Ville et revolution*. Paris: Anthropos.

— 1990. Foreign architects in the Soviet Union during the first two five year plans. In *Reshaping Russian architecture: Western technology, Utopian dreams*, W. C. Brumfield (ed.), 176–214. Cambridge: Cambridge University Press.

Kopylov, V. A. 1976. Sotsial'no-demograficheskaya situatsiya i perspektivy razvitiya gorodov Moskovskoy oblasti. In *Russkiy Gorod (Istoriko-metodologicheskiy sbornik)*, 203–13. Moscow: Izdatel'stvo MGU.

Korcelli, P. 1975. Theory of intra-urban structure; review and synthesis. A cross-cultural perspective. *Geographia Polonica* 31, 99–131.

Koroteyeva, V. V. 1988. Reproduktivnoye povedeniye naseleniya krupnogo mnogonatsional'nogo goroda. In *Problemnyye Situatsii v Razvitii Goroda*, O. I Shkaratan (ed.), 119–54. Moscow: Institut Sotsiologii.

Kostinskiy, G. 1990. Regional preferences and concepts of Soviet youth. *Soviet Geography* 31(10), 732–52.

Kotkin, S. 1991. *Steeltown, USSR: Soviet society in the Gorbachev era*. Berkeley: University of California Press.

— 1993. Shelter and subjectivity in the Stalin period: a case study of Magnitogorsk. In *Russian housing in the modern age: design and social history*, W. C. Brumfield & B. A. Ruble (eds), 171–210. Cambridge: Cambridge University Press.

Kotlyar, A. Ye. (ed.) 1978. *Zanyatost' v Nebol'shikh Gorodakh (ekonomicheskiy-demograficheskiy ocherk)*. Moscow: Statistika.

— 1982. *Dvizheniye Rabochey Sily v Krupnom Gorode: Problemy Regulirovaniya*. Moscow: Finansy i Statistiki.

Kotsar', A. 1987. Khozyaystvo krupnogo goroda: puti sovershenstvovaniya. *Planovoye Khozyaystvo*, No.7, 96–100.

Kovalenko, P. S. 1980. *Razvitiye Gorodov*. Kiev; Nauk. Dumka.

Bibliography

Kozybayev, M. K. (eds) 1983. *Alma Ata Entsiklopediya*. Alma Ata: Glavnaya Redaktsiya Kazakhskoy Sovetskoy Entsiklopedii.

Kunchina, I (ed.) 1981. *Problemy Razvitya Sistemy Rasseleniya i Rayonnoy Planirovki v Respublike.* Vil'nyus.

Kutyrev, V. P., (ed.) 1986. *Sotsiologicheskiye Issledovaniya Problem Goroda i Zhilishcha 1970–1980gg.* Novosibirsk: Nauka SO.

Lappo, G. M. 1978. *Razvitiye Gorodskikh Aglomeratsii v SSSR*. Moscow: Nauka.

— 1987. *Goroda na Puti v Budushcheye*. Moscow: Mysl'.

Lappo, G. M. & F. M. Listengurt 1988. *Problemy Izucheniya Gorodskikh Aglomeratsii*. Moscow: IGAN SSSR.

Lavrov, S. B. & M. N. Mezhevich 1983. Marksizm o sotsial'no-ekonomicheskoy obuslovlennosti rasseleniya (stat'ya pervaya). *Izvestiya VGO.1* **15**(6), 481–91 (for second article, see: N. T. Agafonov & M. N. Mezhevich).

Lavrov, V. A. 1977. *Razvitiye Planirovochnoy Struktury Istoricheski Slozhivshchikhsya Gorodov*. Moscow: Stroyizdat.

Lavrov, V. [A.] 1979. *Preobrazovaniye Sredy Krupnykh Gorodov i Sovershenstvovaniye ikh Planirovochnoy Struktury*. Moscow: Stroyizdat.

Leningrad: Istoriko-Geograficheskiy Atlas 1981. Moscow: GUGK.

Leningrad i Leningradskaya Oblast' v Tsifrakh 1961. Leningrad: Lenizdat.

Lewis, R. A., R. H. Rowland, R. S. Clem 1976. *Nationality and population change in Russia and the USSR: an evaluation of census data, 1897–1970*. New York: Praeger.

Liiber, U. 1988. On the demographic situation of the Estonian small towns and its relationship with the level of social infrastructure. In *Estonia: geographical researches*, J-M. Punning (ed.), 127–35. Tallinn: Academy of Sciences of the Estonian SSR.

Lipyavkin, A. F. 1971. *Volgograd*. Volgograd: Nizhne-Volzhskoye Knizhnoye Izdatel'stvo.

Lissitzky, El 1984. *Russia: an Architecture for World Revolution*. Cambridge, Mass.: MIT Press.

Listengurt, F. M. (ed.) 1976. *Gradostroitel'stvo: Sbornik Nauchnych Trudov k XXIII Mezhdunarodnomu Geograficheskomu Kongressu*. Moscow: TSNIIP Gradostroitel'stva.

Litovka, O. P. 1973. Aktual'nyye problemy prostranstvennogo razvitiya gorodskikh poseleniy. In *Planirovaniye Sotsial'nogo Razvitiya Gorodov*, Vyp.1, A. N. Alekseyev & O. I. Shkaratan (eds), 152–65. Moscow: Institut Sotsiologicheskikh Issledovaniy et al.

— 1976. *Problemy Prostranstvennogo Razvitiya Urbanizatsii*. Leningrad: Nauka LO.

Liyber, Yu. & R. Roozve 1984. Tipologiya mikrorayonov g. Tallina na osnove dannykh usloviy zhizni, povedeniya i otsenok. In *Prikladnyye Sotsial'no-geograficheskiye Issledovaniya*, T. Raitviir (ed.), 266–9. Tartu: Kafedra Ekonomicheskoy Geografii Tartuskogo Gosudarstvennogo Universiteta et al.

Lodder, C. 1983. The Costakis collection: new insights into the Russian avant-garde. In *Russian avant-garde art and architecture*, C. Cooke (ed.), 34–49. London: Academy Editions.

Loginov, S. & V. Lyubovnyy 1975. Problemy malykh i srednikh gorodov Rossiyskoy Federatsii. *Planovoye Khozyaystvo*, No.2, 47–55.

Lopatina, E. 1959. *Leningrad*. Moscow: Geografgiz.

Lubetkin, B. 1933. Town and landscape planning in Soviet Russia. *Journal of the Town Planning Institute* **19**(4), 69–75.

Lukhmanov, D. M. 1989. Gorod na severe: nekotoryye sotsial'nyye problemy urbanizatsii. In *Geografiya i Problemy Regional'nogo Razvitiya*, S. S. Artebolevskiy & G. A. Privalovskaya (eds), 149–59. Moscow: IGAN SSSR.

Lyubitseva, O. A. 1985. Territorial'nyye aspekty razvitiya avtomobilizatsii (na primere USSR). *Ekonomicheskaya Geografiya* **37**, 59–63.

Lyubovnyy, V., R. Bespechnaya, E. Vaynberg 1984. Ekonomika malykh i srednikh gorodov. *Planovoye Khozyaystvo*, No.11, 109–15.

Macfadyen, D. 1970. *Sir Ebenezer Howard and the town planning movement*. Manchester: Manchester University Press.

217

Makayed, N & N. Udovenko 1987. Intensifikatsiya gorodskogo khozyaystva (na primere Minska). *Planovoye Khozyaystvo*, No.12, 102–105.

Males, V. N., Ye. G. Panchenko, V. I. Senchenko 1978. *Kompleksnoye Planirovaniye Ekonomicheskogo i Sotsial'nogo Razvitiya Gorodov i Rayonov*. Moscow: Mysl'.

Manakov, A. G. 1991. Ispol'zovaniye metoda ball'noy otsenki v issledovanii vospriyatiya chelovekomgorodskoy sredy. *Vestnik Moskovskogo Universiteta Seriya 5 Geografiya*, No.5, 44–51.

Manakov, N. & N. Petrov 1949. *Gorodskoye Khozyaystvo Leningrada*. Leningrad.

Markov, S. V. 1984. Otsenka territorial'noy struktury goroda. *Vestnik Leningradskogo Universiteta*, No.24, 99–102.

Markov, Ye. M. 1983. *Razvitiye Malykh i Srednikh Gorodov*. Moscow: Znaniye.

Markov, Ye. M. & V. S. Ryazanova (eds) 1975. *Planirovka i Zastroyka Malykh Gorodov*. Moscow: Stroyizdat.

Markov, Ye. M., V. P. Butuzova, V. A. Taratynov, V. V. Musatov, 1984. *Gradostroitel'nyye Osnovy Razvitiya Malykh Naselennykh Mest Nechernozemnoy Zony RSFSR*. Moscow: Stroyizdat.

Marksoo, A. 1988. On the development concept of small towns in the Estonian SSR. In *Estonia: geographical researches*, J-M. Punning (ed.), 110–26. Tallinn: Academy of Sciences of the Estonian SSR.

Mashinskiy, L. O. 1951. *Ozeleneniye Gorodov*. Moscow; AN SSSR.

Matthews, M. 1978. *Privilege in the Soviet Union*. London: Allen & Unwin.

—1986. *Poverty in the Soviet Union*. Cambridge: Cambridge University Press.

—1990. *Passports and freedom of residence in the USSR*, Lecture sponsored by the John M. Olin Foundation, Hoover Institution, Stanford.

Matveyeva, L. L. 1986. Vzaimosvyaz' migratsionnykh protsessov i razvitiya planirovochnoy struktury vneshikh zon krupnykh aglomeratsii. In *Sotsiologicheskiye Issledovaniye Problem Goroda i Zhilishcha 1970–1980 gg.*, B. P. Kutyrev (ed.), 24–31. Novosibirsk: Nauka SO.

Medvedkov, O. (see also Medvedkova, O. L.) 1989. *Soviet urbanization*. London: Routledge.

Medvedkov, Yu. B. (ed.) 1977. *Gorodskaya Sreda i Puti yeye Optimizatsii*. Moscow: IG AN.

Medvedkov, Yu. V. 1978. *Chelovek i Gorodskaya Sreda*. Moscow: Nauka.

Medvedkov, Yu. V. & I. V. Kantsebovskaya (eds) 1979. *Geograficheskiye Issledovaniya Gorodskoy Sredy*. Moscow: IG AN.

Medvedkova, O. L. 1979. Strukturnyye osobennosti gorodov kak mnogofunktsional'nykh tsentrov. *Izvestiya AN SSSR Ser. Geog.*, No.1, 53–71.

Mel'nikov, D. I., B. E. Slepak, L. A. Shul'man 1979. Prognozirovaniye sprosa naseleniya na tekhnicheskoye obsluzhivaniye i remont legkovykh avtomobiley. In *Avtomobilizatsiya i Rasseleniye (Voprosy sistemnogo analiza): Sbornik Trudov*, Vyp.1, S. S. Artem'yev (ed.), 57–61. Moscow: VNII Sistemnykh Issledovaniy.

Mezhevich, M. N. 1979. *Sotsial'noye Razvitiye i Gorod. Filosofskiye i Sotsiologicheskiye Polozheniya*. Leningrad: Nauka LO.

—1984. Teoreticheskiye voprosy issledovaniya urbanizatsii. In *Sotsial'naya geografiya SSSR (Problemy Metodologii i Teorii)*, A. A. Anokhin (ed.), 58–72. Leningrad: AN SSSR; GO.

Mezhevich, M. N. & L. I. Spiridonov 1973. Kompleksnoye issledovaniye sotsial'nykh problem razvitiya goroda. In *Planirovaniye Sotsial'nogo Razvitiya Gorodov*, Vyp.1, A. N. Alekseyev & O. I. Shkaratan (eds), 84–95. Moscow: Institut Sotsiologicheskikh Issledovaniy et al.

Miliutin, N. A. 1974. *Sotsgorod – the problem of building socialist cities*. Cambridge, Mass.: MIT Press.

Min'kova, M. A. 1984. Arbat, Sretenka i drugiye. *Gorodskoye Khozyaystvo Moskvy*, No.1, 31–2.

Minsk: Entsiklopedicheskiy Spravochnik 1980. Minsk: Glavnaya Redaktsiya Belorusskoy Sovetskoy Entsiklopedii.

Minsk: Entsiklopedicheskiy Spravochnik, 2nd ed. 1983. Minsk: Izdatel'stvo Belorusskaya Sovetskaya Entsiklopediya.

Mironov, V. P. 1977. *Gorod, v kotorom my zhivem: popul'yarniy ocherk o gorode Donetske*. Donetsk: Donbas.

Mitrikas, A. et al. (eds) 1981. *Gorod kak Sreda Zhiznedeyatel'nosti Cheloveka: materialy vtoroy nauchnoy konferentsii sotsiologov Pribaltiki.* Vil'nyus: Institut Filosofii, Sotsiologii i Prava AN LitSSR; Pribaltiyskiy otdel Sovetskoy Sotsiologicheskoy Assotsiyatsii.

Mizhega, N. Ya. (ed.) 1984. *Trudovyye Svyazi v Krupnom Gorode.* Kiev: Vishcha Shkola.

Mogilevskiy, R. S. 1987. *Problemy Kachestva Zhizni Krupnogo Goroda (Opyt Sotsiologicheskogo Issledovaniya).* Leningrad: Izdatel'stvo Leningradskogo Universiteta.

Mokerov, I. P. (ed.) 1986. *Osobennosti Vosproizvodstva i Migratsii Naseleniya na Urale.* Sverdlovsk: AN Ural'skiy Nauchnyy Tsentr.

Mokeyev, G. Ya. 1982. Sistęmnyye elementy planirovki drevney Moskvy. *Arkhitekturnoye Nasledstvo* **30**, Moscow, 5–12.

Morton, H. W. 1980. Who gets what, when and how? Housing in the Soviet Union. *Soviet Studies* **32**, 237–9.

Morton, H. W. & R. C. Stuart (eds) 1984. *The contemporary Soviet city.* London: Macmillan.

Moskva Entsiklopediya 1980. Moscow: Izdatel'stvo Sovetskaya Entsiklopediya.

Moskva: Kratkiy Adresno-telefonnyy Spravochnik 1974. Moscow: Moskovskiy Rabochiy.

Moskva v Tsifrakh (1966–1970gg.): Kratkiy Statisticheskiy Sbornik 1972. Moscow: Statistika.

Moskva v Tsifrakh za Gody Sovetskoy Vlasti (1917–1977 gg): Kratkiy Statisticheskiy Sbornik 1977. Moscow: Statistika.

Moskva v Tsifrakh 1989 1989. Moscow: Finansy i Statistika.

Mumford, L. 1938. *The culture of cities.* London: Secker and Warburg.

Narodnoye Khozyaystvo SSSR v 1962g. 1963. Moscow: Gosstatizdat.

Narodnoye Khozyaystvo SSSR za 70 let 1987. Moscow: Finansy i Statistika.

Narodnoye Khozyaystvo SSSR v 1988g. 1989. Moscow: Finansy i Statistika.

Narodnoye Khozyaystvo SSSR v 1989g. 1990. Moscow; Finansy i Statistika.

Narodnoye Khozyaystvo SSSR v 1990g. 1991. Moscow: Finansy i Statistika.

Nikol'skiy I. V. 1982. Territorial'naya organizatsiya torgovli v krupnykh gorodakh. *Vestnik MGU Seriya Geograficheskaya*, No.2, 62–8.

Novikov, V. I., G. B. Sheleykhovskiy, A. L. Eygorn, (eds) 1934. *Proyektirovaniye Sotsialisticheskikh Gorodov.* Khar'kov and Kiev: Giprograd.

Ogarkov, A. 1984. Ratsional'no ispol'zovat' zemli otvodimyye pod zastroyku. *Planovoye Khozyaystvo*, No. 6, 80–85.

Opolovnikov, A. V. 1974. *Restavratsiya Pamyatnikov Narodnogo Zodchestva.* Moscow: Stroyizdat.

Osborn R. J. & T. A. Reiner 1962. Soviet city planning: current issues and future perspectives. *Journal of the American Institute of Town Planners* **28**(4), 239–50.

Palamarchuk, A. M. 1987. Struktura krupnogo goroda kak obshchestvenno-territorial'noy sistemy. *Izvestiya AN SSSR: Seriya Geograficheskaya*, No.3, 65–75.

Pallot, J. 1979. Rural settlement planning in the USSR. *Soviet Studies* **31**(2), 214–30.

Parkins, M. F. 1953. *City planning in Soviet Russia.* Chicago: University of Chicago Press.

Pashkov, A. S. (ed.) 1988. *Obraz Zhizni Naseleniya Krupnogo Goroda.* Leningrad: Izdatel'stvo Leningradskogo Universiteta.

Pchelintsev, O. S. & N. N. Nozdrina 1986. *Problemy Razvitiya Sotsial'no-Demograficheskikh Grupp i Sotsial'no-territorial'nykh Obshchnostey; Sbornik Trudov*, Vyp.4. Moscow: VNII Sistemnykh Issledovaniy.

Perevedentsev, V. I. 1975. *Goroda i Vremya.* Moscow: Statistika.

Pertsik, Ye. N. 1971. *Osnovy Rayonnoy Planirovki.* Moscow: Izdatel'stvo Moskovskogo Universiteta.

— 1973. *Rayonnaya Planirovka.* Moscow: Mysl'.

— 1980. *Gorod v Sibiri.* Moscow: Mysl'.

Petrov, V. A. 1981. *Sotsial'no-demograficheskaya Struktura Gorodskogo Naseleniya i yego Zanyatost'.* Moscow: Finansy i Statistika.

Pityurenko, Ye. I. 1983. *Sistemy Rasseleniya i Territorial'naya Organizatsiya Narodnogo Khozyaystva.* Kiev: Naukova Dumka.

Pokshishevskiy, V. V. 1957. Nekotoryye voprosy mikro-geograficheskogo izucheniya gorodov SSSR. *Geograficheskiy Sbornik* **11**, 90–109.

Polyan, P. M. 1988. *Metodika Vydeleniya i Analiza Opornogo Karkasa Rasseleniya.* Moscow: AN USSR.

Popov, M. K. 1973. Nekotoryye problemy sotsial'nogo razvitiya gorodov. *Problemy Nauchnogo Kommunizma*, Vyp.7, 98–129.

Portnov, B. A. 1974. Zhilaya sreda gorodskogo tsentra: orientatsiya na potrebnosti naseleniya. *Sotsiologicheskiye Issledovaniya*, No. 4, 30–37.

——1991. Gorodskaya sreda: fenomen prestizhnosti. *Sotsiologocheskiye Issledovaniya*, No.1, 69–74.

Posokhin, M. V. 1974. *Cities to live in.* Moscow: Novosti.

Potapova, T. V. 1988. Okhrana kul'turnoy sredy v Moskovskom regione (arkhitekturnyy aspekt). *Voprosy Geografii* **131**, 142–50.

Pravotorova, A. A. 1986. Kharakter osvoyeniya prostranstva krupnogo goroda zhitelyami aglomeratsii. In *Sotsiologicheskiye Issledovaniye Problem Goroda i Zhilishcha 1970–1980 gg.*, B. P. Kutyrev (ed.), 19–24. Novosibirsk: Nauka SO.

Problemy Prognozirovaniya Sotsial'no-ekonomicheskogo Razvitiya Gorodov 1976. Nauchnyye Zapiski Leningradskogo Fin.–Ekon. Instituta, Vyp.44, Leningrad.

Problemy Razvitiya Gorodov 1976. Kiev: SOPS UkSSR.

Promyslov, V. 1972. Osnovnyye printsipy sovremennogo gradostroitel'stva i razvitiya gorodov v interesakh ikh zhiteley. In *Urbanistica Contemporalis*, J. Hantos (ed.), 387–405. Budapest: Aedes Scientiarum Hungaricae.

Pryde, P. R. 1991. *Environmental management in the Soviet Union.* Cambridge: Cambridge University Press.

Puchin, E. E. 1977. Etalon skhemy razmeshcheniya zhilishchnogo i kul'turno-bytovogo stroitel'stva v malykh gorodakh Latviyskoy SSR. *Voprosy Gradostroitel'stva: Voprosy Stroitel'stva* **6**. Riga: Zvaygzne.

Raitviir, T. 1979. Obraz zhizni naseleniya ESSR i yego regional'nyye razlichii. *Uchenyye Zapiski TGU*, Vyp.490, 81–107, Tartu.

——(ed.) 1984. *Prikladnyye Sotsial'no-geograficheskiye Issledovaniya: tesisy dokladov respublikanskogo seminara-soveshchaniya.* Tartu: Kafedra Ekonomicheskoy Geografii TGU et al.

——1988. Factorial ecological structure of Tallinn. In *Estonia: geographical researches*, J-M. Punning (ed.), 136–48. Tallinn: Academy of Sciences of the Estonian SSR.

Ratiya, Sh. Ye. & K. P. Dogina 1952. *Okhranyayte Pamyatniki Arkhitektury.* Moscow: Gosudarstvennoye Izdatel'stvo po Stroitel'stvu i Arkhitektury.

Reiner, T. A. & R. H. Wilson 1979. Planning and decision-making in the Soviet city: rent, land and urban form. In *The socialist city: spatial structure and urban policy*, R. A. French & F. E. I. Hamilton (eds), 49–71. Chichester, England: Wiley.

Richardson, W. 1991. Hannes Meyer and the General Plan for the Reconstruction of Moscow. *Planning Perspectives* **6**(2), 109–24.

Romanenkova, G. M. & V. V. Boyko (eds) 1983. *Demograficheskoye i Ekonomicheskoye Razvitiye v Regione.* Moscow: Finansy i Statistika.

Rowland, R. H. 1976. Urban in-migration in late nineteenth-century Russia. In *The city in Russian history*, M. F. Hamm (ed.), 115–24. Lexington: University of Kentucky Press.

Ruble, B. A. 1990. *Leningrad: shaping a Soviet city.* Berkeley: University of California Press.

——1992. Reshaping the city: the politics of property in a provincial Russian city. *Urban Anthropology* **21**(3), 203–33.

Rukavishnikov, V. O. 1978. Etnosotsial'nyye aspekty rasseleniya v gorodakh Tatarii. *Sovetskaya Etnografiya*, No.1, 77–89.

——1980. *Naseleniye Goroda.* Moscow: Statistika.

Ruskin, J. 1889. *The seven lamps of architecture*, 6th edn. London: George Allen.

Rutkevich, M. N. 1987. Nekotoryye osobennosti razvitiya sotsial'no-klassovoy struktury gorodskogo naseleniya. In *Sotsialisticheskiy Gorod kak Ob'yekt Issledovaniya i Upravleniya*, I. I. Sigov (ed.),

89–98. Leningrad: Nauka LO.

Rutkevich, M. N., O. I. Shkaratan, N. A. Aitov, et al. 1977. *Perspektivnoye Planirovaniye Ekonomicheskogo i Sotsial'nogo Razvitiya Goroda: Metodologicheskiye Rekomendatsii*. Moscow:Profizdat.

Ruzhzhe, V. L. 1974. Sotsial'noye kachestvo zhiloy sredy. *Sotsiologicheskiye Issledovaniya*, No.1, 38–43.

Ryan, M. 1990. *Contemporary Soviet society: a statistical handbook*. Cheltenham, England: Edward Elgar.

Sagars, M. 1991a. News notes: geographic distribution of private car ownership in the USSR; recent developments in the passenger car industry. *Soviet Geography* 32(1), 61–8.

—— 1991b. News Notes: Soviet truck production in precipitous decline. *Soviet Geography* 32(6), 436–7.

Sarkisyan, G. S. 1983. *Narodnoye Blagosostoyaniye v SSSR*. Moscow: Ekonomika.

Saushkin, Yu. G. 1964. *Moskva*. Moscow: Mysl'.

Saushkin, Yu. G., G. L. Vasil'yev, V. G. Glushkova 1984. Gorodskoy geograficheskiy kompleks Moskvy. In *Sovetskaya Geografiya*, 155–67. Leningrad: Nauka.

Savarenskaya, T. F., D. O. Shvidkovskiy, F. A. Petrov 1989. *Istoriya Gradostroitel'nogo Isskustva Pozdniy Feodalizm i Kapitalizm*. Moscow: Stroyizdat.

Savchenko, A. B. 1986. Mekhanism prostranstvennogo rosta i evolyutsiya ispol'zovaniya territorii Moskvy. In *Geograficheskiye Problemy Razvitiya Khozyaystva Moskovskogo Regiona*, V. G. Glushkova & N. P. Matveyev (eds), 44–55. Moscow: Moskovskiy Filial VGO.

Savchenko, I. P. & A. F. Lipyavkin 1970. *Osnovy Rayonnoy Planirovki*. Moscow: Vysshaya Shkola.

Savkin, K. M. 1989. Istoricheskiye elementy i proyektirovaniye gorodskoy sredy. In *Sredovoy Podkhod v Arkhitekture i Gradostroitel'stve*, A. A. Vysokovskiy (ed.), 106–111. Moscow: VNIITAG.

Sazonov, B. V. & L. F. Strashnova 1988. Sotsial'naya kontseptsiya razvitiya Moskvy: podkhody k yeye razrabotke, strategii razvitiya regiona. In *Problemnyye Situatsii v Razvitii Goroda*, O. I. Shkaratan (ed.), 84–118. Moscow: Institut Sotsiologii AN SSSR.

Schmidt, A. J. 1989. *The architecture and planning of classical Moscow: a cultural history*. Philadelphia: American Philosophical Society.

Segedinov, I. & A. A. Tomsen 1968. Otsenka gorodskoy territorii. *Ekonomika Stroitel'stva*, No.4, 43–4.

Semakov, S. N. 1981. Partiynoye rukovodstvo razvitiyem zhilishchnogo i kommunal'nogo stroitel'stva v novykh industrial'nykh tsentrakh Podmoskov'ya v gody pervoy pyatiletki. In *Russkiy Gorod: Moskva i Podmoskov'ye* 4, 5–25. Moscow: Izdatel'stvo Moskovskogo Universiteta.

Senchenko, V. I. (ed.) 1980. *Teoriya i Praktika Kompleksnogo Razvitiya Goroda*. Kiev: Naukova Dumka.

Sevast'yanov, L. I. 1986. Opyt prognozirovaniya razvitiya rayona (na primere Sovetskogo rayona g. Novosibirska). In *Sotsiologicheskiye Issledovaniye Problem Goroda i Zhilishcha 1970–1980 gg.*, B. P. Kutyrev, (ed.), 90–98. Novosibirsk: Nauka SO.

Shaw, D. J. B. 1978. Planning Leningrad. *Geographical Review* 68(2), 183–200.

—— 1980. Achievements and problems in Soviet recreational planning. In *Home, school and leisure in the Soviet Union*, M. Perrie & A. Sutton (eds), 195–214. London: Allen & Unwin.

—— 1983. The Soviet urban general plan and recent advances in Soviet urban planning. *Urban Studies* 20, 393–403.

—— 1985. Spatial dimensions in Soviet central planning. *Transactions of the Institute of British Geographers* NS 10, 401–12.

—— 1987. Some influences on spatial structure in the state socialist city: the case of the USSR. In *Soviet geographical studies in our time*, L. Holzner & J. M. Knapp (eds), 201–27. Milwaukee: University of Wisconsin–Milwaukee.

—— 1991. The past, present and future of the Soviet city plan. *Planning Perspectives* 6(2), 125–38.

Shelley, L. 1980. The geography of Soviet criminality. *American Sociological Review* 45, 111–22.

—— 1981. Internal migration and crime in the Soviet Union. *Canadian Slavonic Papers* 23, 77–87.

—— 1984. Urbanization and crime: the Soviet experience. In *The contemporary Soviet city*, H. W. Morton & R. C. Stuart (eds), 113–26. London: Macmillan.

Shepelev, N. P. 1986. Transportno-sotsial'nyye aspekty v osvoyenii gorodskoy territorii. In

Bibliography

Geograficheskiye Problemy Razvitiya Khozyaystva Moskovskogo Regiona, V. G. Glushkova & N. P. Matveyev (eds), 34–43. Moscow: Moskovskiy Filial VGO.

Shkaratan, O. I. 1970. Problemy sotsial'noy struktury sovetskogo goroda. *Filosofskiye Nauki*, No.5, —(ed.) 1986. *Etnosotsial'nyye Problemy Goroda*. Moscow: Nauka.

Shkaratan, O. I. & V. O. Rukavishnikov 1974. Sotsial'naya struktura naseleniya sovetskogo goroda i tendentsii yeye razvitiya. *Sotsiologicheskiye Issledovaniya* 2, 36–49.

Shpakovskaya, Ye. S. 1980. Problema vzaimodeystviya unikal'nykh elementov kul'tury i prostranstvennoy sredy v krupneyshem gorode. In *Nekotoryye Problemy Urbanizatsii i Gradostroitel'stva (sotsial'no-ekonomicheskiye aspekty)*, A. S. Akhiyezer, M. N. Nochevnik, O. N. Yanitsky, L. B. Moskvin (eds), 142–9. Moscow: AN USSR.

Shul'ga, V. A. 1988. Voprosy realizatsii planov kompleksnogo ekonomicheskogo i sotsial'nogo razvitiya krupnogo goroda (po primere Moskvy). *Voprosy Geografii* 131, 95–108.

Shvarikov, V. A. 1939. *Planirovka Gorodov Rossii XVIII i nachala XIX veka*. Moscow: Izdatel'stvo Vsesoyuznoy Akademii Arkhitektury.

—(ed.) 1945. *Gradostroitel'stvo*. Moscow: Akademiya Arkhitektury SSSR.

—1954. *Ocherk Istorii Planirovki i Zastroyki Russkikh Gorodov*. Moscow: Gosudarstvennoye Izdatel'stvo Literatury po Stroitel'stvu i Arkhitektury.

Shvedov, S. S. 1976. Tsentr krupneyshego goroda i nekotoryye sotsial'no-kul'turnyye kharakteristiki povedeniya gorodskikh zhiteley. In *Razvitiye Gorodskoy Kul'tury i Formirovaniye Prostranstvennoy Sredy*, L. B. Kogan (ed.), 21–9. Moscow: TSNIIP Gradostroitel'stva.

Shvidkovsky, O. A. 1971. *Building in the USSR 1917–1932*. London: Studio Vista.

Sidorov, D. 1992. Variations in perceived level of prestige of residential areas in the former USSR. *Urban Geography* 13, 355–73.

Sigayev, A. V. 1972. *Avtotransport i Planirovka Gorodov*. Moscow: Izdatelstvo Literatury po Stroitel'stvu.

Sigov, I. I. (ed.) 1982. *Planirovaniye Kompleksnogo Razvitiya Krupnykh Gorodov: Opyt i Puti Sovershenstvovaniya*. Leningrad: Nauka.

Sigov, I. I., et al. 1983. *Sotsialisticheskiy Gorod kak Ob'yekt Issledovaniya i Upravleniya* (Papers of first conference). Leningrad: Nauka.

—(ed.) 1985. *Urbanizatsiya i Razvitiye Gorodov v SSSR*. Leningrad: Nauka.

—1987. *Sotsialisticheskiy Gorod kak Ob'yekt Issledovaniya i Upravleniya* (Papers of second conference). Leningrad: Nauka.

—1988. *Sotsialisticheskiy Gorod kak Ob'yekt Issledovaniya i Upravleniya* (Papers of third conference). Leningrad: Nauka.

Skinner, F. W. 1986. Trends in planning practices: the building of Odessa, 1794–1917. In *The city in late Imperial Russia*, M. F. Hamm (ed.), 139–59. Bloomington: Indiana University Press.

Sklyar, M. I. 1958. Obshchaya kharakteristika sovremennogo Saratova. In *Sbornik Statey Aspirantov*, N. N. Baranskiy & N. A. Gvozdetskiy (eds), 91–130. Moscow: Moskovskiy Gosudarstvennyy Universitet, Geograficheskiy Fakultet.

Smirnov, N. V. 1978. Stadii razvitiya demograficheskoy struktury naseleniya bol'shikh gorodov. *Vestnik MGU*, No.1, 73–7.

Smith, D. M. 1988. *Geography, inequality and society*. Cambridge: Cambridge University Press.

—1989. *Urban inequality under socialism*. Cambridge: Cambridge University Press.

Smith, G. 1986. Privilege and place in Soviet society. In *New horizons in human geography*, D. Gregory & R. Walford (eds), 320–41. London: Macmillan.

Snytko, M. K. 1971. Nekotoryye osobennosti promyshlennoy struktury i velichiny gorodov tsentral'no-chernozemnogo rayona. In *Geografiya Tsentra*, Vyp.3, Ye. M Pospelov (ed.), 82–5. Moscow: Moskovskiy Filial Geograficheskogo Obshchestva SSSR.

Sokolova, M. P. 1986. Resursy s tochki zreniya ekonomiki. *Gorodskoye Khozyaystvo Moskvy*, No.12, 14–15.

Solofnenko, N. A. 1973. *General scheme of settlement on the area of the USSR*. Moscow: Central Scientific Research and Design Institute of Town Planning.

Solzhenitsyn, A. 1975. *The Gulag Archipelago*, vol 2. London: Collins/Fontana.

Bibliography

Sosnovy, T. 1954. *The housing problem in the Soviet Union.* New York: Research Program on the USSR.

Stanislavskiy, A. I. 1971. *Planirovka i Zastroyka Gorodov Ukrainy.* Kiev: Izdatel'stvo Budivel'nik.

Starr, S. F. 1976. The revival and schism of urban planning in twentieth-century Russia. In *The city in Russian history,* M. F. Hamm (ed.), 222–42. Lexington: University Press of Kentucky.

State of Natural Environment and Nature Protection Activities in the USSR in 1989. 1990. Moscow: The USSR State Environmental Protection Committee.

Stepanenko, A. V. 1981. *Goroda v Usloviyakh Razvitogo Sotsializma.* Kiev: Naukova Dumka.

Strizhakova, Ye. M. 1981. *Razvitiye i Razmeshcheniye Proizvodstva v Malykh Gorodakh i Poselkakh Gorodskogo Tipa Rostovskoy Oblasti.* Unpublished deposited MS, Rostov-na-Donu.

Sverdlovskaya Oblast' v Tsifrakh 1986–1990. 1991. Yekaterinburg: Sredne-Uralskoye Knizhnoye Izdatel'stvo.

Szelenyi, I. 1983. *Urban inequalities under State socialism.* Oxford: Oxford University Press.

Tarkhov, S. A. 1981. Metod klassifikatsii konfiguratsii krupnykh gorodov SSSR. *Izvestiya AN-SSR Seriya Geograficheskaya,* No.4, 75–82.

—1986. Sravnitel'no-geograficheskiy analiz struktury setey gorodskogo transporta Moskvy i Leningrada. *Izvestiya VGO* **118**(2), 133–41.

Thiede, R. L. 1976. Industry and urbanization in New Russia from 1860 to 1910, In *The city in Russian history.* M. F. Hamm (ed.), 125–38. Lexington: University of Kentucky Press.

Thomas, M. J. 1978. City planning in Soviet Russia (1917–1932). *Geoforum* **9**(4–5), 269–77.

Timofeyenko, V. I. 1984. *Goroda Severnogo Prichernomor'ya vo Vtoroy Polovine XVIII veke.* Kiev: Naukova Dumka.

Timyashevskaya, M. V. 1986. Sotsiologicheskoye issledovaniye obraza zhizni v novom zhilom obrazovanii dlya praktiki yego perspektivnogo stroitel'stva. In *Sotsiologicheskiye Issledovaniye Problem Goroda i Zhilishcha 1970–1980 gg.,* B. P. Kutyrev (ed.), 113–21. Novosibirsk: Nauka SO.

Tolokontsov, N. A. (ed.) 1988. *Okruzhayushchaya Sreda Krupnogo Goroda.* Leningrad: Nauka.

Tolokontsev, N. A. & G. M. Romanenkovaya (eds) 1980. *Demografiya i Ekologiya Krupnogo Goroda.* Leningrad: Nauka.

Tomsen, A. A. 1975. *Opyt Sotsial'no-ekonomicheskikh Issledovaniy v Stroitel'stve.* Saratov: Izdatel'stvo Saratovskogo Universiteta.

Toshchenko, Zh. T. 1980. *Sotsial'naya Infrastruktura: Sushchnost' i Puti Razvitiya.* Moscow: Mysl'.

Trifonov, A. A. & I. Ye. Makarova, 1989. Ekologicheskiye aspekty razvitiya Moskovskogo regiona i problema kontsentratsii rasseleniya. In *Problemy Uluchsheniya Ekologicheskoy Situatsii i Ratsional'nogo Prirodopol'zovaniya v Moskovskom Regione,* B. S. Khorev, V. L. Baburin, V. G. Glushkova (eds), 36–52. Moscow: Moskovskiy Filial GO SSSR.

Trofimov, V. G. 1981. *Moskva: Putevoditel' po Rayonam.* Moscow: Moskovskiy Rabochiy.

Trotskovskiy, A. Ya. 1985. *Razvitiye Sela v Usloviyakh Urbanizatsii na primere Zapadnoy Sibiri.* Novosibirsk: Nauka SO.

Trube, L. L. 1985. Krupnyy gorod kak sistema konsentrirovannogo rasseleniya. *Izvestiya VGO* **117**(4), 365–9.

Trushkov, V. V. 1983. *Naseleniye Goroda i Prigoroda.* Moscow: Finansy i Statistika.

Tulayev, A. Ya. 1989. Nuzhnyye korennyye izmeniya v planirovke ulichnoy seti gorodov. In *Voprosy Planirovki i Zastroyki Gorodov: Tezisy Dokladov k Zonal'noy Konferentsii 25–26 maya 1989,* 6–7. Penza: not known.

Tverskoy, L. M. 1953. *Russkoye Gradostroitel'stvo do Kontsa XVII veka.* Leningrad and Moscow: Gosudarstvennoye Izdatel'stvo po Stroitel'stvu i Arkhitekture.

Uchet Migratsionnykh Protsessov i ikh Osnovnyye Kharakteristiki v Rossii. 1993. , Working paper 6, Statistical Office of the European Communities.

Valentey, D. I. (ed.) 1979. *Krupneyshiye Goroda – ikh Nastoyashcheye i Budushcheye: SbornikStatey.* Moscow: Statistika.

Valentey, D. I., et al. (eds) 1987. *Gorodskaya i Sel'skaya Sem'ya.* Moscow: Mysl'.

223

Valesyan, A. L. 1990. Environmental problems in the Yerevan region. *Soviet Geography* **31**(8), 573–86.

Vanagas, Yu. 1984. Tip zhiloy sredy i anomaliy gradoekologicheskikh kharakteristik v krupnom gorode (na primere Vil'nyusa i Kaunasa). In *Prikladnyye Sotsial'no-geograficheskiye Issledovaniya*, T. Raitviir (ed.), 175–7. Tartu: Kafedra Ekonomicheskoy Geografii TGU et al.

Vanagas, Yu. S. 1986. Osobennosti funktsionirovaniya novykh zhilykh rayonov Vil'nyusa. In *Sotsiologicheskiye Issledovaniye Problem Goroda i Zhilishcha 1970–1980 gg.*, B. P. Kutyrev (ed.), 64–9. Novosibirsk: Nauka SO.

Vand, L. E. & G. A. Gol'ts 1977. Gorodskaya sreda kak sistema determinatorov. In *Gorodskaya Sreda i Puti yeye Optimizatsii*, Yu. V. Medvedkov (ed.), 109–19. Moscow: Institut Geografii AN SSSR.

Vardosanidze, V. G. 1986. Urbanologicheskiy analiz novogo goroda Madneuli. In *Sotsiologicheskiye Issledovaniye Problem Goroda i Zhilishcha 1970–1980 gg.*, B. P. Kutyrev (ed.), 36–41. Novosibirsk: Nauka SO.

Vardosanidze, V. G., L. B. Kogan, A. A. Pravotorova 1976. Sotsial'no-kul'turnyye issledovaniya v gradostroitel'stve. In *Gradostroitel'stvo: Sbornik nauchnykh Trudov*, F. M. Listengurt (ed.), 83–93. Moscow: TSNIIP Gradostroitel'stva.

Varlamov, V. S. 1961. Novyye goroda-sputniki v Velikobritanii i drugikh kapitalicheskikh stranakh. In *Goroda-Sputniki; Sbornik Statey*, V. G. Davidovich & B. S. Khorev (eds), 137–49. Moscow: Geografgiz.

Vasenina, L. F. 1989. Problemy zhilogo stroitel'stva v malykh i srednikh gorodakh Leningradskoy oblasti. In *Razvitiye i Sovershenstvovaniye Planirovochnoy Struktury Istoricheskikh Gorodov*, A. I. Naumov (ed.), Leningrad: Leningradskiy Inzhenirniy-Stroitel'nyy Institut.

Vasil'yev, G. L. 1985. Sotsial'naya otsenka gorodskoy territorii. *Goroda i Sistemy Rasseleniya* **6**:*Dostizheniya i Perspektivy* **43**, 59–66.

Vasil'yev, G. L. & O. L. Privalova 1982. Sotsial'no-geograficheskaya otsenka vnutrigorodskikh razlichiy. *Vestnik MGU Seriya Geograficheskaya*, No. 4, 9–15. Translated as: A socio-geographic evaluation of differences within a city. *Soviet Geography* **25**(7), 488–96 [1984].

Vasil'yev, G. L., D. A. Sidorov, S. Ye. Khanin 1988. Vyyavleniye potrebitel'skikh predpochteniy v sfere rasseleniya. *Vestnik MGU Seriya 5 Geografiya*, No. 2, 41–7.

Vasil'yeva, E. K. 1978. *Sotsial'no-ekonomicheskaya Struktura Naseleniya SSSR (Statistiko-demograficheskiy Analiz)*. Moscow: Statistika.

Vaytekunas, S. 1985. *Territorial'naya Organizatsiya Sotsial'noy Infrastruktury*. Vil'nyus: not known.

Veselovskiy, B. B. 1950. Rost Moskvy v Stalinskuyu epokhu. *Voprosy Geografii* **19**, 81–110.

Veshninskiy, Yu. G. 1988. Sotsial'no-esteticheskiye predpochteniya moskvichey (otsenka gorodskoy sredy razlichnykh chastey territorii Moskvy). In *Sotsial'nyye Problemy Arkhitekturno-gradostroitel'nogo Razvitiya Moskvy*, M. V. Borshchevskiy (ed.), 91–103. Moscow: TSNIIP Gradostroitel'stva.

Vilenberg, B. & C. Loginov 1961. Kryukovo – pervyy "gorod-sputnik" Moskvy. *Voprosy Geografii* **51**, 52–7.

Visharenko, V. S. & N. A. Tolokontsev 1982. *Ekologicheskiye Problemy Gorodov i Zdorov'ye Cheloveka*. Leningrad: Obshchestvo "Znaniye" RSFSR.

Vladimirov, V. V. 1977. Kharakteristika demograficheskoy yemkosti territorii v rayonnoy planirovka. In *Gorodskaya Sreda i Puti yeye Optimizatsii*, Yu. V. Medvedkov (ed.), 187–91. Moscow: Institut Geografii AN SSSR.

—(ed.) 1986. *Rayonnaya Planirovka*. Moscow: Stroyizdat.

Vladimirov, V. V., Ye. M. Mikulina, E. N. Yargina 1986. *Gorod i Landshaft*. Moscow: Mysl'.

Vodarskiy, Ya. Ye. 1972. *Promyshlennyye Seleniya Tsentral'noy Rossii v Period Genezisa i Razvitiya Kapitalizma*. Moscow: Nauka.

Voprosy Gradostroitel'stva; Voprosy Stroitel'stva 1977, No. 6. Riga: Zvaygzne.

—1980, No. 7. Riga: Zvaygzne.

Vorob'yev, V. V. & K. N. Misevich 1979. Problemy naseleniya i trudovykh resursov rayonov novogo osvoyeniya. In *Geografiya Naseleniya v Sisteme Kompleksnogo Ekonomicheskogo i Sotsial'nogo Planirovaniya*, N. T. Agafonov & O. P. Litovka (eds), 67–73. Leningrad: GO SSSR.

Vosilyute, A. 1984. Modeli povedeniya gorodskikh zhiteley vo vremya otpuska (na primere g.

Shaulyayi). In *Prikladnyye Sotsial'no-geograficheskiye Issledovaniya: tesisy dokladov respublikan-skogo seminara-soveshchaniya*, T. Raitviir (ed.), 143–6. Tartu: Kafedra Ekononomicheskoy Geografii TGU et al.

Vsya Moskva 1990/91 Informatsionno-reklamnyy Yezhegodnik. Moscow: Sovetsko-Zapadnogerman-skoye Sovmestnoye Predpriyatiye "Vsya Moskva".

Walker, A. R. 1988. Urban planning in Siberia: problems of implementation. *Sibirica* **4**, 11–17.

White, J. F. 1962. *The Cambridge Movement: the Ecclesiologists and the Gothic Revival*. Cambridge: Cambridge University Press.

White, P. M. 1979. *Soviet urban and regional planning: a bibliography with abstracts*. London: Mansell.

Wixman, R. 1980. *Language aspects of ethnic patterns and processes in the north Caucasus*. Research Paper 191, Department of Geography, University of Chicago.

Yanitskiy, O. N. 1986. Territorial'nyye obshchnosti v ekologicheskoy strukture goroda. In *Problemy Razvitiya Sotsial'no-Demograficheskikh Grupp i Sotsial'no-territorial'nykh Obshchnostey: Sbornik Trudov*, Vyp.4, O. S. Pchelintsev & N. N. Nozdrina (eds), 68–75. Moscow: VNIISI.

Yanitsky, O. 1986. Urbanization in the USSR: theory tendencies and policy. *International Journal of Urban and Regional Research* **10**, 265–87.

Yankova, Z. A. & I. Yu. Rodzinskaya 1982. *Problemy Bol'shogo Goroda (Opyt Sotsiologicheskogo Issledovaniya)*. Moscow: Nauka.

Yanowitch, M. & W. Fisher 1973. *Social Stratification and Mobility in the USSR*. White Plains, New York: International Arts and Sciences Press.

Yefimov, V. T. & G. I. Mikerin 1976. Avtomobilizatsiya v razvitom sotsialisticheskom obshchestve. *Sotsiologicheskiye Issledovaniya*, No. 1, 128–38.

Yerevan za 40 let v Tsifrakh: Statisticheskiy Sbornik 1960. Yerevan: Statisticheskoye Upravleniye g. Yerevana.

Yevstratov, N. F. & S. M. Matveyev 1967. Razvitiye i rekonstruktsiya Moskvy v perspektive. *Izvestiya Akademii Nauk SSSR: Seriya Geograficheskaya*, No. 5, 63–73.

Yurkovskiy, V. M. 1987. Podsistema mestnogo obsluzhivaniya krupneyshogo goroda (na primere Kiyeva). *Ekonomicheskaya Geografiya* **37**, 94–100.

Zablotskiy, G. A., L. A. Shevchuk, Ye. S. Kuts et al. 1975. *Sotsial'nyye Osnovy Razvitiya Gorodov (Sotsiologicheskiye Problemy Rasseleniya)*. Moscow: Stroyizdat.

Zakharov, V. I. 1983. *Gorod Kalinin; ocherk-putevoditel'*. Moscow: Moskovskiy Rabochiy.

Zaslavskiy, I. N. 1984. Metod analiza territorial'noy differentsiatsii interesov naseleniya (po dannym podpiski na periodicheskiye izdaniya). In *Metody Issledovaniya Slozhnykh Sistem*, Yu. S Popkov (ed.), 131–6. Moscow: VNIIS.

Zastavnyy, F. D. (ed.) 1985. *Rasseleniye: Voprosy Teorii i Razvitiya (na primere Ukrainskoy-SSR)*. Kiev: Naukova Dumka.

Zayonchkovskaya, Zh. A. 1972. *Novosely v Gorodakh: Metody Izucheniya Prizhivayemosti*. Moscow: Statistika.

Zhidkova, L. F. 1980. K voprosu o razvitii goroda Dubny. *Russkiy Gorod (Problemy Gorodoobra-zovaniya)* **3**, 5–22. Moscow: Izdatel'stvo Moskovskogo Universiteta.

Zvonkova, T. V., et al. 1971. Geograficheskiye osnovy territorial'noy organizatsii promyshlennogo uzla (na primere Tol'yatti-Zhigulevskogo uzla). In *Problemy Prikladnoy Geografii*, V. V. Vorob'yev (ed.), 33–41. Irkutsk: AN SSSR SO.

Zhelezko, S. N. 1986. *Naseleniye Krupnogo Goroda*. Moscow: Mysl'.

Zhidkova, L. F. 1980. K voprosu o razvitiya goroda Dubny. In *Russkiy Gorod (Problemy Gorodoobra-zovaniya)* **3**, V. L. Yanin (ed.), 5–22. Moscow: Izdatel'stvo Moskovskogo Universiteta.

Zhiromskiy, V. B. 1988. *Sovetskiy Gorod v 1921–1925gg: Problemy Sotsial'noy Struktury*. Moscow: Nauka.

Zholkov, A. S. & V. M. Zuyev 1984. *Razvitiye Sotsialisticheskogo Goroda*. Moscow: Ekonomika.

225

INDEX

Chersonesus 10
Chimbay 125
Chita 148, 149
Chuvash Autonomous Republic 56
"City of Socialist Man" 3–4, 5, 29–49, 177, 178, 195, 196–204
"City on Springs" 39
class, social (*see* layers)
collective markets 115–16, 127
Commission on the Building in Stone of St. Petersburg and Moscow, 1762 16
Commonwealth of Independent States (CIS) 2
communal apartments 57, 97, 137, 138
communal living 37–8, 43, 81, 93
Communist Party 1–2, 42, 134, 204
Party Congress, 27th, 1987 102
commuting 91, 174
company towns 109, 122–7
conservation
conservation of historic buildings 177–94
conservation areas 142, 186–7
conservation parks 187
Constructivism 30, 32, 34, 35, 39, 44, 45, 49, 52
construction industry 101–2
container traffic 160
cooperative housing 136–7

council, town (*see* local government)
counterurbanization 200
crèche 63
crime 121–2, 174, 176
Crimea 106, 120

dacha 89–90, 175
Danilov Monastery, Moscow 189
declining towns 124–7
density (*see* population)
Department of Museums and the Preservation of Ancient Monuments 179
department stores 111–12, 174
Derbeshkinskiy 127
Disurbanists, Deurbanists 35–7, 39, 40, 196
Dmitrov 19, 184
Dnepropetrovsk 104
Donbas industrial region 22, 25, 57, 74, 156
Donetsk (Stalino) 102, 109, 167
Donskoy Monastery, Moscow 189
dormitories (*see baraki*)
Dubna 89, 117, 167
duma 16, 22
Dushanbe 150

education 134
elektrichka (electric suburban train) 174
Elista 149
elite (*see nomenklatura*)
embassies 24, 142, 144
employment in towns 65, 90–92, 125–6, 134, 173 (*see also* occupations)
enterprise urban management 94, 108–9
environmental conditions 118–121, 144
Enyedi, Gyorgy 5, 203
Estonia 2, 90, 98, 103, 126, 127, 154, 164
ethnic problems 151–7, 201
conflict 155, 204
diversity 139, 153–7
mobility 149–51
patterns 151–5
exchange of accommodation (*see* housing exchange)

facadism 59
factory settlements 20, 22, 24
fairs 26
street fairs 113–15
family as unit of society 29, 81
Far East 66
farm workers 135
Five Year Plan 35, 51–4, 62, 108
First 3, 41–2, 51
Fourth 57
Eleventh 101
Twelfth 171
"Flying City" 39
forest-park zone (green belt) 64, 65, 88, 103, 104
fortress-towns 10, 13, 14, 24
Futurists 33

Gachechiladze, R. 119
garage facilities (*see* cars)
garden city 24, 31, 32, 35–6, 41
garden co-operatives 90
Garden Ring, Moscow 11, 58, 65, 144, 186
gastronom (supermarket) 81, 112, 174
Gel'freykh, V. G. 49, 58
General Plan for Moscow, 1775 19
Genplan (general plan, master plan) 95
General Scheme for the System of Settlement 70–2, 74, 93
General Statute, 1870 22
Georgia (Georgian SSR) 2, 6, 9, 90, 121, 148, 151, 152, 155–6, 164, 188, 204
gigantism 48, 49, 76

228